1993

ADVOCACY
RISK AND REALITY

ADVOCACY
RISK AND REALITY

Mary F. Kohnke, R.N., Ed.D., F.A.A.N.

Associate Professor, New York University,
Division of Nurse Education,
New York, New York

Illustrated

The C. V. Mosby Company

ST. LOUIS • TORONTO • LONDON   1982

MOSBY

A TRADITION OF PUBLISHING EXCELLENCE

Editor: Alison Miller
Assistant editor: Susan R. Epstein
Manuscript editor: Stephen C. Hetager
Book design: Susan Trail
Cover design: Suzanne Oberholtzer
Production: Mary Stueck

Printed in the United States of America

The C.V. Mosby Company
11830 Westline Industrial Drive, St. Louis, Missouri 63141

Library of Congress Cataloging in Publication Data

Kohnke, Mary.
   Advocacy, risk and reality.

   Bibliography: p.
   Includes index.
   1. Nurse and patient. I. Title. [DNLM:
1. Patient advocacy—Nursing texts. WY 87 K78a]
RT86.K63   362.1'0425   82-6460
ISBN 0-8016-2721-4   AACR2

AC/VH/VH 9 8 7 6 5 4 3 2 1   03/D/371

To

MARY

PREFACE

This book is written for those who by inclination or position find themselves functioning in the role of advocate. In particular it focuses on nurses, since they have either chosen or been placed in the role, but the principles discussed in this book will serve anyone who is involved in advocacy. Another reason why this book focuses on nursing is that I am a nurse; nursing is what I know the most about. I discuss the risks and hazards of advocacy from the point of view of nurses, but these risks and hazards are common to all advocates. The risks faced by an advocate in one setting are only variations of those faced by an advocate in another setting. Therefore the types of knowledge needed to cope with risk are similar for all advocates.

I use the term "cope" advisedly, because cope you will. Nurse advocates in a sense set themselves up to be criticized by all who disagree with the decisions a client makes. It is much easier for an advocate's fellow professionals to make a scapegoat of the advocate, for supporting those decisions, than to attack the decisions of the client directly, especially if the client is sick, poor, or not knowledgeable enough to act for himself.

Advocacy is not a new idea. Lawyers have engaged in advocacy for years, but for pay. Certain organized groups, such as Common Cause, have set themselves up as consumer advocates. Cities have set up offices of consumer advocacy, hospitals have hired ombudsmen, and even police departments have been forced to create civilian review boards.

However, it is when a lone individual gets involved in advocacy that the problems inherent in the activity become most obvious. The early years of the career of Ralph Nader offer some good examples of these types of problems. Nevertheless, the role of advocate has become more and more an individual role. This is especially true in the profession of nursing. In the literature the nurse is encouraged to be the patient's advocate, and many nurses (and other health care professionals) have found that the public, too, expects this to be part of the nurse's job.

Despite this social pressure to go out and "rescue the Holy Grail," we nurses rarely find anyone telling us how to do so and how to avoid the risks involved. As a result we see either very little advocacy or more reports of failures than reports of successes. It was with these thoughts in mind that I ventured onto the somewhat precarious course of writing a book on the practice of advocacy.

How one approaches the study of advocacy is presented in Chapter 1, along with my view of what advocacy basically entails. The rest of the chapters are devoted to some of the essential categories of knowledge one needs to consider in the enactment of the role of advocate. They are set up in an order that permits a reasonable learning style, but one can skip around. I may be accused of leaving out more than I have included and of being superficial, especially in the areas of ethics and legalities. However, so many excellent books and articles have been written in both these areas that to condense them here would be an injustice not only to the reader but also to the authors. But no one has written on advocacy itself. This omission has left many in the position of having to enact a role about which they have little or no knowledge. This book helps to fill that gap. Rather than call this a "how to do" book, however, I call it a "how to think, analyze, and survive" book.

What I would most like you to remember as a result of having read this book is that advocacy is the act of loving and caring. As such, it is not to be approached as something that we all do, because we don't. It is not something that we are born with, because we aren't. If we were, it would be more common. Advocacy, like caring, is something that we do because we either experienced it from others as we grew or learned it because it was valuable and right for us to do. Loving and caring are not automatic; they involve an act of free will, a choice of a way to behave and to see ourselves in relation to others. Some say that loving and caring require a self-imposed discipline; others say that they result from a natural gift. But as is true of all disciplines and gifts, one must learn how to use them, not only for the sake of others but also for one's own sake. Thus, this book is intended to show you how to perform your social duty and survive at the same time.

This is the point in a preface where an author generally admits, "I had help." But before I acknowledge the people who helped me and duly thank them, I would like to say a bit about the risk and reality of asking for help—from the points of view of both the helper and the asker. When you ask for help or consultation—in other words, seek out an advocate—you are generally going to get what you asked for. However, you may not always like what you get. Writing a book is like producing a baby: like any mother, you believe your baby is perfect. God help anyone who points out that the baby has six toes, crossed eyes, or blemishes—that, in fact, your product may not be quite perfect.

Brave and diplomatic indeed must be the helper who swims in these waters. Seeking help, the most mild-mannered of authors can suddenly become a shark defending prized territory. One might assume that the more experienced an author is, the less sensitive he is. However, it is just as likely that the reverse will be true.

The people I asked for help gave it kindly and graciously. I, *of course*, accepted it in a like manner. I accept full responsibility for everything that appears in this book. My helpers tried to keep it clean, clear, and somewhat literate. If there are passages that are less than that, they probably resulted from my more sensitive, sharkish moments—when the helpers swam for the shore.

Let me briefly mention the five people who helped me the most with the manuscript—and a sixth, my brother John, who also assisted me. I wrote the book while on sabbatical leave in Florida. John appeared almost every day, late in the afternoon at cocktail time, with, I am sure, two purposes in mind. The first was to remind me that there was a real world with real people in it outside the glass walls of "The Refuge" and the narrow focus of my typewriter. The second was to maintain, or at least to check on, the sanity of his sister. He was usually successful on both counts, since his arrival generally stopped the writing process for that day.

At The C.V. Mosby Co. there were three people who suffered me patiently. My editor Alison Miller and her assistant Susan Epstein were always available to me, but they may have wished that they had been on vacation certain days when I called. Also, there was Steve Hetager, who edited my manuscript. I don't know what I would have done without him. How seldom we authors acknowledge the debt we owe people like these.

At the very start of this project, before my sabbatical leave, I had a research assistant, Peggy Garbin (soon to be Dr. Peggy Garbin). Peggy's assistance in helping me separate reference materials that were essential from those that were not was invaluable. A bright and scholarly young woman, she had the intellect, humor, and political expertise necessary to make justifiable criticisms of the literature and of some of my ideas as well.

Every author needs a devil's advocate. For a book like this and an author like me, an especially astute one was needed. I found just such a person in Dr. Mary Duffy. She was my primary reader of the first draft, and those of you who are familiar with my first drafts will know what a chore that must have been. I asked her to respond to the manuscript in two ways: Was it clear? Was I ever in error? You will notice that I did not ask her, "Am I right?" or "Do you agree?" Like the fine consultant and diplomat she is known to be, Dr. Duffy limited herself to the former two questions in her written critiques. In our conversations, however, she did volunteer some answers to the two questions I did not ask her, and although I took these comments into consideration, I did not always act on them. So in no way is she to be held responsible for my sins of commission or omission. But I do hold her responsible for having provided me with thoughtful and scholarly comments and support. It is that kind of no-nonsense support that anyone who embarks on the writing of a book needs. As an advocate, I would like to advise you to go out and find a Dr. Mary Duffy, a Peggy Garbin, and people like those I found at Mosby. They make the publishing process survivable.

I must add that I had a friend who was with me all the time. I do not hold this friend responsible for any of the content of this book; the responsibility for that is all mine. But this friend's inspiration, quieting influence in times of desperation, and patience with me were always present. For these things I am eternally grateful and say simply, "Thank you, Lord."

One final word before you embark on this journey into the role of advocate: I have attempted to keep footnotes and supporting documentation to a minimum. I have occasionally included footnotes to clarify particular points or to provide bibliographic information. At the ends of chapters, I have often included lists of supplemental readings as well as comments about their value to the subjects under discussion.

Mary F. Kohnke

CONTENTS

ADVOCACY
RISK AND REALITY

Chapter 1

ADVOCACY: WHAT IT IS

Every few years a particular term or concept becomes very popular. Presently "advocacy" is one of these popular buzzwords. Everybody talks about advocacy and seems to be doing it. The term involves such connotations as "protect" and "rights" and conveys the idea that it is something that "good guys" do. Advocacy also seems rather simple, that it is something anyone can do. In nursing education we tell our students to be the patient's advocate. We do not, however, tell them very much more about it, except that it is a "good thing." We seldom deal with questions such as "Is advocacy risky or troublesome?" or "Can advocacy be hazardous to your health?" The answer to these questions is yes; advocacy can be risky and even hazardous. But nonetheless, it is a good thing, and like most good things should be done.

In order to be an effective advocate, you need to know what advocacy is, how to do it, and how to do it well and safely. For just as you cannot venture into a minefield without a mine detector, you cannot venture into advocacy without knowledge and foresight. In the words of the New Testament, advocates should be "as wise as serpents and as gentle as doves."

DEFINITIONS

Let's start with definitions. The definition in most general dictionaries is that advocacy is "the act of defending or pleading the case of another." This definition is applicable to a courtroom situation, and it describes the situation that exists when the other person is very young or unconscious, when he is not present to defend himself, or when he is not able to act in his own behalf. This definition does not apply to advocacy in general or to most of the situations that the practicing nurse encounters. Nurses do not always deal with the very young patient or the unconscious patient. Most of their clients are conscious and able to speak or act. Therefore, what is the role of the advocate in this vast majority of cases? Briefly, the role of the advocate is to *inform* the client and then to *support* him in whatever decision he makes. This type of support differs from the support provided by a lawyer. In the practice of law, the lawyer advocate actually presents the client's case and either pleads for justice or defends the client from accusation. In the nurse advocate role, however, support means that when the client makes a decision, the nurse abides by it and defends his right to make it. The role of advocate comprises only two functions: to inform and to support.

These two functions seem on the surface to be relatively simple. Perhaps this is why most nurses do not study advocacy further. Most educators of nurses do not teach advocacy per se. They teach ethics, ethical codes of behavior, and the intricacies involved in ethical dilemmas. The literature is filled with articles and books on various aspects of ethics and the ethical dilemmas facing a professional. I am not saying that ethics is unimportant, but rather that ethical codes change from profession to profession, culture to culture, and time to time. Professionals must practice within the ethical codes of their professions. But these codes are only one aspect of the larger knowledge base of advocacy and the role of the advocate. Advocates must act ethically, but ethics does not teach one the role of advocate.

The same applies to the legalities of professional practice. Professionals must practice within the legal restraints of their license and the law. They must be aware of the laws governing their practice—not only for the client's safety but also for their own. But again, these laws change from state to state and from time to time. They are even more fluid than ethical codes. Though the advocate works within the confines of the law, the law does not teach a person how to be an advocate. Laws are written to act as protective devices. It is indeed wise to keep abreast of the laws that affect one's practice, for they are a valuable part of one's knowledge base as an advocate—but only a part.

Thus it is a mistake to think that all an advocate needs to know is some ethics or some law. The advocate role is action filled. It has many complexities and needs to be treated as a totality in and of itself.

There are many risks and hidden hazards in advocacy for both the client and the advocate. The most important attributes for the advocate to possess, for the safety of both, are a state of open-mindedness and a broad knowledge base about people, society, and the social order. Open-mindedness allows the advocate to listen to, and hear, what the client is saying. This attribute demands that the advocate have a knowledge of self, which includes an understanding of one's own attitudes, values, and beliefs. Such self-knowledge allows the advocate to hear and understand the attitudes, values, and beliefs of others without identifying with them. The advocate allows others to have different values and beliefs. Open-mindedness is extremely important, for the advocate must be able to present information as objectively as possible and to allow clients to make their own decisions, even when those decisions differ from the advocate's personal judgment.

VIEWED AS A GESTALT

Proficiency in many areas of knowledge is needed to create this open-mindedness, an essential ingredient for learning the advocate role. For purposes of discussion in this book, I have divided these areas of knowledge into ten major categories: (1) informing and supporting, (2) systems analysis, (3) social ethic, (4) ethics, (5) issues, (6) medical-industrial complex, (7) social laws, (8) politics, (9) professional education, and (10) professional practice.

As you can see, advocacy entails many areas of knowledge. Rather than view advocacy according to its parts, however, it is better to view it as a gestalt or picture.

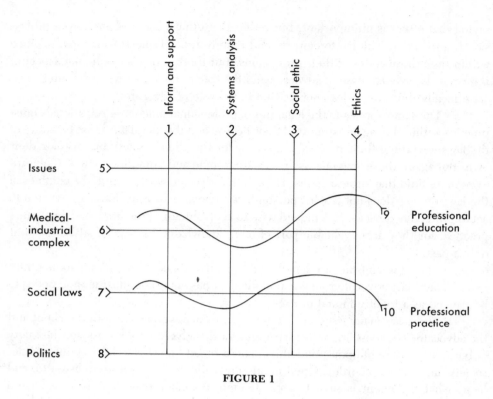

FIGURE 1

Since each part intertwines with every other part, the study of one does not give you a picture of the whole. You must look at each part, but then you must put them together. No one logical sequence fits for everyone. The sequence you follow depends on your learning style and what you bring to the study. It may help if I pictorially present what I am about to verbally describe. But keep in mind that this diagram (Fig. 1) is only one approach to the study.

The vertical lines (1, 2, 3, and 4) represent the first four categories of knowledge: informing and supporting, systems analysis, social ethic, and ethics. The horizontal lines (5, 6, 7, and 8) represent the next four categories: issues, medical-industrial complex, social laws, and the politics of society viewed on a broad basis. The wavy lines (9 and 10) represent the last two categories, professional education and professional practice. At this point a little imagination is in order, for you, the reader, must take this two-dimensional diagram and view it in a four-dimensional way so that movement and pattern are depicted. You will then be able to visualize all the lines intersecting each other and interrelating at any one point along this time-space continuum.

EXAMINED IN DETAIL

Now that you have an overall picture of how the categories intertwine, let's look at each category in greater depth. Although all ten categories of knowledge are needed, the first four categories are what I call fundamentals or basics, for these are the areas of advocacy that do not change over time, but remain essentially the same. The first category deals with the types of knowledge that are involved in the informing and supporting functions themselves. Providing others with information has many facets. One must either have the information or know where to get it. The advocate must want the client to have the information (we don't always want people to know too much). The client must agree to knowing the information (he has a right not to know). The knowledge must be presented in a way that is meaningful to the client. Finally, the advocate must cope with the fact that there may be many persons who do not want the client to have the information. For example, hospital administrators, other professionals (physicians, nurses, and so on), even families and friends, may view informing in a somewhat negative way, as if the client were "the enemy." The act of informing, which on the surface seems simple, can have some complex ramifications.

The same is true of the act of supporting. An advocate must know how to support without falling into a defending and rescuing position, in which responsibility for decision making belongs to the advocate and not to the client. The advocate must understand that supporting a client's right to make a decision does not mean giving approval for the decision. Even clients may demand more of the advocate than support. They may want the advocate to fight their battles for them. Finally, as in the act of informing, there will be people who do not approve of the advocate's supporting the client. They may view such support as the height of disloyalty—to the hospital, to fellow professionals, and to the client's family members, who, after all, say they have the client's best interests at heart. Therefore, what starts out as a simple act turns into a rather complex undertaking.

The second category of knowledge deals with how one examines or analyzes a system. The better an advocate knows the people with whom he or she deals and the systems within which they work, the better the advocate can lessen the risks and hazards involved in advocacy. Therefore, the advocate must have some knowledge of self, clients, families, the health care professions, and health care institutions. In short, the advocate must look at the stated and the unstated goals of self and others. The unstated goals, which are often disguised, are the ones that play the biggest role. The advocate must learn to listen with an educated ear in order to determine what the unstated goals are in a particular situation. Knowing these goals assists the advocate in developing strategies to deal with the risks inherent in informing and supporting. This knowledge also helps to effect needed changes in systems without causing total disruption and failure in the achievement of goals. Essentially, systems analysis involves following a logical sequence of steps and arriving at alternatives. The advocate then examines each alternative with a fair degree of knowledge of its potential success or failure. Put simply, systems analysis can be called process of gaining understanding.

The third category in the knowledge base is information about what I call the social ethic of the group of people with whom one is dealing. This category does not differ much from systems analysis except that it is more specific in its focus. The term "ethic" as used here is borrowed from John Gardner's book *Excellence*. Gardner believes that the ethic of a group or an institution can be viewed in terms of a continuum, with egalitarianism on one end and libertarianism on the other. Although people may not have a conscious awareness of where they fall on this continuum, they have all formed opinions about the rights of others and about what is owed them or not owed them by society. Some knowledge of the social ethic of a group of people will, as in systems analysis, help an advocate to identify the risks involved in his or her actions and the alternatives that must be considered. Assessing the social ethic is an integral part of the systems analysis process.

The fourth category of knowledge, ethics, flows from the third. There is in most societies a general code of ethics to which everyone at least gives lip service. Within each profession there is a more formal code that is supposed to govern professional behavior in general and specific acts in particular.

Ethics is the study of the nature of right and wrong; it is a vast and intricate field. In this book I will deal with the following aspects of ethics: how ethical positions can affect decision making, how ethical positions are related to developmental stages, and how ethical positions are changeable over time.

The next four categories of knowledge comprise the current broad problems that society has not completely resolved and that influence the individual as well as the group decision-making process. The fifth category is what I call issues: racism, sexism, ageism, and access to education and to health care. These issues have an important effect on the advocate and the risks inherent in the role of advocate. For example, an advocate may work with people who do not believe that persons of another race or color have the same rights that they have. They may believe that blacks, Puerto Ricans, or Chicanos, for example, should take and accept what they get from the system, which is likely to be controlled by whites who "know what is best." A female patient may face a similar situation, especially if her physician is a male who believes women are basically emotional, have no brains, and therefore cannot be expected to make decision for themselves, and if she is unlucky enough to have a husband or male family members who hold the same beliefs. The advocacy process then becomes very complicated. More and more frequently, this same situation is also becoming true for the elderly. If an elderly person disagrees with the professionals, he is labeled "senile"; and if he disagrees with his family, the same result can occur, especially if he is seen as an inconvenience by both groups. The problem is compounded if the person is also a woman and black. The issue of access to education and health care is closely related to these three "isms." Prejudice influences a person's ability to acquire knowledge or adequate health care. The advocate faces risks in the informing and supporting role for an individual client; when an advocate moves to help certain groups of people acquire the knowledge needed to advance or gain access to health care, the risks may increase.

The sixth category of knowledge is the role of the medical-industrial complex, as some call it, in the health care of the population as a whole. What, if any, special interest groups affect the nature of health care? How do these groups influence the advocate's role? Pharmaceutical companies, for example, make money by selling drugs. If an advocate informs people of alternate methods of maintaining health—sleep without drugs, bowel regularity without laxatives, healthy diets without vitamin supplements, and so on—the advocate is not going to be the drug companies' favorite person. If hospitals need full occupancy to remain solvent, and an advocate helps people to maintain themselves at home, then while the advocate is saving money for the client, he or she is losing money for the institution. If an advocate helps a client improvise equipment at home rather than buy expensive supplies, the supply companies lose money. These groups are tied together to remain viable. If one suffers as a result of an increase in knowledge on the part of consumers, they all are threatened. These groups are joined by other, larger groups, who have special stakes or financial interests in them in the form of stock in a company or a job to maintain in an institution. One could say the bottom line is this: there is no money in health care, but lots of it in "illness care"; so don't rock the boat!

The seventh category consists of the social laws—in other words, laws dealing with social issues—that are passed to protect the population as a whole or segments of the population. How do these laws affect the groups for whom they are passed, and how do they affect others? What are the ramifications of laws enacted to correct past wrongs? Do they, in fact, affect in an adverse fashion the population as a whole or other segments of the population? For example, how do welfare laws affect people? Do the rules governing eligibility for welfare benefits keep people dependent for fear of losing them if they work but cannot make enough to support themselves? Do these rules dictate to people what they will do and, in reality, take away free choice? Does welfare instill an element of fear into a person's decision-making process? Does remaining docile become a requirement for receiving benefits? What if an advocate provides people with knowledge that allows them to question the system? Will the officials who give out the "goodies" like being questioned about their methods? Who will they retaliate against—the welfare recipient or the advocate who started the questioning? These kinds of questions can be raised about many types of laws; the advocate must be aware of the implications involved.

The eighth category of knowledge is the effect politics plays in resolving issues. The discussion of this category will be geared more to the raising of questions than to the proposing of solutions. Politicians—from running for office to getting elected to remaining in office by means of reelection—depend upon public support at the polls as well as for financing campaigns. The politician is caught in a double bind, for his constituency is composed of consumers of health care as well as special interests in the medical-industrial complex. These two groups, more often than not, are on opposite sides of issues. The politician must weigh the interests of one group against those of the other. How he does this will determine whether he will succeed in politics. What does this mean for the advocate? Here, the advocate will be working in a larger arena—the community—but the dangers are the same. Exerting too much pressure in an attempt to do good poses risks for an advocate, just as it does when he or she works with individual patients in an institution. Politicians can enact laws that help defuse the risk in advocacy, or they can create barriers to the process. Again, the role of the wise but gentle dove is necessary if an advocate is to step on others' financial toes and have them say, albeit with gritted teeth, "Thank you, I know it's best."

An in-depth study of any of the four categories just discussed is beyond the scope of this book. What is important is that you have a sense of how each category is relevant to the advocacy process on both the individual level and the community level.

The last two categories of knowledge are professional education and professional practice. It is necessary that both the advocate and the consumer understand what professionals are educated to do and how the realities of their practice fields enhance or inhibit their ability to function. The focus will be on nursing, since that is the field I know most about. Many of the questions raised, however, are applicable to all professional fields. The discussions of these two categories focus on what I consider to be the current issues in education and practice. Of course, issues—and the importance assigned to them—vary from time to time. The major point is to be aware that education and practice issues do have an effect on advocacy. The variables involved in the lives of human beings are many and ever changing. An awareness of this fact and an alertness to it are what is desired. Such an awareness is part of what I call the armamentarium of the advocate, for one does not go out to inform and support in ignorance. Success in any role is not guaranteed, but failure can be armed against.

LEVELS OF ADVOCACY

A person needs to know the boundaries of any role that is part of what I call "risk defusement." There are risks in riding a bike, water skiing, or even walking down a street, but they decrease in proportion to the knowledge a person brings to the activity.

Advocacy exists on three levels: advocacy for yourself, advocacy for clients, and advocacy for the larger community of which you are a part. Just as you cannot love others if you cannot love yourself, you can never be an advocate for others if you first have not learned to be one for yourself. In order to follow the age-old admonition "Love thy neighbor as thyself," a person first must be able to love himself. To the extent that a person can love himself, he can love others. Being an advocate involves a similar sort of process. First, a person must be informed. He must acquire the necessary knowledge and know himself before he can make an informed decision. He must look at all choices and all consequences. Then, in accepting authority over self, he must make the decision and accept the responsibility for its consequences.

Here in this first, simple level of advocacy one can see an obvious problem. Who can say that he always holds no one but himself responsible for the decisions he makes, that he never blames others or seeks a way out or equivocates? Who can honestly claim that he never tries to "con" others into making decisions for him, that he always can say, "I did it, no one else is at fault, I did it knowingly. I was informed." It seems, rather, that the statements "But no one told me," "You didn't tell me," or "I didn't know" are more common. This is human behavior. We have all acted this way to some extent and will seek to do so again whenever we can. Therefore, as an advocate you must realize that putting clients in the position of making their own decisions is not going to be easy. If a client makes his own decision, who can he blame later if the decision doesn't look so good? That human trait, combined with the natural desire of the nurse to be a "know best" helper, makes the role of advocate a difficult one. For you are placed in combat not only with the patient, to get him to make his own decision, but also with yourself, to keep your mouth shut. We give lip service to the view that all nurses should be patient advocates, but do we really know what is involved—the retraining, the re-education, the self-discipline? Once a nurse is aware of what is involved and begins to think as well as to act as an advocate for both self and others, advocacy quickly becomes a part of a life-style. If a nurse is a consumate game player, however, and thrives in such a role, becoming an advocate is harder.

In advocacy for self, the support aspect of advocacy should be allowed to take over. In other words, a person does not have to experience a "guilt trip" after he has made a decision. If a decision does not work out well, he learns from it and goes on. He supports himself and says, "I'll know better next time."

The second level of advocacy—advocacy for the patient—I have discussed in describing advocacy per se. I can only add this advice: do not be too eager to rush about looking for patients for whom you can act as an advocate. Every day small amounts of advocacy come your way. Patients are always asking you to help them make decisions. "Should I bathe before or after breakfast, before or after occupational therapy, before or after the doctor comes?" These problems may seem small to us, but to a patient in the hospital they may be the most important events in his day. They give us opportunities to help him learn to make decisions for himself, so that when a really big decision comes along he will have had practice. (This is how we should be raising children and dealing with students and young staff nurses as well.) Furthermore, helping patients to learn to make seemingly small decisions provides us with practice in the advocate's role of providing information and then supporting a decision. We also learn to teach a patient how to accept a poor decision and how to make a better one next time.

The third level or arena advocacy is the community. You, as a knowledge-able professional, have information that consumers need, be they members of the local Parent-Teacher Association, participants in environmental groups, or members of other organizations. You have an obligation and a right as a member of the com-munity to share your knowledge. Since you are a member of that community, you will be working both for yourself and for the larger community. One could almost say that advocacy for the larger community is a combination of the first two types of advocacy—advocacy for self and advocacy for others. You need to ask yourself what your responsibility is to the community and to recognize the ways in which your needs and its needs coincide. How can you best fulfill this responsibility? Certainly not by taking over and making decisions for members of the community because you "know more." It should be a cooperative venture, your educating them to make decisions in which you also will have a part. You must avoid having community members say, "We made these decisions because the professionals told us it was best." Thus, you are a part of the total action. As you inform yourself and others, you and they together make decisions that affect everyone. Responsibility is jointly held, not by you alone or by a community group alone.

In being an advocate on a community level, you must always be aware of what compromise, in the finest sense of the word, means. One does not compromise on basic principles, but one must compromise and not insist on having one's own way, especially if doing so means infringing on the rights of others. I recently saw a television program about the most orthodox section of Jews in Israel. This group wanted no one to drive on the Sabbath and threw rocks at Jews living nearby who believed differently and therefore wanted to act differently. How then can the mem-bers of one such group meet their needs without infringing on the needs of the members of the opposing group? Sometimes it is almost impossible to compromise, because some people want to uphold their principles and rights even if they infringe on yours. This you must be alert to; you must not be pushed into an uncompromising position of your own just because other people are intransigent. More directly re-lated to the nursing world is the dilemma involving people who for religious reasons do not want blood transfusions. St. Barnabas Hospital in New York City, among others, has set up a whole system to help these people get the necessary help with the least infringement on their religious beliefs. Yet the bottom line is that you, as a member of the community, have a responsibility to share your knowledge with such clients and to share in the decisions made.

•   •   •

In describing advocacy as a gestalt, I have attempted to use a framework in which the ten categories intersect each other at any point on a time-space continuum. It is impossible to state that any one category has more importance than another along this continuum. Therefore, you will find that the following chapters do not necessarily discuss the categories in a specific order. Nor is the placement of one chapter before another any indication of its importance. You may very well move from Chapter 5 to Chapter 3 or from Chapter 4 to Chapter 6. If you want to complicate things further, you may combine one chapter with parts of another.

Writing a book, which involves forcing subject matter into a logical sequence of chapters, imposes restraints on both the writer and the material. Since one needs to start somewhere, I will discuss the fundamental areas of knowledge in Chapters 2, 3, 4, and 5. Some of the issues relevant to advocacy I will integrate into a chapter on the social ethic, and others will be discussed in separate chapters. The categories of professional education and professional practice will be discussed in separate chapters. It is left to you, the reader, and your memory to integrate the material as best suits you.

Advocacy is complex. It is not a simple "should." One must not embark on it without familiarity with the essential areas of knowledge. I do not make these statements to scare you away from the role, but only to introduce you to its intricacies. Advocacy is not to be entered into without both knowledge and foresight. The following chapters will attempt to provide some of each for you. The rest is up to you, for learning from books cannot be separated from life experience. Again a gestalt.

Chapter 2

INFORMING
AND
SUPPORTING

ALTHOUGH THIS CHAPTER WILL DEAL with two major subjects—informing and supporting, which are the heart of the role of the advocate—one other matter is directly related to enacting the role. This is the subject of rescuing versus advocacy. Together these three topics form the framework of the actual work of the advocate with clients. Informing and supporting involve not only knowing how to think but also knowing how to do. The "how to do" of anything is important, but of even more importance is the knowledge that supports that how to do. In other words, the how to do is the simple part; it is the knowing that supports the action that one must never venture forth without.

Informing and supporting are filled with risks. You are cautioned not to become discouraged at this point. I decided to describe the advocate's role at the start in what one might call its worst light. Material in this chapter and the other chapters will then deal with how you can carefully and successfully overcome most of the risks. Many of the risks involved in advocacy occur when an advocate moves out of the advocacy role into a rescuing role. This problem will be discussed and demonstrated.

INFORMING AND ITS RISKS

One of the first principles of advocacy is that the advocate must deal with himself before coping with clients. You must decide that the role of advocate is warranted and that you want to assume it. In other words, you must decide that you *want* the client to know. This is not as simple as it sounds. Although it is true in the long run that it is easier to deal with a knowledgeable client, in the short haul you must face the problems of making that client knowledgeable, and what this may mean to you personally. So first you must ask, "Do you know what to inform the client about?" The client is supposed to be informed about all treatments, medications, and procedures, as well as about all their ramifications. You must also know what alternatives the client has and what their ramifications are. If you do not have this information, you must seek it out. This is true in any field. You must know your product, the products of others, your service, and the service of others in order to be knowledgeable in the informing process. Attaining such knowledge is not easy in the present times, which are bursting with new information. This is certainly true for nurses, who are constantly being introduced to new drugs, treatments, and procedures. It is especially true for nurses who work in general medical-surgical areas, where they must be knowledgeable about a large variety of illnesses. A nurse must either possess the requisite knowledge or know where to get it. Otherwise he or she runs the risk of

Some of the material in this chapter appeared in a much condensed form in an article of mine entitled "The Nurse as Advocate," which appeared in the American Journal of Nursing 80 (November 1980): 2039-2040.

giving information that is incorrect or out of date. You may find yourself involved in activities that are clearly dangerous to the patient and, as a result, dangerous to you. The courts do not smile upon the professional who claims ignorance in his or her area of practice. So knowing is necessary not only for the person who chooses to act as an advocate but also for the professional who chooses to practice a profession with the added dimension of advocacy.

Finding the time to properly inform clients is an important concern for the advocate. First, consider the time it takes for a nurse to become informed and to remain informed not only about his or her own practice but also about the practices of others. Being informed requires that you be engaged in a state of constant learning. It is not enough to practice what you have learned in school. You must keep up-to-date all the time, and your facts must be accurate. This will require your seeking consultation, going to continuing education classes, and delving into the current literature on your own. If you do not do so, you will run the risk of being labeled incompetent, out of date, and/or lazy. It is the last label, "lazy," that is the danger here. It is bad enough to be accused of not knowing what you are doing, but to be accused of not knowing because you could not or would not take the time to know constitutes an even greater danger. Many nurses wriggle out of the position of not knowing by telling clients to ask their physicians. They deny their ignorance by saying that they do not have the right to impart certain information to clients. This tactic may have served some years ago, but today the nursing literature is proclaiming that it is the nurse's right and duty to inform clients in all areas. Furthermore, the courts are also declaring this to be true. The old cop-out will no longer work. Whether a nurse wants to be an advocate or not, he or she is at least forced into knowing, and therefore into taking the necessary actions to guarantee that knowledge base.

A second problem involving time is the time it takes to inform a client. You are faced with two questions: Do you want to take the time? Do you have the time to take? They go together and constitute a question of priorities. Let's say you do have the time—that is, you do not have other clients waiting, but you do have a desire to extend a coffee break, to make a phone call or two, or just to chat with fellow workers. These activities may be important; we may in fact enjoy the people we work with more than the work we do. The reality, however, usually is that you do not have the time to take, because of other professional obligations. Will you be able to complete all the work you have to do today if you give more time to Mrs. Jones to inform her of what she can expect when she goes to x-ray? How does that task rank in comparison to the desirability of walking Mrs. Smith because this is her first time out of bed?

A shortage of time is a very real problem that all professionals face. Some of the problem is self-imposed, as a result of how they set their priorities. For example, for some professionals the larger the volume of clients seen, the more money made. Sometimes the problem is imposed by others, but for much the same reason. There is a difference. When we set our priorities for purely selfish reasons—monetary gain, for example—we are responsible for the consequences. However, when priorities of which we do not approve are set for us, we must act to change them. If we have not taken the time because an institution does not allow us to and we have not taken any action to change a situation or to change jobs, then we have, by default, agreed to the conditions. This may not seem fair to many, but in fact that is how it will be viewed by others. The defense that we were forced, by the authorities we worked for, to omit actions that are accepted professional behavior will not be found very acceptable by outside observers—especially if there is no evidence that an attempt was made to bring the situation to the attention of the proper officials. So unless we act in some way to resolve this question of time, we can be caught in a greater bind than if we had not acted.

A third problem concerning time is the time involved answering clients' questions that result from the information you have given them. The difficulties and risks involved are the same as those involved in taking the time to inform clients in the first place. But another difficulty is involved here: not being able to answer the questions. You can inform about what you know as well as have the time to do so. But what about the human element of simply being unable to answer a question you have been asked? Most people would agree that not having all the answers is not a great defect. Nevertheless, to some people this is a problem. To be able to say "I don't know but I'll find out" is perfectly acceptable, but you must have reached the point in personal development where you find it so. Furthermore, you must be able to face the possibility of ridicule from others, who may say, "What do you mean you don't know? What kind of a nurse are you?" The risk here is only as great as your self-esteem. You must know in your heart that it is okay not to know as long as you can go about finding out. You must realize that there are people who, because of their own anxieties about not knowing, will make remarks about your not knowing. This situation is part of the human condition; one learns to live with it and not take it to heart.

This factor of time thus has a great influence on the informing process. So when we say "Do you want the client to know?" we are asking many subquestions.

Another question must be faced here. If you decide that you want a client to know, and you have the time to inform him, you must be aware of the possibility that, as a result of his new knowledge, he will say "No." "No, I won't have surgery; no, I won't take the medication; no, I won't have the treatment. *No, no, no.*" You face the very real problem of being told by others, and knowing yourself, that if you had not informed the client in the first place, you would not have a problem now. But remember—if you do not inform a client before the fact, you may be in much greater trouble later, when it is too late to take the treatment back.

A client's refusal to take a medication, or to have a treatment done or a major procedure undertaken, is often of less consequence to himself and to others than undergoing the treatment in ignorance of its ramifications. Assume, for example, that a woman refuses chemotherapy after a radical mastectomy that reveals lymph node involvement. This client's rationale is that the surgery by itself has rid her of all presently detectable cancer, that it is hard enough to live with the physical mutilation of the surgery, that she could not go through the further debilitating effects of the chemotherapeutic agents, and that she thus will take a chance. She believes that the quality of life is more important than the quantity and that refusing the extra margin of safety that the chemotherapy might provide is worth the risk. She assures you that she knows and understands all the ramifications of her choice. Such a client would be making an informed decision. Now let us assume that the situation is different—that this client is not informed of the side effects of chemotherapy or that she is led to believe that there are none or that they are slight. She therefore agrees to treatment. Later, when she is experiencing severe side effects, she comes to believe that she has been lied to and decides to sue the health care professionals involved, on the basis of a lack of informed consent.

This problem involves, at the basic level, the question of who is going to accept the responsibility for a person's life and the decisions about that life. If a client does not have the proper information, the professional accepts, by default, that responsibility. No matter how much you may plead that the client knew and signed the consent forms, you know in your heart that he really did not know—and more important, the courts and others know this, too!

After you have answered the question "Do you want the client to know?" you are faced with a further question, "Does the client want to know?" This question is not as foolish as it may seem. Many clients do not want to know. They will say to you, "Just go ahead and do it; don't tell me about it" or "I'll be too scared to go through with it if I know." Many a patient has spoken in such a way to his physicians and nurses. The role of the advocate becomes a careful balancing act between trying to determine what the patient does not need to know and what he must know, in terms of informed consent. A surgeon may be much more skilled at dealing with this problem than the average nurse, because he faces it more often. Some surgeons manage to tell patients just enough to superficially fill the requirements of informed consent and no more. However, they do run the risk of telling too little and facing irate and uncooperative patients after surgery. Some physicians take this "too little" route as a matter of personal choice, whether the patient wants to know or not. It saves the time that would be wasted if the patient decided not to have the procedure and the time required if he asked for further discussion and information.

It is important for the advocate to remember that the patient—in other words, the client—has a right not to know. But equally important is the fact that the advocate has the right to protect himself from the results of the client's not knowing and from the possibility that others will accuse him of allowing action to be taken without informed consent. The best road to follow is to engage in a knowledgeable and honest exchange with the client concerning the problem. The advocate must confront the client with the realities of not knowing—what the consequences will be not only for the client but also for the advocate himself, if he is accused of not informing the client of what is going to happen. This kind of discussion usually ends with the client agreeing to know certain things and not others. It allows the advocate to protect himself by stating in writing what the client has been told, what he has not been told, and why. The advocate is obligated to honor, as best he can, the client's right not to know, while still protecting himself.

Danger can lie in an advocate's unspoken desire not to get involved in the risks inherent in the informing process. The tendency not to become involved can be strengthened when a client says, "I don't want to know." An advocate can latch on to this statement without further exploration of the situation. It's a great temptation. Many clients are quick to say "I don't want to know about it; just get the thing done." When professionals are in a hurry or have other things on their minds, they frequently accept such statements without considering the consequences. A simple (although tangential) example: A person buys a carpet and wants it laid now. Later he discovers that it does not wear well in heavy traffic areas, that it requires a special cleaning process, and that he must buy extra in order to match the pattern. He goes back to the salesperson and says, "Why didn't you tell me?" The salesperson says, "But you said you didn't want to know." The customer says, "You should have told me anyway; you *knew* I was in a hurry and didn't mean that." Carpeting is one thing; a customer's not wanting to know may hurt only his pocketbook. But medical care is another thing. A client's not wanting to know the side effects of medications or procedures involves more than a question of money; it affects his life. Some clients deal with problems related to their medical care in the same way they deal with the purchase of carpeting. The advocate must be alert to the client with such behavioral patterns as opposed to the client who genuinely does not want to know. In dealing with clients who have at first told me they do not want to know, I have taken the time to explore this statement with them. Rarely have I found a case in which the problem of not wanting to know has not been resolved to the satisfaction of both the client and the advocate. In the few cases in which clients have really not wanted to know, I have taken the precaution, for my own protection, of informing client, family, and physician of the situation. In addition, the decision and the situation were recorded in the patient's chart. The point is not to make a federal case of a client's desire not to know, but rather to act in a manner that is quiet, informative, and prudent.

In the process of informing, information must be presented in a meaningful way to a client, and the nurse must be sure the client understands the information. This aspect of the nurse-patient relationship is the one that is most vital to the patient. The information must be presented in a manner that allows the patient to fully listen to it without having to listen to the hidden feelings of the nurse that may distort it. In other words, the patient must not be put in the position of having to "psych out" the nurse to find out the nurse's personal views and then be subtly intimidated by them. The patient should not have to say to himself, "I hear what she is saying, but what does she really mean?" Students constantly ask themselves this question about instructors, and employees ask it about bosses. So the responsibility for providing information in an effective manner lies with the professional, if he or she wishes to be an advocate in the true sense of the word.

People make decisions for all kinds of reasons, some of which have nothing to do with the immediate situation facing them. So the advocate must constantly take care not to be swayed by the unstated reasons that go into the making of a decision and thereby subtly support a decision that is not based on an objective view of the facts. For example, clients may make decisions that are based on the need to please others, that are contradictory to what they themselves want. So an advocate's opinion of what is best must be put aside in deference to the task of informing clients of the consequences of their choices. In other words, an advocate must state that if "A" is chosen, then "B" will follow, and so on. This must be a consistent pattern in everything an advocate says.

A decision a client makes is his own, even if it is, in your opinion, not the best he could make. It is in fact his decision, no matter what his reasons for making it. He must be allowed to live with it, in the best sense of that expression, since he made it freely and without pressure. This is reality in the finest sense of the word. Respecting a client's decision is hard for us as professionals, who "know best," especially when we sense the reasons behind a decision have nothing to do with reality, at least as we see it. But this attitude is necessary if we expect people to grow and if we respect their right to make decisions that may be wrong in our view. We do not always grow because of the right things we do but often because of our mistakes. We often justify our unseemly intervention on the basis of life and death, without realizing that life and death have different meanings for different people. What to us is life may be a living death to others. It is difficult, to say the least, for us to allow others to make decisions that seem to be wrong. However, the question we must ask ourselves is "Do we have the right to prevent others from freely defining and determining their destiny—especially if they have made their decisions in a knowledgeable manner?" The answer is clearly "no."

I have said that information must be presented in a manner that the client can understand. Words and phrases must be used that are within the vocabulary of the client. A question arises here: how do you deal with a client who does not have a good grasp of your language? He may not speak your language at all, or it may be a second language in which he is not fluent. A translator may be necessary, but care must be taken in the use of a translator—especially if he does not have a good grasp of English. A translator should be fluent in both languages. If he is not, you will have to be very careful that he fully understands what you are saying before he tries to convey it to the patient. Even if the translator is fluent, the same care must be taken.

It is best to first talk with the translator alone, before you begin a three-way conversation. In this preliminary interchange you have time to establish what the translator knows and understands before you join the client. During this preparation have the translator repeat back to you what you said, and encourage him to ask questions so that clarity can be established. When this is not done first but instead is done with the client present, you may find that the client becomes anxious and wants to know what is being said. It is then that confusion can occur. Meeting with the translator ahead of time, though time-consuming, is much more satisfactory in the long run. The client can usually ask more pertinent questions, which can be more easily answered by the advocate, since the translator has a better grasp of the topic under discussion and therefore functions better.

Working with clients who do not speak English is difficult enough, but you have the added variable of how the translator has conveyed the information. This you cannot judge adequately. If the translator is a friend or a member of the client's family, the problem can be even more difficult, since you cannot screen out whatever special interest he may have in the client's decision-making process. Some hint of this interest, however, can be gathered in the preliminary session. You can only hope that your own personal integrity and care will be reflected in how the translator performs his role as your surrogate. (I recommend that nurses who work extensively with clients who speak another language should know that language themselves.)

Finally, in the informing role one must deal with the problem and potential risk posed by persons who may not want the patient informed. These persons fall into three categories: physicians; nurses, other professionals, and hospital administrators; and family or friends. I have placed physicians in a separate category from other professionals because they have a great tendency to see the patient as their exclusive domain. Unfortunately, this myth that the patient is their exclusive property has a sound foundation in reality. In our institutions one sees this in the most obvious way. The physician is the one who admits the patient, determines treatment, and sets the time for discharge. There are, of course, times when the physician collaborates with others in these functions, but generally they are the physician's alone. The physician makes the diagnosis and thereby determines the medications, treatments, and other procedures. Many a physician therefore believes that he or she alone has the right to determine what the patient will be told or not told and who will do the telling.

In the past very little telling was done, and even today what is done tends to be sketchy. Fortunately for patients, many consumer and patients' rights groups, along with the courts, have made changes in this behavior—or should we say lack of behavior. Physicians who do not comply with the requirements of informed consent in all areas of treatment are in much greater danger of being censured than ever before. The censure rarely costs them their licenses or results in the loss of clients, but it does cost them money because of malpractice suits. In addition, because the public is better informed, patients are suing not only physicians but hospitals and nurses as well. Therefore professionals are becoming more conscious of individual responsibility and liability. The advocate who keeps this fact in mind has a measure of protection against being blamed for informing patients when others do not want them informed.

Despite these changes, the physician-controlled situation still exists, and other health care professionals still have a tendency to believe and to go along with the idea that the patient is the physician's alone. Old ways of thinking and behaving die slowly.

Nurses have been told for years in their schools and textbooks that they are to teach patients and to explain to patients what to expect during certain procedures. But when they enter the working world they soon discover that there are certain things they are not to tell patients and that certain physicians do not want them to tell patients anything. Moreover, they find that they can never be sure of just what these things are or of which physicians want what. Many physicians and other health care professionals believe that a nurse should not inform a patient of his temperature, pulse rate, respiratory rate, and blood pressure, much less what pill or injection he is receiving. And discussions of more involved topics—treatments, operative procedures, and alternatives—are definitely out of the question. Some may say, "But those days are gone forever." The reality, however, is that those days are still very much with us, especially in the minds of physicians and many nurses. Advocates thus will have to overcome old ideas themselves and be prepared to cope with them in physicians and others.

Many physicians do want their patients well informed. They inform patients, and they encourage nurses to do so as well. But equally as many physicians do not keep their patients informed or want only some things told to them. There are many reasons for this attitude, some of which also explain the behavior of nurses who do not want to inform. Informing takes time; patients then ask more questions, which require time and knowledge to answer. The worst possibility is that an informed patient may refuse the orders of the physician. The term "orders" is used deliberately here, since that is what they are called and that is how the physician perceives them. No physician wants orders disobeyed. Many do not even want their suggestions to be ignored. When either happens, problems occur. The nurse who assumes the role of advocate and informs patients runs the risk that the patient will bother the physician in some or all of the ways just mentioned. Such a development may not be looked on favorably by the physician. The nurse may be seen as a troublemaker who is either to be silenced or to be gotten rid of. How an advocate copes with these problems will be discussed in later chapters of this book. For now it suffices to say that of those who do not want patients to be informed, the physician usually leads the group. In addition physicians have the most power to reward or punish persons who inform patients.

The second group that may not want patients informed consists of nurses, other professionals, and hospital administrators. The members of this group may take their lead from the physician, but they also may have reasons of their own for withholding information. They all, in some measure, fear that they may suffer repercussions from the physician because of a nurse advocate's behavior—a sort of guilt by association. They fear being told that the advocate would not have done whatever he or she did, if they (being people with some measure of authority) had not either allowed it or encouraged it. They fear that physicians will ask the question "What are you going to do about *her*?" Other reasons why members of this group do not inform patients are more personal in nature and much like those of physicians: "The patient will ask questions, and that takes time; we may not have the answers, and that's terrible; the patient may refuse treatment, and that's a mess, for everyone." So the advocate will be told to mind his or her own business and shut up.

Other nurses sometimes do not want to take care of patients an advocate has taught, because those patients ask too many questions and want to do things their way rather than the nurses' way. "We haven't got time for that nonsense" is too often a nurse's reaction. An advocate's argument that the patient has a right to know can fall on deaf ears, especially when nurses are tired, short of help, and not up-to-date enough to answer patients questions. Advocates also hear nurses say, "If patients want to know so badly, let them ask their physicians, and if they don't know what to ask, well, that's okay. What you don't know can't hurt you." This attitude represents the most dangerous fallacy we have to deal with in the entire health care arena. It is totally opposed to everything we teach about how to stay healthy. Having such an attitude is like saying, "It's okay for you to know all that when you're away from us, but when you are here in the hospital you don't need to know, because we know. We will take care of you." But "taking care of" is not the same as "caring for," nor is taking responsibility for a life that is not one's own the same as caring for a person. Taking over decisions from others is the fastest way possible to create dependency and to slow the growth and development of responsible people, be they children or patients. We tend to confuse the categories of children and patients in our behavior in our institutions. It is sometimes difficult to tell, on the basis of a health professional's behavior, whether a patient is 4 years old or 40 years old.

The risks posed by other nurses, other professionals, and hospital administrators are obvious. You are asking them to take the time to answer questions and deal with potential noncompliance caused by your informing. On a deeper level you are going against the whole social system that governs how patients are viewed and therefore treated. The superficial reactions will consist of objections to the problems, often involving time, that you have created. But a deeper, unspoken reaction may be resentment at your unwillingness to concur in their complete rejection of patients as responsible people who can make their own decisions. Look at the way in which parents react to the independence of their children. Some fight it every inch of the way. Why then should the same situation not exist, even if on a subconscious basis, in the hospital environment, where patients are placed in a child's role? Reprisals against an advocate who questions this role can range from psychological and social isolation from a peer group to outright dismissal from an institution. The former occurs more often than the latter—probably because an isolated person is unable to tolerate the isolation for long, and quits the situation. I wonder how this phenomenon is related to the high staff turnover we see among better educated young nurses.

Families and friends constitute the third group that may not want patients to be properly informed. Family members and friends are grouped together for two reasons. First, some patients do not have families, only friends who are very close. Second, some patients have both family and friends. In such a situation, the two groups may be equally influential in their relationships with the patient. The reasons why family members and friends may not want a patient to be informed vary, but a common one is the desire, perhaps unconscious, to make decisions for another person, to keep him from growing into an independent person and not needing them. This phenomenon occurs in relationships between husbands and wives, parents and children (even grown children). It also happens all too frequently among friends. This fear of granting independence to another person is a powerful force. That independence does not mean a loss of love is unimportant; that we fear it will mean a loss of love is very important. Therefore woe to the person who seems to be taking someone from us. We have all experienced the wrath that results from this real or imagined fear.

Another reason why families and friends may not want information given to a patient is simple. They may not want to be bothered with the patient's questions, and they may want to avoid the problems that can result from the patient's noncompliance with treatments. You have heard family members or friends make statements such as "Come on, cut the hassle and just go ahead and get it over with" or "We have enough problems without you creating more" or "What are you paying them for? They know what is best for you." Such an attitude is characteristic of the "hurry up already" disease of our society, with the too frequently heard aftereffect represented by the question "Why didn't you tell me?" The risk here to a health professional falls into the category of absence of informed consent, with the result of "I'm suing because they didn't tell me what to expect; if they had, I'd have never agreed." That the blame may be equally shared between the patient and the professional does not have much effect in court. Informed consent is part of the law all professionals are expected to know and follow.

A third reason why family members or friends may not want information given to a patient is often not readily apparent. A family member or friend may want a patient to undergo a treatment or an operation for the family's sake, and not for the good of the patient. He may want to do anything to prolong the life of the loved one. The well-known Tuma case is an example. Jolene Tuma, a registered nurse, had an elderly female patient who was acutely ill with myelogenous leukemia, a cancer of the blood cells. The physician explained the need for chemotherapy, and its side effects, to the patient and her family. The patient agreed to take the drugs but later told Tuma about her negative feelings about taking them. Tuma told the patient about several alternative forms of treatment, one of which was the use of Laetrile. The patient asked Tuma to explain these treatments to her son. She did, but without informing the physician of what she was doing. The patient's son (Tuma says he was angry and fearful of the death of his mother) told the physician. The physician brought charges against Tuma with the state board of nursing, and Tuma was found guilty of "unprofessional conduct." After appeals Tuma was eventually cleared; the judge said the definition of what constituted "unprofessional conduct" was not clear in the board's guidelines. (Much has been written about this case. Several references dealing with it will be included in the readings listed at the end of this chapter for those who seek more details. These references include Tuma's letter in *Nursing Outlook* regarding the case.)

It seems the son wanted the mother to have chemotherapy for his sake. She did not want it. He thought it would prolong the mother's life, and he could not face losing her. His attitude was similar to the view that no matter how awful a person may feel as a result of treatment or surgery, any life at all is better than no life. In effect he was saying, "I cannot bear to lose you, even if you cannot bear to live." It would be too harsh to say that love is not involved in such an attitude; it is. But at best it seems rather selfish. However, is not much of love selfish? We all can identify with this kind of love and too often condone it in others as we condone it in ourselves. What needs to be said is that an advocate who *unknowingly* interferes in such a situation faces great risk.

What generally happens was demonstrated in the Tuma case when the nurse informed the patient of alternatives. The son immediately went to the physician and said, in effect, "Look what the nurse is doing not only to me but to you as well. She is usurping our authority and influence with Mother." Unfortunately, the physician heard that his authority was being usurped and did not listen to the deeper message—that the son had his own reasons for wishing his mother to undergo treatment. The physician then went about the procedure of making the nurse pay for her sins of advocacy.

This is one example of the risks an advocate can face in this type of situation. Other risks follow much the same theme, but with variations. The family member usually appeals to some authority to stop the nurse from telling the patient what he does not want the patient to hear. The risk to an advocate depends on whom the family member tells and on how that person in authority reacts to the information. Some hear only the complaint and go out immediately to act on it. They do not really listen with what is often called a "third ear." I call it thoughtful listening. In other words, they do not ask, either aloud or silently, "What is going on here? What lies behind this complaint? Exactly what is the situation?" Some accept the complaint as a true statement of fact and act on it; trouble usually arises from such a reaction. Others thoughtfully listen and investigate before acting. The latter response is safer for the advocate. In these situations the nature of the risks of advocacy depend on the knowledge and behavior of the advocate. His is not a defenseless position; his defense lies in knowing the potential risks.

A final problem involving family and friends (there are many others) is that posed by well-meaning and loving family members or friends who decide that a patient cannot deal with certain information. This situation is most often seen when a diagnosis of cancer is made. One wonders if the physician does not make the first mistake when he or she tells the family the diagnosis before telling the patient. The physician may not know the patient well enough, at that time, to decide what the person's strengths are; therefore he or she accepts the judgment of the family. Perhaps if physicians went by the rule that a person's diagnosis is his privileged information and that it is up to him to tell it or not to tell it to others, fewer of these problems would occur. But that generally does not happen. The family members usually wait to see the physician right after surgery, when the patient is still under the effects of anesthesia. They demand to be told all, and they often are told all. Their reaction is "Oh, don't tell Joe. He'll kill himself." Then the web of lies develop. Everyone sticks to the same story. For example, the patient is told by the physician, "We got it all, and the pain you are having now, six months later, is arthritis." This lie is maintained despite the fact that the patient is losing the ability to function and is dying. Nurses and others dodge the patient's questions by saying, "Ask your physician," and the physician continues the false story until the patient simply gives up and accepts it, even in the face of evidence to the contrary. Anyone who has lived with this kind of situation knows its horrors. It is certainly written and complained about enough.

The risks the advocate faces in telling a patient the truth are manifold. Nurses are told not to do so, and they are given reasons; the least valid reason is the one used most often. They are told, "If you tell the patient the truth, he won't be able to bear it and will commit suicide." This argument generally stops most people, despite the number of articles that declare that the suicide rate among knowledgeable terminal cancer patients does not differ from that of the population as a whole. The will to live is very strong, no matter for how long or under what conditions. Many books have been written about this desire to fight and to live.

There is a way in which you as an advocate can handle this situation, once the lie has developed and you are faced with a patient who keeps asking if they really "got it all" or if he has cancer. Rather than being driven to lying, you can refuse to answer the question directly. You can change the subject slightly and tell the patient that if he really does question the diagnosis, he should and must ask the physician outright and demand to see his chart. A patient who is determined to know will do whatever is necessary to find out. When a patient's will to know becomes apparent to a physician, he usually complies with the patient's request, realizing that he has been led astray by well-meaning family members. He recognizes that he has not assessed the will and desire of the patient well enough. This tactic usually works and is safe. I have never had a patient kill himself; instead, most patients and family members sigh with relief that honest communication has been restored and that they can now cope as a family unit. However, if the patient does not follow through and demand honesty, then you can assume he doesn't really want to know—and that, too, is his decision, whether we like it or not.

· · ·

It must be obvious to you by this time that the informing process is not simple. It involves many risks and ramifications, only a few of which have been mentioned. At this point let us move to a discussion of the supporting aspects of the role of advocate. There is a bridge between informing and supporting. It is the decision-making process of the client. Decision making will be dealt with in part in the discussion of supporting. It will be discussed further in the section on rescuing versus advocacy.

SUPPORTING AND ITS RISKS

Supporting requires several actions and some self-controlled non-actions. The actions fall into two main groups. The first consists of assuring a patient that a decision is his and that he has the right and responsibility to make it. In many cases this assurance is not necessary, since the patient will let you know that he has been making his own decisions all his life. Many people, however, either have not been in the habit of making decisions for themselves or have not had to face many major decisions. If a person with such a background becomes a patient, the habit is reinforced by the very nature of the patient role, which typically does not involve substantial amounts of decision making. Such a situation may put an advocate into a patient-teaching role. For example, a patient often will ask a nurse to make all decisions for him. Should he bathe before or after breakfast? Should he get up before or after the physician comes? Should he walk before or after the family comes? A nurse may even be asked to decide whether he should have milk or coffee with meals. If the advocate uses these situations to help the patient learn to make decisions, when the big decisions arrive the process will be easier. You might say in this case that advocacy is a combination of teaching and supporting. One of the problems is the same as a problem involved in informing: it is time-consuming to help patients learn to make decisions. It is faster and easier, at the time, to simply tell them what to do. It is only later that an advocate sees the results of, and benefits from, the time taken to have the patient make the decision. The benefit to the advocate is clear: the patient will have no one to blame but himself if the decision is not well made. That being a consequence of all decision making, it is easy to see why people may back away from decision making. Many of us do so all the time.

The reactions of others to your supporting patients, much less teaching them to make decisions, present an obvious risk. Fellow professionals, families, and others may prefer that patients remain dependent—especially when they are in the hospital. This desire to keep other people in the role of children, which was discussed in the section on informing, also poses risks to the advocate in the area of supporting. It is bad enough that you have rocked the boat by informing the patient, but now you are going to turn it over by supporting decisions the patient makes.

This leads directly into the second aspect of the action role: reassuring the patient that he does not have to give in to pressure from others to change his decisions if he does not choose to. This may mean that you have to interfere in the actions of others who are trying to undermine the client's confidence in his decision-making ability. Let me hasten to add here that preventing others from interfering with patients' decisions should be done very carefully and probably not at all, unless you are in a position of authority over the one doing the interfering. I might even go so far as to say it would be very poor judgment to attempt to deter a client's physician or family member from saying what he wants to say to the client. Do not forget that you are dealing with the physician's patient and the family member's relative. The prudent thing to do is simply to continue with your quiet but firm support of the patient in your own interactions with him. When you are not in a position of authority to interfere with the harassing behavior of others, if you do so you may be moving out of the advocacy role and into the rescuing role of fighting patients' battles for them. There is a big difference between governing the behavior of those who work under your direct supervision and governing the behavior of those who do not.

The second part of the supporting function is what I call the non-action part. It is often harder not to act than to act. This aspect of supporting demands that you keep yourself from subtly undermining a patient's decision—especially if it is a decision with which you do not agree. You must never nag or say, after the fact, when things go wrong, "See, I told you so." Also, you must not indicate in a nonverbal way that you are displeased with a decision. Nonverbal communication may be more important than verbal communication. How often have we said to ourselves, "Oh well, I may as well do it; I can't stand his sulking; I'll do it just to put an end to that behavior." Sulking, pouting, and silence are weapons we all use to get our own way; we do not refrain from such behavior easily just because we are professionals.

We are also generally not allowed to escape patients' decisions by saying, "I won't have anything more to do with them." There may be cases in which the situation is such a serious affront to a nurse that she must remove herself, but these are rare. It is better if a nurse can simply be honest with a patient and say, "I don't approve of your decision, but I do approve of your right to make it. It is that right I will respect and abide by." Such a statement can be used in a subtle way to undermine a decision, but it is better to have the nurse's position out in the open than to continue a silent battle with the patient. When I was recently a patient, I was being constantly nagged to stop smoking postoperatively, I finally had to tell my naggers to stop. I said that I knew they disapproved but that it was my decision and therefore my responsibility and that I would hear no more of it. They stopped. The word "responsibility" plus my firmness finally got through to them. There is no need to subject patients to this kind of harassment; they have enough problems without more being added. Once the responsibility of informing has been met, leave it and move into a supporting role. Approving of patients' decisions is not required by the advocacy role; you are required only to accept their right to make them.

Other people may try to pressure you into making a patient change his mind about a decision. They will want you to talk to the patient and convince him that he is wrong. This situation is especially likely to develop if you are the patient's nurse and have a close relationship with him. The risks involved in refusing to comply are again the same as those involved in the informing process. You will take the chance of alienating the physician, other professionals, and family members. They can seek retribution in any of the ways previously discussed, depending on how serious they perceive the situation to be. It is possible to cope with all these risks. But first you must be aware of them. (Coping will be discussed in Chapter 7.)

One other topic must be mentioned in connection with informing and supporting. In the literature it is called "value clarification." One article that discusses this subject as it affects the nursing role is "An Approach to Ethical Decision Making," by Muriel B. Ryden.[1] I suggest you look at this article because it presents a reverse perspective from mine. There are others who also hold a positive view of value clarification. This particular article is directed to the nurses' role in what appears to be an advocacy situation. It is in the advocate role that I object to the use of value clarification. The above-mentioned article describes the case of a patient who refused to have his pacemaker replaced. He said his wife had died and he was therefore lonely and had nothing to live for; so he chose not to prolong his life with a new pacemaker. This is where value clarification comes in. The article suggests that it becomes the role of the nurse to discuss with the patient the value he has placed on human life, his own in particular, that lead him to behave in the manner he does. What seems obvious is that others do not like, approve of, or accept the patient's decision. Rather than discuss or even argue with the decision per se, they go about this in a more subtle manner. They explore with the patient his values. Rather than attack the decision itself, they go at the underpinnings of the decision-making process. This tactic is very clever and certainly can be successful. It is used by many of us

[1]Muriel B. Ryden, "An Approach to Ethical Decision Making," *Nursing Outlook* 26, no. 11 (November 1978):705-706.

in all walks of life, even in the teaching profession. But in the teaching role one is not acting as the students' advocate but instead is engaged in teaching them something that is thought to be *right* for them to learn. However, the proponents of value clarification will deny that they are teaching values; rather, they say, they are only helping a client to clarify the values he already has. It is necessary in the assessment process for an advocate to have an open mind and to understand and be understanding of others' values. That is very different from engaging in an almost psychotherapeutic dialogue with a client to help him clarify his values. There is a fine line between clarification and subtle manipulation; I wonder how often it is crossed.

The professional nurse makes an assessment of a patient in terms of where he has been, where he is now, and where he wants to be in the future. The nurse discusses the patient's situation with him and explains his options concerning medications, procedures, and so on. When a nurse has done these things, he or she has more than fulfilled the advocacy role with the patient—without engaging in what might turn out to be subtle manipulations of the patient's decision-making process. From what I can gather from the situation described in the Ryden article, this may not have been the case. The client may have made a decision without having adequate information. The fact that a client has not been given adequate information does not justify a nurse's assuming the posture of a value clarifier. Rather the nurse simply does an adequate assessment of the client and supplies any information he has not received or corrects misinformation. One may call this hair-splitting, but using great subtlety to influence the decisions of others often is hardly distinguishable from what some may call simple information giving. For example, how often have we said, "What do you mean Joe decided that? I know Joe; he would never make that decision. What did you say to him?" The typical response is, "Nothing, I just gave him the facts." Then when we go to see Joe, we find that something other than a little fact giving occurred. It is this type of situation that the advocate must be on guard against. Value clarification in the advocacy role carries with it too much of the "I know best" posture of all professionals. The value clarifier is, in effect, saying, "If he only knew what I know, he would never have made that decision." Maybe he would have; maybe he would not have. A sense of personal integrity in respecting the free will and guarding the decision-making process of others is the greatest weapon advocates have in restraining themselves from exerting undue influence on the decisions others make.

RESCUING VERSUS ADVOCACY

For persons in the so-called helping professions, advocacy is psychologically very difficult. It is almost in direct conflict with their image of themselves as people who "know best"—experts who are paid to know and to make decisions based on their "superior" knowledge. They more often than not see themselves as the rescuers of mankind or at least that portion of mankind that is sick and in need of rescuing. The very fact that clients come to them for help reinforces this image. They say, "But we are only trying to help them." The rescuers then put themselves in the position of making decisions for others; the bottom line is that they end up accepting the responsibility for the decisions. This fact is often displeasing to professionals; they try to ignore it. They are all too willing to make the decisions, but they are not equally willing to accept responsibility for having done so. They attempt to "weasel out" by saying, "Well, you had a choice" or even worse, "You gave permission." They even obtain permission in writing and then say it is proof of free choice on the client's part. Not only does making decisions for others rob them of their responsibilities and rights, but it also places the professional in the very awkward position of being blamed if all does not come out well. Since most of us inherently know this, we attempt to have clients make the decisions we want them to make, under the guise of having done so themselves.

We are only fooling ourselves if we believe that clients do not know what is going on. Fooling ourselves may be alright if all goes well, but seldom does all go well. When it is possible for something to go wrong, it seems that it often does go wrong—as Murphy's Law predicts. Then when clients blame us we act startled and surprised and say, "How can you blame me?" Furthermore, we accuse them, either openly or silently, of being ungrateful—never admitting for one minute that we got ourselves into the mess by our insistence of the "we know best" attitude.

This type of conflict has been discussed in the literature and labeled the "games triangle" or Karpman's triangle.[2]

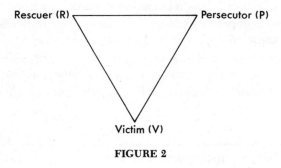

Rescuer (R)   Persecutor (P)

Victim (V)

FIGURE 2

[2]S.B. Karpman, "Script Drama Analysis," *Transactional Analysis Bulletin* 7, no. 26 (1968):39-43.

It is shown in Fig. 2 as the rescuer-victim-persecutor triangle. Karpman developed the concept out of his knowledge of games, the major roles played in gaming, and the fluidity in the changing of roles. How the process works will be demonstrated by example. A two-person example will be presented first. Keep in mind, as indicated in Fig. 3, that a person can move from role to role—from rescuer to victim to persecutor and back again.

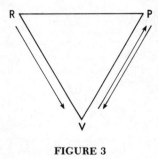

FIGURE 3

The victim is a 67-year-old female patient who turns on her signal light at 3:00 AM and yells, "Help, help, I can't breathe, I have pain." A nurse-rescuer runs to her room to help. When the nurse gets there, the patient says, "It's okay now, it went away." This behavior is repeated each night, and sometimes it occurs more than once a night. The nurse begins to see herself not as the rescuer of patients in distress (Fig. 4) but as a victim who is being persecuted by a patient (Fig. 5).

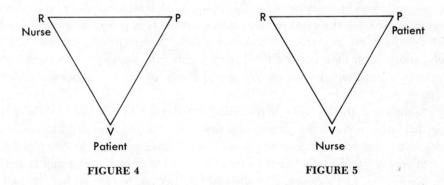

FIGURE 4   **FIGURE 5**

No one wants to be a victim—especially a nurse who sees herself as a rescuer. Therefore the nurse finally tells herself, "I'm going to put a stop to this nonsense." So the next time it happens the nurse tells the patient, "You had better stop this behavior because no one is going to rush to answer your light. If you don't stop, when you are really in trouble you will receive no help at all." The patient cries and says, "No one understands me." The nurse leaves the room triumphant that she has gotten out of the role of victim but somewhat disturbed that she has now assumed the role of persecutor and made the patient a victim (see Fig. 6).

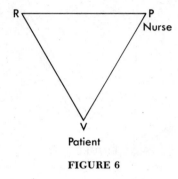

FIGURE 6

The nurse, who is a rescuer by choice, had not liked seeing herself in the position of a victim, but in her attempt to extricate herself from this position she has assumed an even worse one—persecutor of the very person she had seen herself as rescuing.

The role changes in the triangle rarely stop. The plight of the nurse brings her to the point of having to ask for help herself. So she may call in a third person. The judgment and knowledge of the third person determine whether he or she also becomes involved in the game or, seeing that a game is in progress, stands outside it and helps the nurse to extract both herself and the patient from the game. Unfortunately, more often than not the third person gets into the game as a rescuer, and then further position changes ensure that a three- or even four-person game develops.

Staying with the same hypothetical situation, let's examine a three-person game that could occur if the patient acts first, because she does not like the victim role. Assume that one morning the patient, not wanting to be told to stop playing her game of crying "wolf," tells her physician that the nurse had been cruel to her the night before and, furthermore, that she had told her not to turn on her light all the time when she was short of breath and in pain. The physician, taking this as a statement of fact, becomes irate because of the nurse's gross lack of consideration for patients and her obvious incompetence. He reports her to her supervisor and wants her disciplined for her behavior. (See Figs. 7 and 8.)

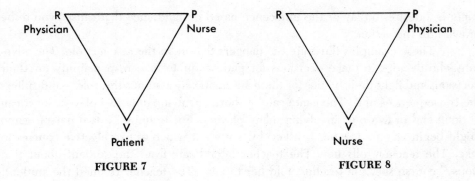

FIGURE 7   FIGURE 8

The supervisor tells the nurse of the situation and lets her explain her behavior—a development that may not always occur. In this case the supervisor chooses to identify with the nurse; she may see herself more as a rescuer of nurses than of physicians or patients, believing that the nurse is being victimized not only by the patient but also by the physician. She has two options. She can tell the physician that the patient had lied and therefore made a fool of him, or she can enlist others above her to do so. In either case the physician then sees himself as a victim—of either the patient (the situation that the supervisor hopes for) or the nurses, but nevertheless a victim (see Fig. 9).

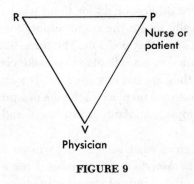

FIGURE 9

Now the same situation that existed for the nurse in Figs. 5 and 8 exists for the physician. He, too, does not want to be a victim; no one really does. So he will act to remove himself from the position, with his actions depending on whom he identifies as the cause of his situation.

The preceding examples allow you to see the game. You can see that any number can play and that the roles are constantly changing. All it takes to enter the game is a desire to play or the innocence based on ignorance that causes you to be drawn into the action.

These examples illustrate the dangers that lie in the rescuer role. The advocate who decides to make decisions for patients or to take responsibility for their decisions and fight their battles for them automatically assumes this role—and suffers the consequences of it. The game can be short, involving only two players, or it can be long and drawn out, involving many players. For example, a two-person game might begin when a teacher is asked by a student which of two elective courses to take. The teacher tells her. The teacher later hears from the student about that "lousy" course she, the teacher, told her to take. The teacher rescued the student, because she "knows best," and made the decision. She later becomes a victim because the student finds the decision not to her liking. The Tuma case involves many players. When Tuma agrees to talk to the son for the mother (I call this fighting the mother's battles), the son calls in the physician, who then calls in the state board of nursing to punish Tuma. The number of players then increases further. Tuma not only calls on the nursing world to defend her but goes to court and appeals court and finally is vindicated for her act of advocacy (or was it rescuing?). These two examples illustrate the well-meaning rescuer role and its results. The game that can ensue can be relatively simple, with little risk involved, or very complex, with great expense and risk involved.

The teacher willingly and maybe even eagerly accepted the role of knowing best and made the decision. The bottom line in both examples is the same—whenever you make decisions for others, or do for them what they should be doing for themselves, you automatically accept the responsibility for the results. In the advocacy role a nurse never gets into this position. The thing that the nurse, as advocate, must keep uppermost in mind is that clients must make choices freely. If nurses do not allow clients to do so, they are not engaging in advocacy as I use the word; they are rescuing. The rescuer role has no place in the life of a professional, except when a client is too young (for example, an infant) or in a coma, and thus is unable to make a decision.

I am sure that much of what I am saying will go against the grain of many professionals' concepts of themselves and their roles. Free will is something to which we give a great deal of lip service but seldom deeply believe in and act on. The "we know best" theme is something we have been taught as children; our parents practiced it with us, and many parents continue to practice it even when their children are 40 or 50 years old. It is reinforced in the school systems, and then if one enters the helping professions it is reinforced again and becomes almost second nature. To be an advocate, as a nurse, requires a reorientation and a constant care not to slip into the "we know best" attitude. It also requires an element of faith—faith in the ability of human beings to make their own decisions and even more in their right to do so.

•   •   •

Advocacy is so important that not only should articles, books, and college courses be devoted to the subject, but continuing education workshops should be created for the nurses who are working with clients every day. One of the current major drives in nursing is not only to enhance nurses' image in consumers' eyes but to correct misconceptions about what nurses really do. Part of this effort has been to encourage nurses to be consumer and patient advocates. But, as I have stated before, nursing educators have neglected to tell nurses how to do so. By now it ought to be obvious to you the reader that this has indeed been a serious omission. Working in high-drama areas such as intensive care units is safer than being at a patient's side acting as an advocate. However, the paradox is that although there is danger in being an advocate, there is equal danger in not being one, since you as a professional are held accountable for what you do as well for what you do not do. The key to the paradox and the secret to success lie in knowing—having the knowledge necessary to fulfill your professional responsibilities.

About now you may be saying to yourself, "This sounds all very grand, but obtaining all this knowledge also sounds very difficult; I'm not sure about this business of being an advocate." Let me assure you that having knowledge and knowing are not as difficult as they may seem to be. Some people may like you to think they are, so that you will become discouraged and they will continue to know more than you do. As you have already seen, there is power in knowledge—and who wants to share power? Be reassured and read on. Knowing is not difficult; in fact, it can be fun.

Systems analysis, the subject of Chapter 3, is an area of the knowledge base that is of vital importance to you, so do not be turned off by the fancy title. In essence, systems analysis is a way of finding out what you need to know in order to predict and avoid risks in the advocacy process.

NOTES ON CHAPTER 2

Articles by Donahue and Abrams provide opposing views on the subject of nurses as patients' advocates. Donahue, on the "pro" side, speaks of the need for nurses to be motivated, skillful, and knowledgeable as the key to being a patient's advocate. She also speaks of the need for nurses to assert their right to be advocates. Abrams, in the "con" article, presents five possible models for advocacy and discusses each. She points out the risks in the role and questions whether it is appropriate for the nurse to be the one to defend the rights and best interests of the patient. It is obvious from these two articles that the role of advocate is not defined the same way by everyone.

Donahue, Patricia M. "The Nurse, A Patient Advocate?" *Nursing Forum* 17, no. 2 (1978):143-151.
Abrams, Natalie. "A Contrary View of the Nurse as Patient Advocate." *Nursing Forum* 17, no. 3 (1978):259-267.

An excellent essay on the role of the nurse as patient advocate has been written by Van Kempen. She defines advocacy in a way not dissimilar to the theme of this book. She provides a sketch of the sociohistorical development of the role of advocate, gives case examples of advocacy, and provides a list of advantages and disadvantages of the role. Her overall attitude is that the nurse should be the patient advocate as well as the educator who informs the health care system about this role.

Van Kempen, Shelly. "The Nurse as Client Advocate." In Clark, Carolyn Chambers, and Shea, Carole A. *Management in Nursing—A Vital Link in the Health Care System.* New York: McGraw-Hill Book Co., 1979, pp. 184-197.

Another article that supports the idea of the nurse as patient advocate, but that is geared more to the community and to the need for nurses to become involved in the social-political environment, is done by Kosik. She believes advocacy is the moral obligation of everyone in the health care system, but she shows how the nurse is often in the best position, or the primary position, to make a difference.

Kosik, Sandra Henry. "Patient Advocacy, or Fighting the System." *American Journal of Nursing* 72 (April 1972):694-698.

In the area of information control, client autonomy, and patients' rights to information, numerous articles have been written by nurses, physicians, theologians, and lawyers, just to mention a few. The three I have selected relate to client autonomy versus paternalism. Dworkin's article deals with free choice and is ethically oriented, relying on Mill for his arguments. Payton's article is a simpler one, and it is easier to locate. Payton draws on Dworkin's work. A short article dealing with helping patients grow in decision-making ability is that done by Braden and Price.

Dworkin, Gerald. "Paternalism." *The Monist* 56 (January 1972):64-84.
Payton, Rita Jean. "Information Control and Autonomy." *Nursing Clinics of North America* 14, no. 1 (March 1979):230-233.
Braden, Carrie Jo, and Price, Joseph L. "Encouraging Client Self Discovery." *American Journal of Nursing* 76, no. 3 (March 1976):444-446.

Articles on information control within the specific area of patients' medical records vary in the positions they express, and the types of people who speak out on the subject also vary greatly. Shenken and Warner say that making records available to patients will improve the system.

Sehnken, Budd N., and Warner, David C. "Giving the Patient His Medical Record: A Proposal to Improve the System." *The New England Journal of Medicine* 289 (Sept. 27, 1973):688-692.

The next article speaks of the benefit of giving patients their records in the rehabilitative process.

Golodetz, Arnold, Ruess, Johanna, and Milhous, Raymond. "The Right to Know: Giving the Patient His Medical Record." *Archives of Physical Medicine and Rehabilitation* 57 (February 1976): pp. 78-81.

In the following article, a young student nurse speaks out on the issue from her experience as a patient.

Casoly, Rose Marie. "Give the Patient His Due." *American Journal of Nursing* 72, no. 6 (June 1972):1101.

Halberstam speads of the physician's right to the privacy of his or her notes—in other words, the patient's chart.

Halberstam, Michael J. "The Patient's Chart is None of the Patient's Business." *Modern Medicine* 44 (Nov. 1, 1976):85-88.

Westin, in *Hasting Center Report*, writes about the legalities involved in the issue and offers some possible models of compromise.

Westin, Alan. "Medical Records: Should Patients Have Access? A Proposal for Dual Record Keeping." *Hastings Center Report* 7 (December 1977):23-28.

Finally, for those deeply interested in the subject, there is McIntosh's article. It is a review of the literature on information control and information seeking, as they relate to cancer, but it covers many areas. The article deals with many studies on all aspects of the problem, and McIntosh furnishes the reader with a huge list of references. The article is followed by an interesting comment by Parkes, a social psychiatrist. Parts of the article deal with why physicians do not inform patients.

McIntosh, Jim. "Process of Communication, Information Seeking and Control Associated with Cancer: A Selective Review of the Literature." *Social Science and Medicine* 8 (1974):167-187.

Any number of articles have been written on the Tuma case. I will mention only four: Tuma's original letter to the editor of *Nursing Outlook*, two articles by a lawyer relating to the case, and a reaction to the case as it relates to ethics. These four pieces should bring most of the facts of the case to the reader.

Tuma, Jolene L. Letter to the Editor. *Nursing Outlook* 25, no. 9 (September 1977):546.
Gargaro, William J. "The Tuma Case." *Cancer Nursing* 1, no. 4 (August, 1978):329-330.
Gargaro, William J. "Update on Tuma Case." *Cancer Nursing* 1, no. 6 (December 1978):467-468.
Stanley, Sister A. Teresa. "Is it Ethical to Give Hope to a Dying Person?" *Nursing Clinics of North America* 14, no. 1 (March 1979):69-80.

Material on Karpman's "games triangle" and on the rescuer role can be found in several sources, including the following.

Karpman, S.B. "Script Drama Analysis." *Transactional Analysis Bulletin* 7, no. 26 (April 1968):39-43.
Steiner, Claude M. *Scripts People Live*. New York: Grove Press, Inc., 1974.

Also, Eric Berne's book, *Games People Play*, should be a must on all advocates' reading lists.

One final reference may not be readily available to readers. In this book, Renee Fox has written a chapter entitled "Training for Uncertainty." Fox mentions two things that I would like to share. The subject of the chapter is the training of young student physicians, and the chapter speaks of the uncertainty that lies in the practice of medicine, especially in the diagnosis and treatment realms. Fox says there are "two types of uncertainty that may be recognized. The first results from incomplete mastery of available knowledge. No one can have at his command all skills and all knowledge of the lore of medicine. The second depends upon limitations in current medical knowledge. There are innumerable questions to which no physician, however well trained, can as yet provide answers. A yet third source of uncertainty derives from the first two. This consists of the difficulty in distinguishing between personal ignorance or ineptitude and the limitations of present medical knowledge." Though this is being said regarding medicine, it can as easily be said about nursing, and advocacy. It is this uncertainty that we must live with and not be afraid to admit to with our patients, if open communication is desired.

In discussing the perceptive powers of physicians, Fox says, "We see only what we look for, we look for only what we know, the famous Goethe axiom goes." One might well paraphrase this warning, for the nurse and the advocate, as follows: "We hear only what we listen to, and we listen to only what we want to hear." Fox talks about narrowing one's scope in an attempt to try to narrow the areas of one's uncertainty. This is understandable, but for the advocate, the risk is greater, if the scope of his or her knowledge is narrow. The advocate must learn to live with the uncertainty. It is about the only sure thing one can predict in the realm of human behavior.

Merton, R.K., Reader, G., and Kendall, P.L., ed. *Student-Physician*. Cambridge: Harvard University Press, 1957, pp. 207-241.

Chapter 3

SYSTEMS ANALYSIS

I AM USING THE TERM "SYSTEMS ANALYSIS" in its simplest sense. By "system" I mean self, other people, or groups of people, such as organizations. By "analysis" I mean the process of discovering the attitudes, values, and beliefs of people and groups. What are their stated and unstated goals? How do these goals relate to their behavior?

This chapter will follow the organization of a systems analysis assignment that students are asked to complete in the early part of the advocacy course at New York University. The assignment was designed by Dr. Patricia Fry, Professor in the Division of Nursing at New York University, and then added to by me. It is meant to teach the process of examining the systems of self and immediate others, and the larger system of which all are a part. It demonstrates the interrelatedness of all three systems based on the goals of the person doing the analysis. Also included in this chapter is a chart that illustrates the process in a slightly different way. Most students find it easier to understand the chart if they have read and discussed the assignment first. The assignment requires the student to write an essay, according to the following guidelines.

Title: *Assessment of the Self and Work Systems and Their Interrelationship*

Identify two of your professional goals. Discuss how these goals are consistent or inconsistent with your personality style and how they all communicated to other people. How do you rate yourself in terms of Rollo May's concept of pseudo-innocence? Support your statements by referring to May. Define and discuss the focal system (that is, the work system) you have chosen in terms of the stated and unstated goals of the persons in it, and describe the communication patterns within the system. Briefly define the ecological system of which the focal system is a part. Describe the ethics of the self, focal, and ecological systems in terms of John Gardner's concept of egalitarianism versus libertarianism. Discuss and explain the functionality of your goals (for example, do areas of conflict exist?)

Grading criteria*

Two goals	10
Consistency with personality	5
How communicated	5
Pseudo-innocent rating of communication	10
Define focal system	5
Goals stated and unstated	15
Communication within system	5
Define ecological system	5
Social ethics of systems	
Ethic of self system	5
Ethic of focal system	5
Ethic of ecological system	5
Discuss and explain functionality of your goals (areas of conflict among focal system, goals, ethics, etc.)	15
Standard of written work—includes documentation, bibliography, relevance of sources, form, clarity, organization of ideas, and grammar	10
	100

*Included here for the benefit of teachers of advocacy.

GOALS OF SELF AND CONSISTENCY WITH PERSONALITY

Identifying and evaluating your goals constitute probably the most difficult part of systems analysis. Most people are not in the habit of setting conscious goals that they can work toward. Rather they have a vague sense of what they are doing and where they want to go. Some do not even have a vague sense of where they want to go, much less why.

Therefore it is at this point that the real work begins—with an assessment of self in order to define your professional goals. A three-step approach that nurses use for patient assessment works fairly well in assessing your self system. First, where are you coming from? In other words, what has gone on in your past to bring you where you are today? What have you done? How have you done it? Why have you done it? Second, where are you now? What is going on now in your professional life, and how do you feel about it? What changes, if any, do you want to make? Third, where do you want to go? This step arises directly out of the second step; the answer to this question becomes your goal. For example, your goal may be to become a patient's advocate, to help or teach others to be patient's advocates, or simply to persuade others to accept your role as an advocate.

Now you have a goal. You must next examine this goal to see if it is consistent with your personality.

Many of us set goals that are not consistent with our personalities. We frequently do not even stop to ask ourselves whether our goals are consistent with our personalities. For example, a person decides to go to school and take two courses while working full time. He therefore must have time to read and study, usually in the evenings or on weekends. This person needs to ask himself if he is the type of person who enjoys learning and reading enough to give up part of his social life for them. Can he stick to it week in and week out? If going to school is expensive, can he give up other things to pay for it? I could go on and on, but the point is that this person must examine his goal before he goes to school. Take a simpler example. A person decides three weeks before Christmas or Easter break that he wants to get away to a warmer climate for a week. At that point he may discover any or all of the following: the planes are booked, he does not have the money, or he cannot spare the time because of work he had saved to do during the break. When asked if the idea of getting away during the break had occurred to him earlier, he says, "Oh yes, I know that I always feel the need at that time of year." However, he had never examined this need in terms of a goal and what he may have to do to make the goal a reality. I might even speculate that planning ahead to meet a need is not consistent with his personality: he does not plan, and needs therefore are not met.

If your goal is to be an advocate, then the examination of this goal, as it relates to your personality, will mean that you must look at everything involved in informing and supporting—the risks as well as the rewards. You must also examine what it may mean to you as a professional person, both in your own eyes and in the eyes of others, if you do not act as an advocate. The informing and supporting process was discussed in detail in the preceding chapter. At this point review that process in relation to your own personality. If that process and your personality are not compatible, in what way are they not compatible? Can this situation be changed in some way to allow you to fulfill the role of advocate? Remember—we are not doomed to continue our lives in the same way we have in the past. We can change. Whether we do will depend on our ability to make an honest assessment of a situation and thus to identify the change needed and on whether we see the situation that would result from the change as being more desirable than the situation that exists now. The success of a change must come from our own desire for self-improvement, not only from a desire to please others. Others are not always with us, but we are always with ourselves. It is true that a support system is very important in helping a person to change, but we should seek one that has some enduring quality.

Now that your goal or goals have been identified—and examined in terms of their compatibility with your personality—one other area of the self system needs to be explored—the way you communicate.

COMMUNICATION AND PSEUDO-INNOCENCE

When we establish goals, it is frequently necessary that we communicate them to other people, especially if they will affect other people. Surreptitious behavior is rarely a successful means of achieving a goal. Such behavior may function very well if the goal or the action involved in achieving the goal does not have any great effect on others, but when it does this type of behavior rarely works to our advantage. The goal of being an advocate, and all that it entails, does involve others. Therefore communication of this goal is necessary. But how do we communicate? Most of us, if asked, would say, "Why, we communicate very openly and honestly." That statement really is not true. We need only to look at most of the major problems in the world to see that it is not true. Communication breakdown is one of the most common problems we face today. It occurs on the international and national levels, within families, and in all the systems in between. It is therefore worthwhile to assess our own communication patterns and what they mean in terms of the achievement of goals.

Communication is a broad and detailed field of study in itself, and much has been written about it. One book that I believe is particularly profound is Rollo May's *Power and Innocence*. May makes some excellent observations about power, communication, and innocence.

May believes that we think of power in only its negative forms, rather than seeing it as the birthright of all human beings. He sees power as the source of a person's self-esteem, which he defines as the knowledge that one is significant. May believes that when we are confronted with our powerlessness, we often deal with it as if it were a virtue. We consciously divest ourselves of power and consider it a virtue not to have it. May calls this stance "pseudo-innocence," which he distinguishes from "authentic innocence."[1]

May describes authentic innocence as follows:

> . . . innocence as a quality of imagination, the innocence of the poet or artist. It is the preservation of childlike clarity in adulthood. Everything has a freshness, purity, newness, and color. From this innocence spring awe and wonder. It leads toward spirituality; it is the innocence of Saint Francis in his Sermon to the Birds. Assumedly it is what Jesus had in mind when He said: "Only as ye become like little children shall ye enter the kingdom of heaven." It is the preservation of childlike attitudes into maturity without sacrificing the realism of one's perception of evil, or as Arthur Miller puts it, one's "complicity with evil."[2]

May says that pseudo-innocence, on the other hand, is the kind of innocence "which does not lead to spirituality but rather consists of blinders." He describes it as follows:

> Capitalizing on naiveté, it consists of a childhood that is never outgrown, a kind of fixation on the past. It is childishness rather than childlikeness. When we face questions too big and too horrendous to contemplate, such as the dropping of the atomic bomb, we tend to shrink into this kind of innocence and make a virtue of powerlessness, weakness, and helplessness. This pseudo-innocence leads to utopianism; we do not then need to see the real dangers. With unconscious purpose we close our eyes to reality and persuade ourselves that we have escaped it. This kind of innocence does not make things bright and clear, as does the first kind; it only makes them seem simple and easy. It wilts before our complicity with evil. It is this innocence that cannot come to terms with the destructiveness in one's self or others; and hence, as with Billy Budd, it actually becomes self-destructive. Innocence that cannot include the daimonic becomes evil.[3]

May likens this kind of innocence to that seen in neurosis: "Often the only strategy available to such persons, learned by necessity in childhood, consists of accepting the overt powerlessness their situation requires and then getting their power by covert means."[4]

It does not take a great deal of imagination to see this type of innocence

---

[1]Rollo May, *Power and Innocence* (New York: W. W. Norton & Co., Inc., 1972.), p. 48.
[2]*Ibid.*, pp. 48-49.
[3]*Ibid.*, pp. 49-50.
[4]*Ibid.*, p. 50.

operational in nursing. Nurses who accept what they believe to be a state of power-lessness revert to covert means of manipulating physicians to get what they want, rather than communicating in an open, honest, factual manner on the basis of the power of their professional knowledge. Such manipulation is what May calls a "common defense against admitting or confronting one's own power."[5] An even more common situation is the way many women deal with their husbands to get what they want. It can be called the "Not tonight honey, I'm too tired" method.

When one looks at the totality of advocacy, its concomitant risks and hazards, and the dearth of information concerning the subject, the stern admonishment to go and be an advocate cannot help but seem to represent a pseudo-innocent attitude—a "denial of danger," a "closing of the eyes to reality," a "utopia" where all "seems simple and easy," to quote May. It is within this framework of the denial of reality and covert means of using power that advocates find themselves. They know they have power based on their professional knowledge. They are concerned about the welfare of other people, and they have the desire to communicate with them. To quote a bit more from May: "That power and love are interrelated is proved most of all by the fact that one must have power within oneself to be able to love in the first place."[6] "We would not communicate unless we valued the other, considered him worth talking to, worth the effort to make our ideas clear." He calls this positive desire to reach out to others "communicating without talking down, without patronizing."[7] It is quite obvious that pseudo-innocent behavior and covert communication have no place in the life of the advocate. In fact, it is highly doubtful that a pseudo-innocent person could ever be an advocate. May suggests this when he says, "Innocence as a shield from responsibility is also a shield from growth. It protects us from new awareness and from identifying with the suffering of mankind as well as with the joys, both of which are shut off from the pseudo-innocent person."[8]

Therefore it well behooves you as a potential advocate to examine the process of how you communicate your goals to others and the way this process may affect your patterns of behavior. Do you see yourself as having power based on your professional knowledge? Do you accept this power and its potential to enhance your ability to care for others? Are you willing to communicate from this power base in order to transmit your goals in a manner that makes them clear and understandable to others? Are you willing to discuss, to talk to other people rather than talk down to them? As a nurse, you must admit to the reality of the general image of powerlessness that nurses have. If you are a woman, you must admit that you may be considered powerless for that reason also. But images can be changed and are being changed. Remember, however, that a change may be tested by others, to see if it is real. That

[5]*Ibid.*
[6]*Ibid.*, p. 114.
[7]*Ibid.*, p. 247.
[8]*Ibid.*, p. 64.

is all part of the reality you must see, accept, live with, and deal with every day.

May's concepts of innocence and power are extremely relevant to the world of the nurse and to the lack of reality that I see in nurses when they deal with the subject of advocacy. I urge you to read May's book in its entirety. It can help you a great deal in understanding yourself and others. His discussion of language, language behavior, and the use of words is excellent. Consider, for example, this observation: "Language arises from an underlying web of potentiality for understanding, an emphatic tie between people, a shared structure, a capacity to identify with another."[9] Since the advocate's prime medium of communication is language, the more you know about its use and misuse the more successful you will be in your role.

Let's now assume that you have learned the steps involved in the analysis of self and your communication system, especially in terms of your communication needs in the advocacy role. We can then move on to an analysis of the focal system.

FOCAL SYSTEM; GOALS STATED AND UNSTATED

The focal system is made up of the people you directly deal with every day, on a regular basis. For example, if you are a staff nurse, your focal system will include the other nurses working in the unit, your direct supervisor, and the physician you may be dealing with in a particular advocacy situation—in other words, anyone who may be directly involved in your achievement of a particular goal on a particular day. This group of people may differ depending on the goal. Some use the term "significant others" to describe the members of a focal system.

The stated goals of the members of this group are the reasons they openly give for being involved or employed as they are. Nurses may say that they want to deliver the best nursing care possible. The physician may want to cure all patients. The patient may want to get well as quickly as possible. The supervisor may want to help the nurses on her staff. Generally, the stated goals are the obvious ones expected of a person in a particular role—or, one might say, the socially acceptable ones. There are situations in which this may not be true: a patient may say he wants to die, a nurse that she wants to find a physician to marry, a physician that he wants to make money, or a supervisor that she wants to keep the peace. When people speak in this way, they are either praised for their candor or accused of blunt selfishness. Most people keep such goals quiet, and they therefore fall into the category of unstated goals. Stated goals are the ones that are open and known to all. They are not difficult to discover, because they are stated and frequently restated to all who want to listen. However, the degree to which they are actually operative will vary.

Unstated goals are rarely admitted, but they are generally the ones that most

[9]*Ibid.*, p. 66.

determine a person's behavior. Because they do have the greatest effect on behavior, they are the most important ones to know. The nurse who says she wants to give the best care possible may silently be saying, "But not if it interferes with my coffee break, lunch hour, quitting time, or weekends." It does not take long for an astute observer to discover these unstated goals. The physician who says he wants to cure all patients, when he really means all who can afford him, is soon found out because of the nature of his clientele and the time he devotes to them. The patient who says he wants to get well as soon as possible, but contributes nothing to the process and in fact makes his condition worse, is easily spotted. Finally, the supervisor who says she wants to help her staff nurses—but adds silently, "only if they don't make waves"—is also easily detected.

Thus, the fact that goals are unstated does not mean they are completely hidden. Usually the person they are most hidden from and the person who will deny them the most is the person who has them. That, perhaps is what makes unstated goals most dangerous. There is no way you can openly confront a person about them, in honest communication, unless you are in a position of authority over him. Even then it is difficult. It becomes a "shape up or ship out" dictum, which does little to change the goals and only encourages the person to disguise them more effectively. If you do not have the authority to neutralize the effects of these goals directly or to use them to your advantage, you must find other ways to deal with them.

Let's take the example of the supervisor who does not want the nurses to make waves. If she sees the advocate's role as a wave-making situation, she will not support a nurse advocate at all. However, if the nurse can convince her that not acting as an advocate will result in bigger waves and will reflect directly on the supervisor, especially if a lawsuit should occur because of the absence of informed consent, then the nurse may make a great support person out of the supervisor. The double-edged sword can cut two ways—it's all in knowing how to swing it. Some may call this manipulation; others call it analysis of systems and use of the resulting knowledge in the most productive way possible. You cannot always directly engage people in doing the right thing if they have hidden fears about it, but you can indirectly engage them by means of a knowledgeable demonstration of what greater fear and danger may result if they do not act properly. The only question that remains is the rightness or wrongness of what it is you want others to do or not to do. (I am assuming that advocacy and the protection of the rights of others fall on the good side.)

I cannot emphasize enough how important an awareness of other people's unstated goals is to success in advocacy. But as an advocate you must also know your own stated and unstated goals, and you must examine them in relationship to each other. You will encounter enough conflict with others without having to face it in yourself as well. If you have the unstated goal of being well liked by your peers and by other professionals, then you must consider whether this goal is compatible with being an advocate. You must be knowledgeable enough in the advocate role to be able to guard against the risks involved and thus to accomplish both your stated and your unstated goals. If you are not knowledgeable enough, you will be asked, in May's words, "Harmless as doves you are, but where is your wisdom of serpents?"[10]

So knowing yourself and understanding the people you work with (and knowing how to cope with them in an effective manner) are equally vital. Assessment always goes before action. It dictates the action we take, how we take it, when, and why. The fact that advocates must live in a world characterized by ever-increasing speed and a narcissistic emphasis on instant gratification means that they must have a great deal of self-discipline in the assessment stage. Despite what some people may believe about the atmosphere of life-and-death situations that supposedly exists in hospitals and the need for instant decisions and actions, this atmosphere is more often a fantasy rather than a reality. More often than not, this atmosphere is a creation of the people who work in these institutions rather than a result of the conditions of the patients. The assessment process in the advocacy role cannot allow itself to be victimized by such an atmosphere. It is a pseudo-innocent stance to accept the fantasy and be pushed into instant decisions. The reality that we generally have the time to think, assess, explain, and decide can be difficult to see, but we must see it if we are to avoid making patients into victims.

Advocates cannot allow themselves to become a part of the "if I had only known" or "if we had only taken the time to think" group. I cannot help but be reminded of the type of person who wants me to hurry so he can get off work at 4:00 PM. When asked where he is going and what he will be doing, he replies, "Well, nowhere special" and "Nothing in particular," but how he rushes to go nowhere and do nothing! This common syndrome of the age we live in represents almost a denial of the life of the present for the sake of the future, which will also be denied when we get there, because it will then have become the present. One of the best ways to learn about the preciousness of the time we have now is to work with the dying. They know the value of time all too well. One might ask then, "Why don't the people who work in hospitals know this best, since they have the greatest contact with the dying?" The answer is quite simple. We live in a time and a culture that deny death, and this denial exists at its height in our hospitals, among the people who are closest to it. A sad paradox. One might call our time "The Age of Pseudo-Innocence."

COMMUNICATION WITHIN FOCAL SYSTEM

Every focal system has a communication system that is unique to it. A hospital may have 20 or more patient units, with the communication system varying

[10]*Ibid.*, p. 56.

from one unit to another. And each communication system may differ from that of the ecological system. The kind of communication system that exists generally depends on the leadership style within the unit—that is, how the leader perceives his or her role. If the leader has an autocratic style—in other words, sees himself as the top decision maker and order giver—then the communication system will assume a straight-vertical-line, top-to-bottom pattern. The leader speaks to an assistant, who then speaks to the staff members, who then speak to the attendants, and so on. The leader may even insist on being the only person who speaks to physicians. Patients usually speak to the nurses who care for them, but they have more freedom to cut across all levels. The rigidity of this communication system is quite obvious, but it has one redeeming characteristic: everyone at least knows who to go to and who is in charge. It is when a focal system is closed to suggestions from anyone other than the leader that errors are most likely to occur and to affect patients adversely. The leader—often a head nurse—sets the tone by indicating what he or she wants to hear or not to hear.

The reverse of the authoritarian style is the laissez-faire style: no effective leadership exists, except in name only. Although this style may seem good since communications are open, one usually finds it quite chaotic. No one seems to know what is going on, and a substantial amount of "buck passing" occurs because authority is not truly accepted by anyone.

The best of these two worlds is what some call a democratic style, but care must be taken in how this term is defined. If it means that all major decisions are made by the group and that the leader has no authority, then it borders on the laissez-faire. The democratic leadership style can be called "collective responsibility," but it can also be called "collective irresponsibility," because, like the laissez-faire style, it allows buck passing. Without authority there can be no placing of responsibility and thus no accountability. If, however, the democratic leader sees the final authority as resting in himself but engages in open communication, then you do indeed have the best of both worlds.

If, as an advocate, you do not know what the communication flow is or what kind of system you are functioning in, you run greater risks than necessary. You will not know to whom to communicate your goals and whose support you will need. If you assume that authority rests with the head nurse, when the leadership style is actually laissez-faire, you may find yourself alone when you most need support. The same result may occur when you have so-called group leadership: a head nurse may agree with your position on some issue or problem but then change her mind because the group is not with her. Not only do you have the possibility of communication breakdown, but you cannot plan strategies for dealing with risk.

The most important question that must be answered is "Who's in charge around here?" The person designated as leader may be a leader in name only. The real power may lie with an assistant or a staff person. Such a situation can be the easiest thing in the world to be fooled by, and many unnecessary mistakes and blunders have resulted. Therefore, since communication patterns depend on the leader, be sure you know who the true leader is.

ECOLOGICAL SYSTEM

The ecological system is that larger system of which the focal system is a part. If the focal system is a unit of a hospital, then the ecological system consists of the entire hospital—the nursing service administration, the hospital administration, the medical board, and all other departments and their staffs. The policies that govern the operation of the focal system are derived from this larger system. The policies and goals of the ecological system may be more or less consistent with those of the focal system. However, you must not forget that the power to change usually lies with this larger system. It determines the policies and goals and usually has the power to see that they are enacted. There is interaction among all the focal systems, and any of them can be the source of new policies and goals. But almost always, any change must be approved by the larger system if it is to become an effective operating mechanism. Revolutions can arise in the focal system, but usually they are not successful unless the ecological system is very weak or very much out of step with society as a whole. But even then it is soon replaced with another ecological system that has power.

Ecological systems that are tolerant of diversity, that do not infringe on the basic operating principles of focal systems, are the most successful. It is only when focal systems step over this boundary that trouble begins. Because the power lies with the ecological system, you as an advocate must know what the ethic of this system is and how it relates to your concept of advocacy and your role as a nurse. You must ask yourself these questions: Does the ecological system view all patients as having the right to determine their treatment? Does it believe that informing patients is a principle that must be upheld? Or does it believe that only certain classes of patients have this right—that is, the paying ones? Does it believe that only physicians should determine who should be informed and who should do the informing? Or does it see these decisions as part of the nurse's role? If the latter is the case, will it transform this belief into action by supporting a nurse against a physician?

You must also determine what kind of pressure is being exerted on the ecological system by outside sources—for example, regulatory agencies, consumers, and professional organizations. How can you use these factors to your advantage? For example, which is more important to the ecological system of a hospital: to maintain tight control over all decision making by both staff and patients or to appear to be in the vanguard of consumer interests? In addition, is the ecological system aware of the consequences of each of these positions?

It is apparent that we do not live in small worlds of self, patients, or focal systems. What seems impossible after an assessment of a focal system can in fact be accomplished, depending on the desires of the ecological system. In addition, the focal systems combined can change the ecological system, especially with consumer support. The advocacy process receives support not only from consumers but also from regulatory agencies and most professional groups. The question is how to use such support. Answering this question may take time and planning; instant gratification is not part of the role of advocate. In advocacy, to paraphrase an old saying, it is often better to lose a battle now so that we can win the war later.

SOCIAL ETHIC OF SYSTEMS

In Chapter 1 I mentioned John Gardner's continuum of egalitarianism versus libertarianism. Egalitarians believe that human beings are equal in every respect and therefore "that no man should be regarded as better than another man in any dimension, and that there should be no difference in status whatever."[11] But the fact is that there are differences in ability and performance. Extremists of the egalitarian view seek to limit or work "against such individual differences, protecting the slow runners and curbing the swift."[12] In other words, egalitarianism has a leveling effect. Libertarians believe that people are "not equal in their native gifts nor in their motivation; and it follows that they will not be equal in their achievements."[13] It also follows that extremists of this view will say quite simply, "Let the best man win."[14]

Both of these views are operational in American culture, and both occur in extreme and moderate forms. The extremists of the two positions are in open conflict with each other on many levels. Gardner believes that this conflict lies at the heart of most of society's problems and dilemmas—including, I would argue, those involving the provision of health care. These problems are complicated by the fact that a person or group may espouse the egalitarian view in regard to the health care system, for example, yet maintain a libertarian admission and treatment policy. Or an institution may claim to be libertarian in its hiring policies yet assume an egalitarian stance in its promotion policies. It may use the argument "a nurse is a nurse is a nurse," thereby ignoring educational preparation. A more detailed discussion of this topic will be presented in the Chapter 4. At this point it is necessary only that you be aware of the conflict and the problems that can arise as a result of it.

As an advocate you must identify the ethic of the focal system, that of the

[11]John Gardner, *Excellence* (New York: Harper & Row, Publishers, Inc.), 1961, pp. 15-16.
[12]*Ibid.*, p. 6.
[13]*Ibid.*, p. 14.
[14]*Ibid.*, p. 6.

ecological system, and your own ethic. Are they compatible? If they are not, how does that fact affect your role? You must determine what risks such a situation holds for you and whether it is possible to practice advocacy at all under such circumstances. The process is similar to identifying stated and unstated goals. Then you must ask yourself whether you can incorporate the various ethics into a strategy for action. Or do the ethics of the focal and ecological systems so conflict with your own that functioning becomes all but impossible for you? The bottom line lies in an assessment of the extremeness of the views held by the people with whom you must work. Can they be moderated?

You also must identify the ethic of the client. What role does this ethic play in the client's decision-making process? Knowing the client's ethic will have little effect on the informing and supporting role itself, but it will help you understand and be more accepting of the client's decisions. Understanding why people behave as they do and make the decisions they make helps you not only to accept their right to determine their own destinies but also to assess your own reactions and to determine your own behavior. I must add here that acceptance of the behavior of others is not equivalent to approval of the behavior. This is a point many advocates forget. There will be times when you must state quite frankly to a client that you understand and accept his right to make a particular decision but that you personally cannot approve of it. You may even have to say why you do not approve.

EVALUATION OF GOALS

When all the parts of the assessment process have been completed, it is time to put them together, to determine whether your goals are functional, whether conflicts exist, and, if so, where. You then plan your strategy to enact the goals, or you decide that the goals are not functional. This kind of assessment must become a working part of the advocate's everyday behavior. At first it may seem time consuming, but as you make it a part of your working gestalt it comes naturally and does not consume much time. Such an assessment can be thought of as a continuous exercise in reality orientation or survival. It can pay large dividends in the working life of anyone, regardless of occupation, but it is essential to persons who participate in high-risk activities that involve others, like advocacy.

• • •

I said earlier that I would present a chart of the assessment (or systems analysis) process. However, the method represented here differs slightly from the procedure we have been discussing. This method of systems analysis is best used when a person is planning to make changes in a large system, such as a hospital. The procedure we have been discussing thus far in this chapter is best used on a more

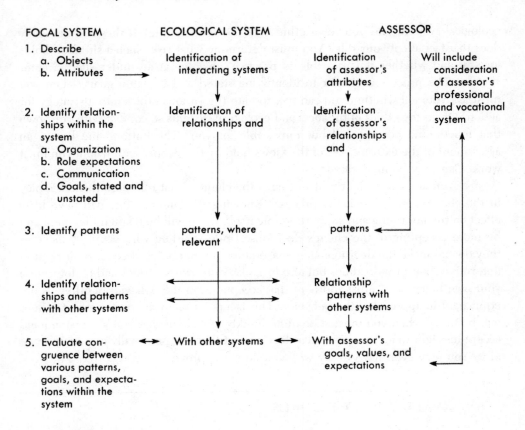

FIGURE 10

Developed by Patricia Winstead-Fry and others in the Division of Nursing at New York University.

personal level—to identify risks that an advocate will face in particular situations. This chart appears as Fig. 10.

The three columns in Fig. 10 represent the focal system, the ecological system, and the assessor (or self system). Running down the side of the chart are six steps in the assessment process. The arrows show the relationships of the steps to the columns and the columns to each other. Step 1 is to describe the three systems. This step sets the scene, and care must be taken not to leave out any significant fact or person. Step 2 is to assess the relationships within the systems and between the systems. Step 3 is to describe organizational or operating patterns. For example, are there rules that govern behavior? Is a system stable? Is there cohesiveness? Are there tangential relationships that affect patterns? Are there territorial prerogatives that must be observed? Step 4 is to examine how the patterns in step 3 are interrelated.

Here you are looking for patterns that overlap from one system to another. The degree to which patterns overlap systems is a good indication of the likelihood that a pattern can be changed in any one system. The more overlapping, the smaller the likelihood of change. For example, if everyone agrees on what the role of the nurse is, it is not likely that the role will be changed. If nurses are seen as physicians' obedient handmaidens by physicians, administrators, and nurses themselves, then it is almost impossible for them to be autonomous professionals who serve as patients' advocates. Needless to say, if a new nurse arrives on this kind of scene and wants to be an advocate, his or her ability to do so will be resisted by all systems. Step 5 is to evaluate the information gathered in steps 1 through 4 and their relationships with each other. Step 6 is to make a decision about the practicality of your goal or goals. At this point you may want to alter the goal. If this is the case, the new goal should be subjected to the same assessment.

Thus the assessment process will lead you to one of three possible conclusions about the goal: "Yes, it's okay," "Alter it," or "No, it won't work." As I stated before, this chart is particularly valuable for examining proposed changes in a system. Too often we think of really good ideas that will potentially benefit everyone only to see them fail. We are left amazed and asking ourselves how something so good could fail so abysmally. Then, in retrospect, we say, "If we had only done . . ." or "If we had only known . . ." The purpose of systems analysis is to avoid that unhappy result, to recognize problems early so that they will not prevent the success of a plan or so that a fruitless plan can be abandoned at the start.

One further point is important to the fulfillment of goals or the implementation of planned change. This point relates primarily to goals or plans that involve others, not just yourself. To put it simply and directly, do you need to receive full credit for the accomplishment of a goal or the success of a plan? In other words, what is most important to you—that the goal or plan succeed or that you receive credit for it? This one point, unless clarified by the assessor at the very start, can cause more heartbreak than any other, because quite often we do not receive full credit for our ideas. Whether we will receive credit can be determined in the assessment stage. We may discover that success will depend on selling the idea to a key person who will not go along with it unless he sees it as his own, and no matter how we may wish it to be otherwise, that is exactly what will happen. So it is better to be forewarned and forearmed than to be regretful and petulant later. This is not to say that it is wrong to want credit for your ideas—it is not. But you must be aware that some goals can be accomplished only if others not only agree with them but also claim them as their own ideas. In other words, you must remember that diplomacy is often the art of letting others have your own way. Therefore it is important that you decide whether the accomplishment of a goal is more important to you than the credit you may receive for the accomplishment. A small point perhaps but certainly a vital one to your peace of mind.

• • •

In this chapter I have touched only briefly on the need to assess the social ethic. An understanding of the social ethic of the focal, ecological, self, and client systems is vital to the planning of strategy and the accomplishment of goals. A knowledge of this ethic and the roles it plays in decision making provides us with a chart into the unknown area of unstated goals. Such knowledge exemplifies the professional attitude of "the more you know the safer you can navigate," as opposed to the head-in-the-sand belief of "what you don't know can't hurt you." With this in mind, let us move on to a discussion of the social ethic.

NOTES ON CHAPTER 3

Gardner's book is excellent on the subject of egalitarianism versus libertarianism. It is a classic in its field, and it is easy to read. I cannot suggest strongly enough that all advocates read it.

Gardner, John W. *Excellence*. New York: Harper & Row, Publishers, Inc., 1961.

I also suggest that if you intend to be an advocate, you read *Power and Innocence*. It deals with power in a very clear fashion.

May, Rollo. *Power and Innocence*. New York: W.W. Norton & Co., Inc., 1972.

Chapter 4

SOCIAL
ETHIC
AND
ISSUES

Egalitarianism and libertarianism, as defined by Gardner, were discussed in the preceding chapter. The purpose of this chapter is to look at how these two ethics and modifications of them apply to some of the major issues and problems facing society today. The subjects I have chosen for discussion are race, age, sex, access to education, and access to health care. Many other problems and issues could be added to this list. The ones I have chosen, which tend to overlap each other, impinge quite directly on the advocacy process. If you refer back to Fig. 1, in the first chapter, you will see that this chapter represents an integration of knowledge area 3, social ethic, and area 5, issues. Area 6, medical-industrial complex, area 7, social laws, and area 8, politics, also impinge on advocacy but in a broader, less direct fashion. These topics will be explored together in a later chapter.

As we examine the ways in which an egalitarian or a libertarian might view each issue, keep in mind the fact that these views may affect your role as an advocate for all people, as well as the decision-making processes of clients and the policies of your focal and ecological systems.

RACE

Although culture and language may be more significant than color and physical features in distinguishing one person from another, unfortunately the latter two criteria seem to carry the most weight. The fact that an American white may have more in common with an American black than with a European white seems to matter little. Color and physical features are still the most prominent factors in identification. It seems that what we see triggers an instant reaction in us that facts or reason cannot quite overcome. Visual evidence of difference is a constant reminder of difference. There is nothing wrong with recognizing differences, but we humans have a habit of defining differences in terms of good and bad. As a result, in the United States, which is predominantly white, persons who are not white have generally been regarded as inferior. The history of this racial prejudice is older than the history of the country, and it still exists today. Despite the many laws that have been passed to remove or to prevent the creation of barriers that support the fallacy of inferiority, that fallacy still exists.

How do egalitarians and libertarians view the question of race, and how do they react to measures designed to eliminate racism? An extreme egalitarian believes that all men are created equal and that no one is better than another. When faced with the reality of difference, he attempts to protect the slow by hampering the fast.[1] He supports policies that take money from the rich and give it to the poor regardless of whether they work. He would allow a person to enter college regardless of his

---

[1]John Gardner, *Excellence* (New York: Harper & Row, Publishers, Inc., 1961, pp. 6, 15-16.

ability to achieve—even prefer an unqualified applicant to a qualified one—and then insist that the person be passed and given a degree. An extreme egalitarian would give people jobs in which they are not prepared to function. In essence he would require that a person put forth little effort in an attempt to achieve. You might say that the extreme egalitarian is a born rescuer and that he refuses to accept the idea that the victim could ever victimize him. When faced with the reality that he indeed has been victimized by a victim, he puts on additional blinders and makes further excuses for the victim, or becomes so disillusioned that he totally drops out, blaming all of humanity for his plight.

An extreme libertarian believes that human beings are not equal in their gifts or motivation and therefore in their achievements. So, he argues, let the best man win.[2] He shuts his eyes to the fact that many differences in the ability to achieve have resulted from racist policies. Rather, he holds on to the belief that if you qualify you receive, and if you do not qualify, you get nothing, regardless of the fact that you were not given the opportunity to qualify to start with. That's not his problem. Not only is he not a rescuer, but he denies that there is any such thing as a victim at all. His denial of reality is just as total as that of the extreme egalitarian. So when the extreme egalitarian places him in the role of persecutor, the extreme libertarian is outraged and cannot understand why he has been so attacked. He becomes even more stubborn and holds even more strongly to policies that say that the best service is given to those who pay, that entrance to college is determined by the kind of high school one went to and the grades one achieved, that jobs are given to those with the best references, and that the rich owe the poor no more than what charity moves them to give—in essence, that a person must pull himself up by his own bootstraps even if he does not have boots. Otherwise, he gets what is available and accepts it without protest. The extreme libertarian attitude could almost be classed with the "we know best" attitude of professionals.

The extremists of both views are blind, not only to each other's positions but also to any common ground where reality could be found. As an advocate you generally will not run into extremists of either kind; rather you will see shades of one or the other. For example, it may be more acceptable to be the advocate of a rich white patient in one setting, while in another setting it may be more acceptable to be the advocate of a poor black patient. (The black patient who is rich represents a toss-up; money in our culture may sometimes speak louder than color.) Furthermore, the advocate must take into consideration how the patients see themselves. Regardless of whether the prevailing social ethic favors them, if they see themselves as victims of society they may choose to act out this role in spite of the choices they are given, thereby setting up a problem that would not have existed if they had not created it. A defeatist attitude may well become a self-fulfilling prophecy, no matter what we may do to help change it.

[2]*Ibid.*, pp. 6, 14.

Advocates who recognize that there is something to be said for both the libertarian and the egalitarian views are in the best position to begin change. They will see that there has been injustice in society and will work to correct it, but they will also see that people do have differing abilities and gifts and therefore cannot be equal in terms of achievement. But advocates also must see that everyone has the right to make his own decisions, regardless of race or achievement. This attitude will be evident in their total behavior in the advocate process—not only in the informing and supporting roles but also in the assessment of how others will perceive their actions. They will use whatever means are at their disposal to inform and support a patient. They will assess all systems in such a way as to reach the goal that is in the patient's best interest, as defined by the patient. Therefore, although the goal of advocacy is always the same, the strategies will differ from one situation to another.

You must be careful about using labels like "liberal" or "conservative," "libertarian" or "egalitarian." Most people do not fall clearly into one category or another. They may tend to lean in a certain direction, but social pressure can often move them or at least neutralize their behavior. As advocates our primary interest is in the neutralizing process, for the purpose of reducing risks. Our goal is not to change the racial prejudices of others. Too often we forget what our original goal is, become distracted by another goal, and end up not being able to achieve either. One further word of caution: racial prejudice is a two-way street; it can be found in any and all combinations. It is therefore prudent that we not jump to what may seem to be the obvious conclusions but instead maintain an open-minded and objective stance. Our assessment of a situation can then help us to avoid major risks in the informing and supporting process.

The existence of racial prejudice itself is not always the determining factor in a person's behavior. That is why the social ethic is so important to assess. A professed egalitarian can be a most prejudiced person, with the egalitarian stance being a defense against or denial of that prejudice. The advocate faces the question of which factor has the greater influence on the person's behavior. I believe that the social ethic will have the greater effect in the short run, unless a major conflict occurs that taps the deep underlying prejudice. It is these major conflicts, present in all the issues we will be discussing in this chapter, that must be avoided. Most people, by the time they reach adulthood, have formed some opinion or belief about these issues. These opinions and beliefs can be altered, but I cannot emphasize enough that this is not the role of the advocate.

AGE

In recent times problems related to aging have steadily become more prominent, and the term "ageism" has surfaced. The population movement from the country to the cities has been a contributing factor. In part it is a question of space and living conditions. For example, there may be no room for the elderly members of a family that lives in a small city apartment. In addition, if all the younger members of the family work, there may be no one at home to care for the elderly. As a result we have seen a vast increase in the development of nursing homes and senior citizens' communities. This, combined with the fact that illness is a great risk factor in the elderly, has often placed a great financial burden on families.

The factor of limited space has often meant that the differing privacy needs and cultural needs of persons of different generations have not been met. The activity and noise that children produce and need may not be compatible with the needs of older adults for some peace and quiet. Parents who are caught between the needs of their own parents and their children can be torn asunder. Add to this the fact that the elderly often are no longer productive and contributing (financially) members of the family, and you are faced with today's dilemma of what to do with the elderly. That a solution must be found is obvious, but what is that solution? Elderly persons who are able to plan ahead for their care may manage quite effectively. For example, they may move to a retirement community, or they may stay in their homes and employ help. But a considerable number are left at the mercy of their children or, if they have none, at the mercy of society.

How then would an extreme egalitarian react to the problems of the elderly and all their ramifications? Since he believes that all must receive equally, he would subscribe to policies that provide equal care to everyone, regardless of ability to pay. He would argue for free hospital care, medical care, nursing homes, and so on, and he would say that the caliber of care should not differ according to a person's finances. He would argue that society must bear the cost. Furthermore, he would say that expensive surgery and medications should be available to all, even if they represent elective procedures that have little hope of success. One hardly can discern any form of ageism in these views.

The extreme libertarian believes that those who can pay deserve the best they can pay for and that those who cannot pay must take what is available. He would not starve the elderly poor, forbid them medical care, or throw them into the street. Instead he would provide them with the bare minimum in food, health care, and housing. He would self-righteously stick to his premise that they should have planned ahead for old age if they wanted better conditions. And he would persist in this attitude even in the face of the reality that saving is impossible for poor people and the fact that in recent years inflation often has eaten up savings that had been carefully built up. Some libertarians go so far as to argue that expensive drugs and treatment should be available only to those who can pay and that others will have to live with the facts of aging as a given in this world. It is difficult to label such an attitude as true ageism—that is, a prejudice against the elderly—since it is applied to everyone, regardless of age.

The social ethic can dictate the kind of physical conditions with which the elderly will live, but the root of ageism lies deeper. So the advocate should be careful not to view libertarians as being against the elderly and egalitarians as being for them, or vice versa.

The problem of ageism originates in individual views of and reactions to the aged. Prejudice against the aged cuts across both the egalitarian and the libertarian ethics. Many elderly people, both rich and poor, have been mentally and socially abandoned by the persons who had been closest to them. The loneliness and despair of the old are not removed by pleasant surroundings. The pain of rejection is rarely mitigated by money. However money can be used to turn the tables against those who reject the aged. For example, many of the communities and apartments where the elderly are in control have strict rules about letting in young people who have children. In areas where housing is tight, such as California, such policies can cause difficulty for young families. The ageist, regardless of social ethic, who wants the elderly out of sight and out of mind would call this discrimination against the young "justice" and approve of it. After all, it meets his need to avoid coping with his own attitude toward the elderly or the aging process.

The ageist who is an egalitarian is in a bit of a pickle. He, too, wants the elderly out of sight and out of mind, but it bothers him to see only the wealthy hidden away in a comfortable style. Therefore he will insist that society provide a comfortable situation for all the elderly. If this costs too much, he will insist on lowering the living standard for all.

This "out of sight, out of mind" goal in regard to the elderly binds the extremists of both ethics together. It is this attitude with which the advocate will have the most difficulty coping. The "out of sight, out of mind" attitude is at the heart of various widely held feelings about the elderly: Because a person is old he is out-of-date, and therefore his opinions and desires are not to be paid attention to—a sort of "we know what's best for you" syndrome, which is very common. Because a person is old, he is no longer productive and has become a burden, so those who must bear this burden are in the best position to decide how to do so. Again, a "we know best" attitude. The elderly have nothing in common with the young; therefore it is best for old people to be with their own kind. (Sound familiar? Racists have been using a similar argument for years. It is easy to replace the sayings of one group of prejudiced people with the sayings of another.) These attitudes result in such remarks as "Mother would be happier in a nursing home with others of her age" or "We have nothing to talk with Mother about when we visit, and that situation disturbs her, so let's not go so often and disturb her" or "It so upsets me to see her this way that I can't hide it, and she knows and gets upset, so I won't go and upset her."

Attitudes like these and the view that the elderly are not capable of making their own decisions can pose real difficulties for the advocate. These attitudes not only are seen in families but also seem to permeate the whole health care system.

What makes the situation worse is that many of the elderly themselves accept these beliefs and assume the role of victim. In fact, some gladly accept this role and even thrive on it. Self-chosen and accepting victims love rescuers. Where injustice and prejudice are also present, the advocate must indeed be wise.

The question of ageism cuts across all levels of American society and can supersede all other prejudices—race, religion, sex, social status, financial status. A culture that places a major premium on youth and looking young, that denies aging and death, will not deal with ageism very easily. The members of such a society will find it hard to deal with it in themselves and therefore will deny it in others. To defend its "out of sight, out of mind" position, this society will come up with the most basically illogical statements ever invented and will fight any and all who try to expose them as illogical. In such a society everyone knows that his own most immediate problem with ageism—that is, his parents—will go away when his parents die. Therefore he will not be quick to attack others who have the same problem. In addition, his denial of the aging process in himself prevents him from identifying with the elderly and seeing his own future in them.

The current increases in longevity, combined with decreases in the birth rate, makes one seriously wonder what solution will be found for the problems related to aging. The recent increases in the degree to which the aged are separated from the rest of society will work against the merging and accommodation we have seen in such areas as race, religion, and sex. The advocate for the aged and for the patient who happens to be elderly has indeed an uphill battle. As long as the view that young is not only beautiful but right is subscribed to, the solution will not lie in moderating the egalitarian or libertarian ethic but rather in dealing with the denial process of each individual and the culture itself.

More space has been devoted to the issue of age than has been devoted to the others because it will affect the nurse advocate more than the others will and because of the great denial factor that accompanies it. That is not to say that attention is not being paid to problems related to aging. The elderly, organized into groups like the Gray Panthers, are having an effect on legislation. There is more openness in the discussion of death and dying than there used to be, which has helped remove some of the denial. Many groups have organized on the national level to deal with the problems of the aged. These are all positive signs and do chip away at the denial process, but with inflation, increases in the aging population, and the myths that still prevail about the usefulness of the aged, the future is not exactly bright and shining.

•   •   •

But enough for now. Let's move on to the area of sex and sexism, and then see how race, age, and sex affect or have a place in the issues of access to education and access to health care.

SEX

The subject of sexism, and the feminist call to eradicate it, has been discussed extensively in the various communications media. The egalitarian view is that all should have equal access to social benefits. Egalitarians do not discriminate according to ability; they also do not discriminate according to sex. Libertarians, too, do not discriminate on the basis of sex. They hold that if you can achieve, you should be allowed to do so; the fact that, because of discrimination, you have not been allowed to prepare to achieve is not relevant.

The views of both groups are much the same as they were in regard to the race issue. The egalitarian would say that a woman and a man deserve equal consideration for a job, even if a woman does not have the ability to perform the job as well as a man. The libertarian would say that a woman deserves equal consideration for a job if she can prove herself qualified, while at the same time denying that, because of past discrimination, the woman may not have had an opportunity to become qualified. The extremist of each view denies reality and accepts myths, just as he does in regard to race.

The myths about the sexes that have grown up over centuries cut across race and age, and they constitute a major problem for the advocate. A person's sex, age, and race are visually identifiable, and sight is the first trigger of prejudicial reaction. But sex discrimination can claim a longer history than the others. Racial discrimination can occur only when a racial group constitutes a minority; and many cultures have venerated the aged. But sex has involved a predetermined role expectation in all cultures and throughout all of history.

The feminist movement is not new; it has been around for some time, but it has become better organized and more vocal in recent years. It is a movement primarily of middle-class and upper-middle-class white women. Black women have not played a prominent role. (Some say this is because black women, like black men, want a complete turnover of the social norms and the power structure, while white women want only to become part of the power structure.) The prevailing myths concerning women do nevertheless affect all racial groups. The myths that the female is weak, unable to be logical in a decision-making process, governed by emotion rather than logic, and therefore should be dominated and dictated to by the male, for her own good, have long been prevalent. These myths often have been accepted by both men and women, regardless of social ethic. Many women, instead of seeing themselves as victims, accept the female stereotype. So even if egalitarians may open opportunities to women, these opportunities may not be taken advantage of, and libertarians may use this fact to buttress their position. Those who gain by the myths are the hidden sexists of either the egalitarian or the libertarian ethic. Again, as in the case of ageism, the social ethic may not be the determining factor in a person's behavior. Thus, it is important for advocates to assess the social ethic, but they also must be alert to underlying sexist attitudes that may affect decision-making processes, especially in regard to female patients. This is hazardous ground indeed for an advocate in the health care delivery system.

This system has three power centers. The two having the most power are hospital administration and physicians. Both of these groups are made up primarily of white men. The third power center is nursing service administration. God help the female advocate who works in an environment in which nurses see themselves as subserviant to a male hierarchy rather than as equals! Should she find herself in the position of advocate for a female patient who is going against the wishes of an all-male group, she often can expect to find little support from her professional colleagues. If the system is predominantly white and the patient is black, and old as well, need I say more? However, all hope is not lost, obstacles that seem insurmountable can be turned to an advocate's advantage. For example, an advocate can claim prejudice not only on the basis of sex but also on the bases of race and age. (More such defensive weapons will be discussed in a later chapter. I only mention them here so as not to discourage potential advocates.)

The myths that prevail not only among men but also among women are the ones that most concern the advocate. These are most central to the decision-making process of the patient. For example, if a female client really believes—even after being properly informed by an advocate—that she does not have the right to make decisions for herself, or that she is unable to do so, the advocate can do little to change this attitude. If the advocate holds a contrary belief, and insists on acting upon it, he or she can be drawn into a dangerous rescuing position. The advocate must accurately assess not only the client's ethic but what the client believes about herself as a result of it. Since sexism can exist in either an egalitarian system or a libertarian system—underground, so to speak—the advocate must be very canny and wise.

•   •   •

A victim who chooses to remain one must be allowed to do so. The informing process must be thorough enough to alert a client to the questions of ageism, racism, and sexism as they affect the client's decision-making process, but the advocate must also be aware of the limitations of the informing process, and not step over the line that separates advocacy from rescuing. The advocate must be prepared to deal with client statements like "I'm only a woman," "I'm black," or "After all, I'm old," followed by "Therefore they must know best." If these remarks are framed as questions and not as statements of resignation, then there is hope. The worst situation would involve an elderly female patient who believes the sexists' line and who has a son who is a sexist and a male physician who is one also. An effort must be made in the informing process, but even in an egalitarian, pro-feminism environment, advocates do not have great success in helping female patients make independent decisions. I am not advocating a defeatist attitude for the advocate but only the careful assessment of reality.

Never forget that the almost happy, accepting victim will almost always prefer his own life to that of the potentially lonely but independent person. For those who cherish independence and the freedom to make decisions, and who have experienced the pleasure and joy that come from this kind of freedom, my advocacy of letting others remain dependent will seem unforgivable. I can only say that experience has taught me that you cannot make others happy by insisting on some course of action that you know is best for them. Do not assume the "I know best" attitude; it is really up to the client to decide right and wrong. You may be forcing him into a freedom he does not want and cannot handle. He may already have made his decision and chosen to live with it. If you try to change it, you become no better than all the other "know righters" in this world.

The issues of racism, ageism, and sexism directly impinge on the issues of access to health care and access to education.

ACCESS TO EDUCATION

The egalitarian's view regarding access to education has been widely published and even embodied in some laws. This view is that people should have equal access to education at all levels, from primary education to graduate education, and to jobs as well, and that "artificial barriers" to educational access should be removed. Egalitarians claim that these barriers, such as grades or test scores, are artificially created by groups who want to prevent access by certain groups of people. They say that school grades do not reflect ability and that test scores are culturally determined and therefore not a fair judge of ability. When barriers are removed and persons who have been admitted without meeting requirements fail, extreme egalitarians say that past discrimination is the reason. So they call for remedial work to help the educationally disabled. This has proved to be very expensive and of dubious worth. The end compromise has been the creation of quota systems for the disadvantaged. However, such systems have met with some negative reaction from the courts. For example, in 1978 the United States Supreme Court found in favor of an eligible white man who was refused admission to a California medical school so that blacks who were less qualified could be admitted. Quota systems have led to the same problem in regard to the job market: attempts to eliminate discrimination against blacks have sometimes led to claims of reverse discrimination.

The libertarian believes that those who qualify for or earn the right to education and jobs should get them. Of course, the libertarian refuses to deal with the fact that, in many cases, those who qualify have benefited from schools and environments that prepared them to qualify.

Extremists of the two positions have not won much favor or support. The egalitarians would hold back the best so that the less qualified could go ahead, even if they cannot achieve. The libertarians would ignore past patterns of outright discrimination and do business as usual, giving no thought to righting the wrongs of society.

Because of the cost of higher education and the need for a high level of performance in jobs, the libertarians would seem to have the upper hand. However, the groups most discriminated against—racial minorities and women—have been influential enough to prevent the libertarian ethic from having its way totally. Some degree of compromise has been established, and laws have been passed to enforce this compromise. One might be tempted to claim that the moderates of both sides have won, but that is not quite the case. The libertarian ethic still is dominant, and that probably will always be true in a capitalist society. Productivity is still the measuring rod. But the more gross injustices have been dealt a blow, and some change is being made.

The most important thing for the advocate to remember is that people must be allowed to achieve according to their abilities. Any truly artificial barriers must be removed. The public schools must all be of high caliber, to allow all students an opportunity to achieve to the best of their abilities. The professions must not be allowed to create barriers of race or sex against entry into their schools or into the job market. Some remedial work may be necessary to correct past wrongs; it must be provided. But who pays for it must be decided. All these things can be done while standards of excellence are still maintained. The leveling or equalizing of achievement that the egalitarian extremist would have is as damaging to the individual as the libertarian extremist's policy of ignoring past discrimination.

The key to an open society that wishes to remain open is access to knowledge and the freedom to use that knowledge to the best of one's ability. The same reasons and barriers that exist to prevent patients from knowing are used to keep knowledge in short supply among the population in general. The more people know, the more they are going to question and get involved in decision making—a development that obviously will not suit those who want to make all the decisions themselves. Keeping people ignorant helps to keep them subservient. Many of the same risks and hazards that an advocate faces in the small system of a hospital also exist in a larger, community situation. People in power do not like consumers, or groups of consumers, who act as advocates. All things of value are protected from people who might wish to share in them.

Considering the barriers that have been placed in the path of knowledge, one would think that more people would be struggling to get it. But perhaps the knowledge of its value has been hidden also. It is the fortunate child indeed whose parents have let him in on this secret by teaching him the *value of knowing,* and thus allowing him to experience the freedom that comes from knowing. However, with freedom goes responsibility, which we often shirk. And so we are back at square one. One wonders, if the barriers to education were all removed, just how many people would rush to get it after the novelty wore off.

ACCESS TO HEALTH CARE

The egalitarian believes that everyone should have equal access to health care or illness care, regardless of ability to pay. The extremist of this view would also say that the type of care and the accommodations should be the same for all. Just as achievers in education would be held back to help persons who are less gifted, so the rich would pay the cost of health care for the poor without receiving more than the poor receive. However, in a thoroughly egalitarian society there would be no rich, and one might even question what kind of health care would be available, since the gifted would be held back from making excellence in health care possible.

The libertarian, on the other hand, believes you get what you pay for. The philosophy of the extremist of this view would be akin to "survival of the fittest" (fitness here being defined in financial terms). Such extremists may institute certain public health measures, but only if those measures are necessary for their own welfare. Humanitarians among the libertarians would certainly not be against charity, but only if someone is moved to spend his money that way. He must not be forced to do so.

It would be hard to say if the presence in the United States of publicly supported hospitals, public health departments, and so on, represents a gain for the egalitarian ethic. Is it simply that libertarians have been seeing that a healthy society is more profitable to them? Perhaps some of both. The recent moves to Medicare and Medicaid and the interest in national health insurance certainly seem egalitarian. The establishment of socialized medicine and health care in various other countries would seem to indicate the same kind of egalitarian movement. In these countries, however, the rich can still obtain more and better health care if they pay extra for it. And the result of free health care has been very high taxes, for the cost of health care in the benefits provided by the health care system is enormous. Many cutbacks have been made in England because of this. The move to enact a total health care insurance plan in the United States has been held back for this very reason, expense. But let's look at what currently exists.

Medicaid is supposed to allow the poor to receive medical care. But the question is what kind of care and from whom? Many physicians will not accept Medicaid patients, nor will some hospitals admit them. The payments are lower than those of other insurance schemes; for example, Medicare and most private insurance plans pay more. Also, when they are admitted to hospitals, Medicaid patients are treated in the same way that patients in public hospitals and in the charity wards of private hospitals are treated. They are placed in the cheapest accommodations, and they usually are treated by the house staff and do not have a private physician, although an attending physician usually does supervise the work of the house staff. Also, they usually may receive only the necessities in treatment, with elective procedures rarely being available to them, unless a house staff member needs practice in a certain procedure, such as a nose job to improve looks, or other types of surgery of the same nature. So Medicaid may appear egalitarian, because it makes health care more accessible, but it is still libertarian in terms of the kind of care offered.

Furthermore, when hospital cutbacks are made for financial reasons, they usually begin in the clinics that serve the Medicaid patients, and with the beds allotted to them. The public hospitals are then asked to pick up the overload. But public hospitals are also expensive to operate. They are paid for by taxes, and the public objects to higher taxes, so even these services are then cut back. New York City is a major example of this situation. In the past few years enormous cuts have been made in the public sector there, and although egalitarians and the poor have been vocal in expressing their dismay, the average taxpayer has been much more silent. This is not to say that health care is not available to the poor in New York City or that it is of poor quality. It is available, and it is generally quite acceptable, especially if the seeker is knowledgeable about what is available.

This brings us back to the old point of *knowledge* and to the advocate role. An advocate may not be able to change a health care delivery system, but he or she can provide knowledge. This will at least help people get the best of what is available. By providing knowledge, an advocate can help people learn how to negotiate the health care system. If an advocate does not become involved in the negotiating process herself—that is, as a rescuer—he or she is fairly safe in this behavior. There are the usual dangers in the informing process. There is much less toleration of patients who demand their rights in the wards or units that treat the poor than in those that deal with paying patients. So whatever risks and hazards are present in advocacy, they will be increased when an advocate deals with the poor. This fact seems sad, since the poor have so few rights anyway, but the old axiom "The less you have, the less you get" still holds. So the advocate who thinks that advocacy for the poor will be admired by all, as a good thing, has a surprise coming. It will not be. Therefore, the assessment of a health care system and its real ethic is very necessary.

I use the term "real ethic" advisedly. The most dangerous situation for an advocate is to misjudge the ethic of a system; a system may state that it is egalitarian, while its policies are really libertarian. The policies speak to the unstated goals, not to the written and spoken philosophy that is put out for public relations purposes. Advocates who have no toleration for this kind of hypocrisy and therefore decide to act on the stated goals, and either get their way or expose the hypocrisy to the world, may lose. They may win small, individual battles, but they may very well lose the war and perhaps their jobs and references as well. For example, they may well be allowed to appear successful and to get policies changed; the system may even praise them at the time. But all the while plans will be under way to prevent them from ever acting this way in the future.

The most effective way a system deals with this situation is to promote nurses to safe areas where they cannot act as advocates, under the pretense that their talents are needed there. This is the smartest way to deal with such situations, especially if the nurses have good reputations and carry some clout. In their new areas, they are given authority in name only or work that turns out to have little challenge. So they will either settle in and become complacent and quiet or look for other jobs, without having any comeback to the system at all. After all, how could they complain? The system not only rewarded them with promotions but praised their behavior. Very clever. One sees this strategy in all systems; hospitals and nursing service groups are only now becoming efficient in its tactical use.

The days of just firing people, especially vocal ones, are passing rapidly. We are becoming much more sophisticated in handling our troublemakers. People who do not go along with unstated goals of systems are labeled troublemakers. If they are low on the ladder of power and a bit careless to boot, they will generally be forced to resign under threat of firing and poor references. For the future-minded, career person the threat of poor references is very effective, more so than the firing. It's a tough world. In many cases the advocate who acts to right wrongs and expose hypocrisy has little chance of success. She may be a harmless dove on the side of good, but she may lack the wisdom to survive.

• • •

Few systems can be changed permanently by overt force. A change must come from within; in most cases it results when someone creates an awareness in those who are in charge that change is necessary for their own survival. Implementing change is therefore slow; it requires knowledgeable assessment and strategies planned on the basis of that assessment. If such planning and patience are not in keeping with one's temperament, it is better to leave a system and find one that is more akin to one's own ethic and style. There is nothing worse than the wasting of good people.

This leads us back to the topic of the assessment of self. What is your ethic? If you are not an extremist, where do you fall on the scale between egalitarian and libertarian? More important, are you consistent, or are you basically egalitarian on one issue and basically libertarian on another? If you find yourself changing your ethic, depending on the issue, just what does this mean? Why the inconsistency? What does this inconsistency say about your basic attitudes and beliefs? In other words, do you have prejudices about some things but not about others? Ah, the terrible truth: are you prejudiced? Be careful here in your answer. Denial will only cause you blindness and trouble in making an assessment. If you have prejudices, face them; and then determine how important they are to you and how they affect your behavior. In other words, fit them into your assessment. Can you consciously control them? If you cannot control them, should you work in situations where they will constantly be brought out? We should be wise enough not to lead ourselves unnecessarily into such situations; and when confronted with them, we should be wise enough to recognize them and act accordingly.

By the same token, we must not deliberately lead others into areas of their prejudices. To avoid doing so, we must perform an adequate assessment of others and the systems of which they are a part. I call it "knowing the path through the minefield." The same questions you ask of yourself, you also ask of others and the system. You cannot always expect another person to face the truth of his ethic or prejudice, but you can develop a strategy to deal with it.

Finally, never be afraid to admit that there will be people and systems that we cannot deal with and that we are better off distancing ourselves from. This is not an admission of defeat but a recognition of simple reality—the reality of one's own strengths and weaknesses. A denial of either is simple foolishness; false humility or false bravery leads only to failure. Denial keeps us from being strong when strength is called for and prevents us from asking for help when help is needed. If we can neither go it alone nor ask for help, we become immobile and useless to ourselves and to others. Denial is not the armor the advocate needs; if it is yours, do not ever be an advocate.

As I have said before in this book, my purpose is not to turn you away from the role of advocacy or unknowingly toward it. You might say that I am simply trying to light up the path so that you can decide. The light is knowledge; if you want to know, you can. The informing process is the same for yourself as it is for patients; they may fear knowing, and so may you. It's okay to be afraid; just admit that you are afraid. The responsibility that goes with knowing and then decision making is the same as that which goes with choosing not to know. You must accept responsibility either way; you make a decision either way. That is the paradox, or what some may call the "joker in the deck." A person may choose not to vote in an election because he likes neither candidate. How angry he becomes when told that his non-vote, in reality, went to the winning candidate. He then says, "But at least I didn't have a part in his winning." Ah yes, but he certainly will be affected by the winner's policies; and he will have no recourse, since he cannot even say that he spoke by ballot against the policies. If he complains, and if he is then asked what he did to prevent the candidate's election, he will be left as silent as he was at the polls. There is nothing sadder than the loneliness of the knowledge that one did not consciously choose.

It seems that I have built a case for being an advocate as well as a case for not being an advocate. Just as there are extremists of the libertarian ethic and of the egalitarian ethic, so one might say there are extremists for and against advocacy. Yes, there can be extreme points of view for or against advocacy, but they are no more sound than those for or against egalitarianism or libertarianism. Rather than be an extremist in the cause of advocacy, carefully and knowledgeably choose a path that allows you to act as an advocate as much as possible, and if you cannot engage in the role yourself, you can at least not interfere with others doing so. Provide support, especially to those who choose to be advocates.

One other area of fundamental knowledge in the advocate's armamentarium needs exploring—ethics. Ethical positions form one of the cornerstones of the social development of an individual or a system. So let us round off the discussion of fundamentals with an examination of ethics.

NOTES ON CHAPTER 4

On the subject of social ethic, Gardner's book *Excellence* is a must. It deals with how the social ethic is conceptualized and operationalized in American culture.

Gardner, John W. *Excellence.* New York: Harper & Row, Publishers, Inc., 1961.

In addition, McClure's article, written from a nurse administrator's point of view in having to cope with an egalitarian position, might bear reading. Her approach is in terms of accountability.

McClure, Margaret. "The Long Road to Accountability." *Nursing Outlook* 26 (January 1978): 47-50.

It is difficult to say what one should read in the areas of the "isms" of race, sex, and age. Many volumes have been written on racism. The person who has never experienced racism directly or even indirectly should refer to the old classic novels of Richard Wright or even to the writings of Malcom X. For the political aspects of the subject, he should refer to Carmichael's and Hamilton's book.

Carmichael, Stokeley, and Hamilton, Charles V. *Black Power: The Politics of Liberation in America.* New York: Vintage Books, 1967.

However, there are other and perhaps better writings on the subject. For persons who have experienced racism and thus are more than sensitive to it and perhaps are advocates of an extreme egalitarianism in all areas of life, I would recommend Gardner for a moderate view and to the works of writers like William F. Buckley for a libertarian view. An advocate must at least be aware of the fact that people take various positions that will affect their behavior. An advocate must be knowledgable about these positions, whether or not they agree with them.

Much as been written recently on sexism, mostly from the feminist point of view. Given the fact that sexism affects more people than racism, the volume of this work may soon equal that of the work on racism. I hesitate to recommend anyone, so I will say only that my students have found Guissum's book valuable.

Guissam, Marlene, and Spengler, Carol. *Womanpower and Health Care*. Boston: Little, Brown & Co., 1976.

Tangential to the subject of sexism is Ashley's book on paternalism. However, for a different view of this topic, read the anti-ERA writers. Let me remind you that ignorance of the law and ignorance of one's opponent's position are inexcusable in a society where both are widely published and accessible.

Ashley, JoAnn. *Hospitals, Paternalism, and the Role of the Nurse*. New York: Teachers College Press, 1976.

Much is also being written about ageism. Usually the topic is referred to in articles that deal primarily with bad nursing homes, poor financial and emotional support of the aged, or the subject of a dignified death. There are many works on the subject of our worship of youth, which is one of the basic underlying motivations for ageism. In general, I would refer you to the writings of the Gray Panthers organization for more definitive work on ageism. Interestingly enough, this is the one "ism" that cuts across boundaries of sex and race. However, in spite of this seemingly broad appeal, it receives the least attention.

The literature on sexism and racism is often geared to the subject of access to education and health care. I merely suggest that one read widely and accept a position that is based more on logic than emotionalism. Our newspapers, magazines (both popular and professional), television programs, and movies all deal with one aspect or another of this issue. The advocate must be knowledgeable about all sides, even if he or she may prefer one side to another.

Chapter 5

ETHICS

THE PURPOSE OF THIS CHAPTER is to describe the relationship between ethics and advocacy. Advocacy is the process of informing people so that they can make decisions and then supporting them in their decisions. Ethics or ethical positions are influenced by attitudes, values, and beliefs. Ethics speaks to what is right or wrong, to duties and obligations. The particular ethical theory one subscribes to will depend on one's attitudes and beliefs. A knowledge of ethical theories will help advocates to understand other people's points of view and thus to develop strategies that will make the advocacy process safer both for themselves and for clients. So although ethics and advocacy are related, they are clearly different.

The distinction between ethics and the law is also relevant to advocacy. In an attempt to synthesize what many writers have said about the relationship between ethics and the law, I have arrived at the following brief opinion: ethics deals with good or bad, right or wrong, and (on a broad, universal basis), justice and injustice; many but not all of these concepts are translated into laws that enhance justice or offer remediation for injustice. The concept of just or injust as it relates to laws is bound into the framework of a particular society, culture, or country, and thus is not universal. Also, within this narrower framework, laws can be just as well as unjust. The law, therefore, is a much narrower concept than ethics. One might say that ethics speaks to how human beings relate to each other in a system or philosophy of fairness, while the law attempts to organize this relationship into a system of compliance in a particular social order. The law attempts to deal with major wrongs against an individual and a society, while ethics speaks to all the wrongs in humans' interactions with each other, which are not always translatable into the law of a society. Some say that if ethics were always translatable into laws, the human ability to interact would be stifled to a ludicrous degree. (One excellent discussion of this topic can be found in John Stuart Mill—see the readings at the end of this chapter.) As ethics and the law are related to advocacy, so they are related to each other. Both are essential for the advocate in the formulation of risk-defusing strategies.

Since ethics is a major part of the advocate's assessment process, as well as a tool that can be used in risk defusement, it is necessary that the advocate be familiar with the more common ethical theories or perspectives. I will present three of these positions in condensed form: the utilitarian, the Kantian, and the situational. There are numerous other theories, and I suggest that you consult a good ethics textbook to become more familiar with them. But for the purposes of this chapter I will deal only with these three, because of their broad influence in Western society. Keep in mind that the discussions of these ethical positions are very brief.

In this chapter I have included Lawrence Kohlberg's ideas on moral development as they relate to ethics, because I believe they will help the advocate in both the assessment process and the risk defusement process. Many ethical theorists believe that views one holds as a youth may change with maturity. This is Kohlberg's position. Kohlberg deals with the way in which changes in one's ethical views reflect one's moral development.

I hope that by providing you with a broad overview of some major ethical theories, and related work like Kohlberg's, I will help you to understand and appreciate the need for a broadening of your knowledge base before you embark on the role of advocate.

Finally, I will present a discussion of how ethical dilemmas relate to the advocate's role. I believe that a familiarity with ethics is necessary to the knowledge base of an advocate. I also believe, however, that because both ethics and the law deal with right or wrong, duties and obligations, they tend to speak to the rescuer in us and therefore tend to make us forget that the role of the advocate is only to inform and support a client in his decision-making process. Regardless of whether we approve of a client's informed decision, we must acknowledge his right to make it.

UTILITARIANISM

To define utilitarianism, which is commonly called a theory of "consequence," I will quote from the work of the philosopher who is most closely associated with this point of view, the nineteenth-century Englishman John Stuart Mill: "All action is for the sake of some end, and rules of action, it seems natural to suppose, must take their whole character and colour from the end to which they are subservient."[1] This statement has commonly been interpreted to mean that the end justifies the means. Some critics of utilitarianism have said that the philosophy means that actions taken for the good of the whole are justified, regardless of their effect on the parts. Other critics call this the doctrine of expediency: it is where you are going that counts, not how you get there. Utilitarians respond by saying that such interpretations result from a poor understanding of the basic premise of utilitarianism. This premise is what Mill and his predecessors call the "happiness theory"—that man's goals are happiness and exemption from pain:

> The creed which accepts as the foundation of morals, Utility, or the Greatest Happiness Principle, holds that actions are right in proportion as they tend to promote happiness, wrong as they tend to produce the reverse of happiness. By happiness is intended pleasure, and the absence of pain; by unhappiness, pain, and the privation of pleasure.[2]

Mill says that utilitarianism is based on a clear moral standard that includes ideas of both pain and pleasure. Mill admits that these ideas may be defined in

[1]John Stuart Mill, *Utilitarianism, Liberty and Representative Government* (New York: E. P. Dutton and Co., Inc., 1951,) p. 2.
[2]*Ibid.*, pp. 7-8.

various ways, but he argues that this fact does not affect the theory of life on which utilitarianism is grounded—

> . . . namely, that pleasure, and freedom from pain, are the only things desirable as ends; and that all desirable things [which are as numerous in the utilitarian as in any other scheme] are desirable either for the pleasure inherent in themselves, or as means to the promotion of pleasure and prevention of pain.[3]

Mill goes on to defend utilitarianism from those who claim that if his philosophy were adopted, human beings would want the lowest types of pleasure and would be like animals. He denies this allegation by arguing that as human beings rank from the lowest to highest, so do their pleasures. He says that the various classes of pleasure appeal, respectively, to the various classes of human beings. He also says that pleasure does not consist in the consideration of one person for himself alone but of men for men, that we want the greatest amount of pleasure for everyone and the least amount of pain for all. Mill argues that the ends of human actions are the basis of morality. He believes that if we wish the best for ourselves and others, the actions required to gain such an end will be in accordance with it. Since the pursuit of happiness is coexistent with the mitigation of unhappiness, such an action takes into account both goals.[4]

Mill also discusses the problem of conflicting obligations. He says that such conflicts exist, regardless of the moral theory under which a person operates, and that they must be resolved. He believes that the concept of pleasure versus pain should be the criterion of judgment. Mill would argue that this is not a selfish attitude, since human beings are so dependent on each other that one person's interest in pleasure would be extended to others.

It may well strike you that utilitarianism is the basis on which large systems do function—systems like government agencies, schools, and hospitals, which out of necessity cannot deal with individuals as such. Policies may be determined on the basis of having to cope with large numbers of people in the most ethical manner possible under the circumstances. However, it has been noted that this utilitarian philosophy conflicts directly with traditional medical ethics, which says that everything possible should be done for the individual.[5]

The most important fact to remember about utilitarianism is that people have taken from it (fairly or not) the idea that if the end is good, the means used to gain that end are justified. I do not believe that all utilitarians would agree with this expression of utilitarian theory, but the theory lends itself to this conclusion as a justification to behavior.

[3]*Ibid.*, p. 8.
[4]*Ibid.*, pp. 8-23.
[5]Ann J. Davis and Mila A. Aroskar, *Ethical Dilemmas and Nursing Practice* (New York: Appleton-Century-Crofts, 1978).

KANTIANISM

Let me quote directly from the German philosopher Immanuel Kant (1724-1804): "Act so as to treat man, in your own person as well as in that of anyone else, always as an end, never merely as a means."[6] In other words, the means must be justified in and of themselves, not merely by the ends they achieve. Kant speaks of maxims being general laws in themselves: "We must be able to will that a maxim of our actions should be a general law. This is the canon of any moral assessment [of our] actions."[7] This point of view does not allow a person to tell a lie and then justify it by arguing that it serves a good end or that the truth would be hurtful. Kant says that a person wills actions as well as ends:

> . . . an action done from duty derives its moral worth, not from the purpose which is to be attained by it, but from the maxim by which it is determined. Therefore the action does not depend on the realization of its objective, but merely on the principle of volition by which the action has taken place, without regard to any object of desire. It is clear from what precedes that the purpose which we may have in view for our actions, or their effects as regarded as ends and impulsions of will, cannot give to actions any unconditional or moral worth.[8]

Kant compares this position to the biblical command to love one's neighbor, even one's enemy. He says that this command calls for a practical action of love, not a psychological one—love not in sentiment but in principles of action.

Some relate Kant's view of man as an end in himself, and not as something to be acted on, to Israeli philosopher Martin Buber's concept of "I-Thou"—as opposed to "I-It," wherein a person is seen as a thing or an object. However, Buber deals primarily with the nature of relationships between human beings, while Kant is concerned primarily with human behavior.

• • •

It is interesting to note that the utilitarians and the Kantians seem to use similar passages from the Bible to support their stands. But the resulting attitudes are not the same. In utilitarians one seems to sense an "I know best" theme creeping in to justify behavior if an end is good, while Kantians are inclined to suffer a bad end rather than violate the principle of free choice. However, Mill himself moved close to a Kantian perspective regarding individual liberty by advocating that such liberty not be violated, no matter what the end. He held freedom of the individual to be inviolate.

[6]Carl J. Friedrich, ed., *The Philosophy of Kant: Immanuel Kant's Moral and Political Writings* (New York: Random House, Inc., 1949), p. 178.
[7]*Ibid.*, p. 172.
[8]*Ibid.*, p. 147.

Both the Kantians and the utilitarians have been divided into various sub-groups by ethical theorists. For a more complete understanding of these ethical schools, and others, I urge you to refer to a work such as that of Frankena.[9]

SITUATIONISM

A third group of ethical theorists subscribes to what is called "situational ethics." They seem to swing between the utilitarians and the Kantians, depending on what they believe a situation calls for. According to a major authority in this area, a theologian named Joseph Fletcher, "situationism is a method, not a substantive ethic."[10] He speaks of it as an approach to ethical decision making:

> The situationist enters into every decision making situation fully armed with the ethical maxims of community and its heritage, and he treats them with respect as illuminators of his problems. Just the same he is prepared in any situation to compromise them or set them aside 'in the situation' if love seems better served by doing so.[11]

Fletcher says that the basis of situationism is love. "The situationist follows a moral law or violates it according to love's need."[12] Here he is using "love" in the Christian sense of *agapē;* he says that situationism has its roots in the classical tradition of Western Christian morality. Ethical principles are derived from the universal law of love, not from laws or rules. "Circumstances alter rules and principles." Fletcher believes that the only principle that is always right and good is love, and he refers to the biblical command to love God and one's neighbor.[13]

Fletcher says that four presuppositions are at work when a person makes a decision: (1) pragmatism, (2) relativism, (3) positivism, and (4) personalism.[14] The situational method then is based on what Fletcher calls six propositions:

1. "Only one 'thing' is intrinsically good; namely, love: nothing else at all."
2. "The ruling norm of Christian decision is love: nothing else."
3. "Love and justice are the same, for justice is love distributed, nothing else."
4. "Love wills the neighbor's good whether we like him or not."
5. "Only the end justifies the means; nothing else."
6. "Love's decisions are made situationally, not prescriptively."[15]

[9]William K. Frankena, *Ethics*, ed. 2 (Englewood Cliffs, N.J.: Prentice-Hall, Inc., 1976).
[10]Joseph Fletcher, *Situation Ethics: The New Morality* (Philadelphia: The Westminster Press, 1974), p. 34.
[11]*Ibid.*, p. 26.
[12]*Ibid.*
[13]*Ibid.*, pp. 29-30.
[14]*Ibid.*, pp. 40-52.
[15]*Ibid.*, pp. 57, 69, 87, 103, 122, 134.

The fifth proposition makes the situationists look like utilitarians at heart, but Fletcher denies that they are. He moves toward a Kantian position to say that ends and means do not exist apart from one another. Fletcher defines situationism as a decision-making method and not as an ethic. Situationists do not adhere to any one ethical rule or theory but fall back on situations and love as the determining factors in a person's behavior.

In some circumstances, situationists seem to be Kantians; in other circumstances, they seem to be utilitarians. In addition, they are like Buber in their belief in people as opposed to things. It is difficult to classify situationists as ethical theorists; they do not adhere to a theory in the same way that Kantians or Utilitarians do. Situationists consider themselves members of a "new morality"; some would call them modernists. They constitute a large group, and advocates would be well advised to at least be familiar with their thinking and influence.

●   ●   ●

Advocates will encounter all three of these ethical positions, and others, in their professional lives and in their reading. People make decisions on the basis of some set of values, whether or not they can articulate what ethical schools the values represent. In fact, most people do not know. To complicate matters even more, a person may hold one set of beliefs about how others should relate to him and another set about how he should relate to others.

It is important for advocates to examine themselves and what they believe in and to establish some consistency in their actions. It is also important that they develop an understanding of the ethical possibilities that exist and of the range of ethical positions that may determine human behavior. Advocates should be familiar with the current philosophers who are authorities in ethics (to this end I suggest you read W.K. Frankena's work on ethics, which I have already mentioned). Advocates should also be familiar with the work of the professionals in their own fields who have specialized in ethics. Two nurses, for example, who have written on ethics are Anne Davis and Mila Aroskar (see reading list). There are others; the nursing profession has, I believe, more scholars who have specialized in the field of ethics than any of the other health-related professions. This says a great deal about nurses' basic committment to human rights.

I believe it would be helpful at this point to present a hypothetical case and to examine how utilitarians, Kantians, and situationists might view it.

Mrs. Adams, who is in her mid-forties and married, and who has two grown children and two children in their early teens, has been told that she has a tumor of the breast. Her physician has told both her and her family that the treatment of choice is a radical mastectomy and that if the lymph nodes are involved, the surgery will be followed by radiation and/or chemotherapy. She is informed about other surgical possibilities (less radical forms) and about possible treatments other than surgery. The physician gives his opinion of the options and what he feels are the consequences of each. He ends by repeating what he believes to be the best choice, a radical mastectomy. After some thought Mrs. Adams decides that she will not have the radical mastectomy. She says that she would rather die than go through life with such a severe bodily distortion; she simply could not live with it. The physician, the husband, the children, and other relatives all want Mrs. Adams to live.

What actions might the physician and the family members take if they were all of the utilitarian ethical position? Utilitarians look for the greatest good for all and for the end result of good. In this case their goal would be to ensure that Mrs. Adams lives. To be fair, we must assume that they would understand how Mrs. Adams feels about the bodily distortion of radical surgery and that they would sympathize with this feeling to an extent. However, they still would not want her to die. As utilitarians, they would argue that her living would result in the greatest good for everyone, that the end of living far outweighs the means of achieving it, in spite of Mrs. Adams' feelings of despair. They might rationalize that she will get over these feelings and that even if she does not, they would rather have her alive than dead. (This is not an unusual case or an unusual way for any family to feel. If the members of a family are of the utilitarian ethic, this feeling will come even more naturally to them).

In this situation an advocate could expect the physician and the family to be united in an attempt to persuade Mrs. Adams to change her mind about the surgery. Their methods may range from appeals to her love for the family to guilt-inducing accusations—for example, that she is selfishly disregarding their feelings and their fears that she may die. Furthermore, they may attempt to engage others in the persuasion process—certainly the nurse who spends the most time with her, and perhaps even her clergyman, if she has one. If everyone banded together, Mrs. Adams would be left on her own to withstand the pressure of all those who are significant to her. If her nurse acted as an advocate and supported Mrs. Adams' right to her own decision, it is easy to see how difficult the nurse's position would be.

Now let us assume that the same situation exists but that the physician and the family members are of a Kantian ethical position. This fact would not change their desire that Mrs. Adams live or their reasons for so desiring. But the Kantians believe that the means of living are as important as life itself and that the good of the individual, as determined by the individual, is as important as the good of others. What then would the physician and the family members do? Again, to be fair, let us assume that they would express their desire that Mrs. Adams live; they would emphasize that their love for her would not change because of a change in her physical appearance. But should she remain adamant in her decision, they would, with reluctance and sadness, honor this decision and even support her in it. There would be a united front with the patient rather than against her, and an attempt to make the best of the situation. The Kantians make the advocate's position much easier, since the advocate's role is to support Mrs. Adams in her decision. The advocate would, in essence, receive no opposition in this support role, and might even be encouraged in it.

Finally, what would happen if everyone took a situationist stance, again assuming that everyone wanted Mrs. Adams to live? Again, a great deal of discussion would go on among the physician, family members, and Mrs. Adams, but in more combinations. In addition, others might be drawn into the discussion for the purpose of reaching a decision about whether to go along with Mrs. Adams' and support her or to try to change her mind. Many questions would be raised: Is Mrs. Adams' decision an emotional decision of the moment? Would having her talk with a therapist help to clarify her attitudes toward herself and others? Does she *really* know enough to make the decision she has made? How badly do the members of her family need her support? Can they continue without her? Does her decision represent a suicidal wish? Is she sane at the moment? Will she become totally dysfunctional as the result of the blow of surgery? In other words, all avenues of inquiry would be explored (an excellent opportunity for the person who practices "value clarification" to step in and have a talk with Mrs. Adams).

Where is the advocate in this process? The advocate may or may not be in a good position, depending on the outcome of the discussion. But during the process the advocate is in a precarious position, because he or she is supporting Mrs. Adams' right to make a decision. The advocate's position is not as precarious as it is with the utilitarians but not as safe as it is with the Kantians. Needless to say, the Kantians are the safest to deal with, in terms of the advocate's role of informing and supporting. This is not to say that they are right.

One factor has not been dealt with in this example. What is the ethical position of the advocate in this situation? Whatever it is, it will certainly affect the way the advocate feels. But it must *not* affect the way he or she acts. The advocate's role is clear: to inform and support, regardless of his or her personal ethical belief. That is not easy, but the role of advocate is not an easy role. It is made more difficult when an advocate has to face risks for a person who may be acting contrary to the advocate's own personal beliefs. In simple language, it is easier to support a person's right to make his own decisions when you agree with those decisions.

One might well ask, what if Mrs. Adams is wrong in her choice? What if she has made an emotional decision, a decision of the moment, perhaps based on vanity, that she will regret later? That very question is what has made situational ethics so strong in modern times. This question is the basis for the bulk of the literature on ethical dilemmas that we see so much of. This literature often leaves us with more questions than answers and actions. I will make no attempt in this book to tell you how to resolve dilemmas, nor do I believe the advocate should attempt to resolve them. The advocate's role is clear: inform and support. To become bogged down in dilemmas will prevent a person from acting as an advocate. Judgment is not part of the role of the advocate; the advocate's duty is only to ensure the right of free will or free choice.

One final note to think about in regard to Mrs. Adams' case: What would the situation look like to the advocate if we introduced the variables of racism, ageism, and sexism? What if Mrs. Adams were black and old? What if her husband, her male physician, and her male children were chauvinists? What if she were in her seventies, being loved but also being suspected of being slightly senile, at least at the time she made her decision? What if she were convinced that, because she is old, black, and female, her decision was made in ignorance and that she would regret it later? Furthermore, what if she presented an interesting surgical case for the teaching purpose of the hospital and the medical establishment? All these variables can tremendously increase the pressure on Mrs. Adams and, needless to say, on the nurse advocate.

•   •   •

At this point you might be seriously questioning whether an advocate can generally have good relationships both with a client and with a client's family. Or how is the concept of holistic care affected by advocacy? Or, to put this question in another context, is there an ethical conflict between the role of advocate and the role of professional nurse, in regard to the delivery of holistic care? Is there a hierarchy of obligations or of roles? The same questions could be asked about the legalities of the role of nurse. How do you divide ethics, legalities, and advocacy into separate entities? That this division must be made is not the question, but how do you do it?

Before we discuss these questions, let us explore one more area of the ethics knowledge base. Keep in mind that the purpose of this chapter is to provide knowledge that can be used in the analysis process and in risk defusement. So let us look at Kohlberg's ideas about ethics as another potentially valuable tool to be used in the assessment process. Then we will move on to the questions of how to differentiate ethics from legal questions, from the role of the advocate, and from the role of the nurse in holistic care, and how to deal with dilemmas.

KOHLBERG'S DEVELOPMENTAL FRAMEWORK

Ethical theories focus on the content and nature of ethical choices. Kohlberg does not propose an ethical theory. Rather, he deals with the developmental process of moral judgment, and its significance in ethical reasoning. His work builds on the work of Jean Piaget, which focused on the use of cognitive-developmental psychology to describe the changes in ethical reasoning that take place during a person's lifetime. This work was part of Piaget's larger work on cognitive functions and development. Using Piaget's developmental model, Kohlberg demonstrated that moral development involves a sequence of stages that a person passes through as he becomes older and more mature and as he is influenced by the environment.

Kohlberg defines three developmental levels, each of which has two stages. He and his colleagues studied and observed these stages not only in the United States but in several cultures in various parts of the world. He found that although the time required to move through the stages varies from person to person and from culture to culture, the sequence remains the same.[16] The following levels and stages are described by Kohlberg:

LEVEL 1: PRECONVENTIONAL   An individual's moral reasoning results from the consequences, usually physical, of his actions—that is, the rewards, punishments, and favors that are given out by the persons who are seen to have authority over him. The individual is likely to respond to labels of good and bad, right and wrong. There are two stages.

STAGE 1   Avoidance of punishment and deference to power are ends in themselves and form the basis for moral decisions. One could say the individual responds more from a fear of punishment than from a respect for authority. This attitude is common in children up to the age of about seven. However, this response can also be seen in persons who are older. One might describe it as primitive.

STAGE 2   The necessity to satisfy one's own needs forms the basis for moral decisions. The needs of others are viewed pragmatically. This stage is characterized by hedonism; actions are based on the concept of "I'll do for you if you do for me." or "What's in it for me? What can I get out of this?" Actions and decisions are based on gain only. This behavior is common in the business world and the marketplace.

One can see Level 1 behavior in grossly immature nurses or patients.

LEVEL 2: CONVENTIONAL   The moral reasoning of the individual results from the expectations of the family, a social group, a community, or a nation. These groups are supported by the individual, and what the group expects is what the individual does. The individual would certainly be considered "other oriented" in terms of values and opinions. He is a conformist. This level also has two stages.

STAGE 3   That which pleases or helps others and is approved by them becomes the basis for moral decisions—a "good boy" way of behaving so that others will like and approve of a person. To conform is good, and frequently if a person does err it is the intention to do good or conform that matters. One would hear comments like "He meant well" or "he was trying to do his best, and that is what is most important." These are the kinds of remarks that one might make about learners or

[16]Lawrence Kohlberg and Elliot Turiel, "Moral Development and Moral Education," in *Psychology and Educational Practice*, edited by G. Lesser (Chicago: Scott, Foresman & Co., 1971).

beginners—for example, a little girl who breaks a glass while helping her mother wash dishes after dinner. Decisions and actions based on the intent to do good are rewarded and/or forgiven. These not uncommon situations can be found in the behavior of professionals, who are not beginners but who may act like good children to superiors, supervisors, physicians, and so on. As long as a person is rewarded, or at least forgiven, it pays to be good. Much incompetence is covered up in just this manner. One will not find an advocate in this stage.

STAGE 4   The basis for moral decisions lies in obeying the rules and the authorities and maintaining the current social order. Law and order are important ends in themselves. "Doing one's duty," "showing respect," and "keeping things in order" are paramount. A person does what is expected of him. I mean to imply not that persons in Stage 4 are incapable of thought or reasoning but rather that they are highly motivated to comply with social norms and to obey rules even though they may secretly question them.

This has been the mode of operation in nursing for years. I call it the "don't think" mode: "Follow the doctor's orders." *Don't think.* "Follow the hospital policies." *Don't think.* If all else fails, "Do what the supervisor says." *Don't think.* This is conformity at its height, and it is duly rewarded by the group and the group standard.

The movement to create knowledgeable, autonomous, professional thinkers in the nursing profession has run headlong into furious opposition in our institutions. This opposition comes from physicians, hospital administrators, and nurses themselves. Much lip service is given to hiring college-educated professional nurses who can think and bring creativity to their jobs. But once they have been hired, they are expected to conform to the norms and rules of the group, which generally adheres to the "obey the orders" philosophy. A nurse who objects is labeled a nonconformist— and worse, a troublemaker—and soon learns his or her place in the hierarchy or finds another job. The key to acceptance is conformity.

Kohlberg believes that the majority of American adults are in this stage of moral development. I would certainly agree that most of the people who are engaged in the delivery of health care or illness care are in this stage; many of those in our educational systems are, too. This latter statement may surprise some, but instructors do not always practice, or are not always expected to practice, what they teach their students. Their goal may be to help students to become independent, knowledgeable thinkers, but society does not want to see too much of this behavior in teachers themselves.

One wonders what then happens to the questionable idea of role modeling. The old adage "Do what I say, not what I do" is the message that teachers often communicate to their students. However, instructors are to be accused of some negligence for not telling students that the behavior they teach them will not be met with many "hoorays" in the marketplace of nursing. The state of moral development of nursing instructors often reminds me of the child who so desperately wants to be grown up and to be treated like an adult, and says so, yet cannot quite help acting like the child he is. The sad part is that nursing instructors, or nurses in general, are not children, and it is time we gave up the toys and behavior of childhood. In the words of the New Testament, "When I was a child I spoke and thought and reasoned as a child does. But when I became a man my thoughts grew far beyond those of my childhood, and now I have put away the childish things." Not only our moral development but our development as professionals and advocates depends on our becoming adults. Subservient obedience to rules set by others is not possible for advocates. They cannot function at this level, and they will receive little support from persons who do.

LEVEL 3: POSTCONVENTIONAL   A person's moral reasoning includes the realization that universal moral principles supersede the authority of groups. The individual makes an effort to move away from the morality of groups and toward a morality that is his own. He attempts to define moral values and principles for himself; they may or may not be similar to those of a group, and they do not rely on group identification for validity. In other words he accepts moral principles that fit his concept of himself. Again there are two stages.

STAGE 5   Personal values and opinions are seen as the basis for moral decisions. However, the individual is seen as a member of a group that democratically makes rules based on the opinions of the individual members. Rules may be altered by the individuals involved. Although the morality is personal, it does depend on the concept of a social contract. Moral action is defined in terms of generally accepted views of individual rights and in terms of standards that have been examined and agreed on by the whole society.

In this stage a person moves from the narrowness of the law to the broadness of ethics. He realizes that whether the law guarantees him certain rights or not, the broader framework of ethics, which is not translated into the law, does give him these rights. One might say that the current lists of patients' rights in various settings, although not legal documents, are nonetheless codes of behavior that one must adhere to. Likewise, the various codes of ethics that professions have set up for themselves are not translated into the law, but rather are accepted as guidelines for professional behavior.

Thus in this stage moral behavior goes beyond the narrow confines of conventional role conformity. Moral action rises above what any one group may decide are the rules; the general consensus of society as a whole becomes the guide to proper behavior. Moral action agrees with the democratically accepted standard of behavior of the larger society, whether this standard has been translated into enforceable laws or not. The boundaries of morality have been extended beyond the immediate group and beyond the written law, to become a social contract that rises above what is written or practiced in any one place.

Stage 5 is probably the world in which most who venture forth into the role of advocate will reside. Their role will be generally accepted by society as a whole but will not be defended or protected by the written law or the rules of the immediate groups in which they work. They may be viewed as nonconformists by their immediate groups. Although they will not be considered lawbreakers, they certainly will be considered to be outside the law, since there will be no clear law they can conform to. Their behavior and their defense will be based on a higher form of social morality and social consensus. That this consensus exists and is firm, clear, and democratically arrived at is certain, but how advocates will be able to function will depend on their assessment abilities and their risk defusement strategies. Again, advocates must combine the "wisdom of serpents," with the "gentleness of doves." It is no wonder that Kohlberg says that only one in five Americans achieves this stage of moral development.

STAGE 6   Moral decisions are based on the universal principles of justice, reciprocity, equality of human rights, and respect for the dignity of human beings as individuals. These principles apply to all human beings and may supersede the rules established by groups. In other words, moral action may go beyond what society thinks is right, even if society has arrived at a point of view by democratic means. In this stage the individual is on his own; he is outside even the broad framework of acceptable societal standards. He develops universal ethical principles. Individual principles of conscience are developed that are comprehensive, universal, and consistent. They tend to be abstract, rather than concrete moral rules. Here the individual must deal only with himself. Life is seen to be sacred and to represent a universal value. Kohlberg believes that such people as Martin Luther King, Socrates, and Abraham Lincoln have demonstrated evidence of this stage in their writings and speeches.[17]

I have presented the essence of Kohlberg's concept of moral development. The preceding summary in no way represents his complete work, nor does it do justice to his breadth of thinking on moral development. I encourage you to go directly to his writings to see how he establishes the validity of his concepts through his research.

[17]The preceding discussion of Kohlberg is based not only on the source given in footnote 16 but also on three other sources: First, David A.J. Richards' paper entitled "Moral Theory: The Developmental Psychology of Ethical Autonomy and Professionalism," delivered at the New York University Colloquium on the Teaching of Ethics and Moral Value, February 20, 1979; second, Ruth Bindler, "Moral Development in Nursing Education," *Image* 9, no. 1 (February 1977): and third, Rosemary Krawczyk and Elizabeth Kudzama, "Ethics: A Matter of Moral Development," *Nursing Outlook* 4 (April 1978):254-257. Any number of authors have written on and interpreted Kohlberg's work. I have chosen these three as representative and also pertinent to my presentation of his work in the context of advocacy. The comments on his stages as they relate to nursing are my own. The articles both of Bindler and of Krawczyk and Kudzama attempt to show how nursing educators can use Kohlberg in the teaching process as it relates to ethical and moral development and to what they call the ethical dilemmas of the nurse. They are valuable readings.

•   •   •

Kohlberg's concept can serve as a guide in the assessment of self, client, or health care system. At this point it would be a good exercise for you to go back to the case of Mrs. Adams and ask these questions: If the nurse were asked by the physician and the family to convince Mrs. Adams to have the surgery, how would the nurse react if he or she were in each of Kohlberg's stages? Why would the nurse act in this manner? You should consider one further question, which is a bit more complex. How do Kohlberg's stages relate to the utilitarian, Kantian, and situational positions? My purpose is not to confuse you but only to point out the many variables an advocate must consider.

Be aware that in spite of the importance of a knowledge of ethics, such knowledge is not a sure guide in the role of advocate. It is only part of the gestalt that must be taken into consideration. Now let us go back to the question of how ethics, holistic care, and the law are related.

ETHICS, ADVOCACY, AND HOLISTIC CARE

Is there a hierarchy in ethics? Does the nurse, in the case of Mrs. Adams, owe less allegiance to the family of Mrs. Adams than she does to Mrs. Adams herself?

Here again we are dealing with questions very rarely mentioned in the literature. We see a great deal written about "holistic care," which is defined as care that is directed not only to the client but also to the client's family. For example, when my partners and I wrote about our private practice in the book *Independent Nurse Practitioner*, we stated that when we accepted a new client we also involved the client's family in our care. Various other books and articles have also argued that nurses should provide holistic care, no matter what the practice modality. But what the literature has not spoken to is the role of the advocate in case of a conflict between the desires of the client and the desires of the family. This kind of conflict does not usually arise, but, as in the case of Mrs. Adams, it can arise. When it happens, what then happens to the concept of holistic care? Is this a classical example of an ethical dilemma? Or does this situation even involve ethics?

Such a conflict can result in an ethical dilemma if you choose to allow it to. Or you can view it in a simpler fashion by asking yourself these questions: what is the nurse's role? How does the nurse interpret this role to others? Despite the advantages of the holistic approach to care, the nurse must keep in mind who the primary client is. This is where the question of priorities comes in. Although the nurse prefers to deal in a holistic manner with the family, the basic reason the nurse is there is that a client needs care. So the priorities are set at the start: first the client, then the family. For without the client there would be no family to consider. Holistic care is only a preferred method of delivering care to a client. In other words, if the care is not holistic, this does not mean that it is not care. The care still exists; it is simply narrower in scope. The nurse may wish to include the family, but if the family members do not want to be included, or later exclude themselves because of a conflict with the patient's desires, this fact does not stop the nurse from delivering care to the client. So the client comes first; he is the central figure in the care delivery design.

If nurses define their role as simply one of delivering physical nursing care, they can exclude themselves from conflicts between clients and families or other people. When asked to support a physician or a family against a client, they can silently do nothing, or they can say, "I'm not getting involved; it's none of my business; I'm only going to do what I was hired to do"—in other words, "Don't bother me, I can't cope." This is a common choice; whether nurses express this decision verbally or not, the result is the same.

If nurses define themselves both as holistic care deliverers and as patient advocates, they must make clear whom they see as the client when priorities come into question—or, better, before they do. If nurses make their role or roles clear at the start, less confusion occurs. The family and the physician know where a nurse stands at the beginning. This stand may not make any difference to them, and they may even be pleased, at least at the stage when there are no problems. When and if problems occur, as in the case of Mrs. Adams, they at least will know what the nurse's position will be. This is not to say that they will not attempt to get the nurse on their side—they probably will. But they will not be completely taken by surprise when the nurse refuses. Clarification of one's role is necessary to one's success in that role, no matter what the role is.

Let us go back to my original question. Is there a hierarchy of ethical considerations? No, the question of ethics is not involved. Rather, it is a question of deciding what role you wish to play and making the client and the family aware of it. The concept of holistic care is not in conflict with the role of advocate unless the family makes it so—or the nurse fails to clarify his or her role to the family and the client. Thus the nurse who chooses to deliver holistic care also acts ethically and as an advocate. The family may refuse holistic care, may not want the nurse to be the client's advocate, or at times may not want the nurse to act ethically, but the client takes priority. What does the client want? If there is more than one client in a family, this does not complicate the situation, since each client is first approached as an individual. The holistic framework the nurse functions in is not changed. Remember, the bottom line of advocacy is that the client makes the decisions, not the nurse advocate. Some may say that there are cases in which the entire family is the client. Generally, this is true only in cases involving family psychotherapy, and in such cases the role of the therapist is clearly defined. In some situations, however, an entire family may be ill. But the professional nurse still approaches each member as an individual client and acts accordingly. While the nurse may see a family as a unit, the unit is made up of individuals. Thus we can allow dilemmas to be created if we forget our role and/or allow others to change it for us.

• • •

There is one other area in which confusion and dilemmas can be created. Just as ethics, advocacy, and the concept of holistic care can be confused and dilemmas can be created, so can ethics, advocacy, and the law (or legalities) be mixed together. Let us now discuss how these concepts are different.

ETHICS, ADVOCACY, AND THE LAW

At the beginning of this chapter I pointed out that the law is a narrower concept than ethics. Ethics speaks to how human beings relate to each other in a framework or philosophy of fairness, and the law attempts to organize this relationship into a system of compliance with a social order. The law speaks only to the wrongs that are recognized as such by a particular society, while ethics speaks to more universal wrongs. The latter may not be translatable into the laws of a particular society. Also, remember that all laws are not just, nor is there any universal stability in laws. They change over time and differ from place to place.

There are general laws that relate to the behavior of professionals and institutions toward clients. There are also laws concerning the licensing of professionals; they speak to the boundaries of the practice and to the relationships between various groups of professionals. Since ethics is a broader concept than the law, one might be reasonably safe in saying that if a person practices ethically, he will also be practicing legally. Of the two, ethics and the law, only the law is readily enforceable.

In a sense, advocacy serves as a bridge between ethics and the law. That is, properly informing a client meets the requirements of the law, and supporting a client meets the requirements of ethics in terms of honoring a person's right to self-determination. So it would seem that ethics and the law should not conflict but rather should complement each other. In general that is true. There are perhaps situations in which the law is somewhat questionable or even downright unjust and in which true conflict thus occurs. But when these areas are brought to light, the law is generally adjusted over a period of time. For example, for many years patients had no access to their own hospital records; they had to accept what they were told. This situation has changed in many states, where access is now considered to be a right.

One might then ask, "How can ethical confusion or dilemmas occur?" A person can become confused if he asks the wrong questions—if he faces a situation and then asks a question that has no relationship to the facts of the situation at all. If a person does not pay attention to these facts, he can be led into a dilemma or a maze, never realizing that the wrongness or even foolishness of the question itself was his first misstep. This is best demonstrated by an example. A person recently said to me, "I have an advocacy question that deals with ethics to ask you." (I was thus geared to think in terms of advocacy and ethics.) This person went on to say, "A nurse, who is also acting as a patient's advocate, has just received a physician's order for a medication that is not in the generally accepted and prescribed dosage. Does the nurse inform the patient of this situation? If she does, is she then in an ethical bind because she has disturbed the patient-physician trust relationship?" It is easy to see in this example how the nature of the question alone can quickly lead one off in a wrong direction. (This is not to say that one would necessarily stay on that path long.) In essence, the question has nothing to do with the situation posed, and the situation, as stated, has nothing to do with either advocacy or ethics as such.

Let's examine the situation. "A nurse received an order for a medication that is not in the generally prescribed dosage." The proper question is "What does she do?" The laws that govern her license provide a ready answer. She is held legally responsible for the medications she gives; she must know the proper dosage or find out that information before giving the medication. She is held responsible or liable for her actions, whether she initiated an order or a physician did. Under the law she must refuse to give a medication she knows to be in contradiction to accepted practice. Therefore the answer to the "correct question" is that the nurse calls the physician, brings the situation to his attention, and either gives the medication or does not give it, based on her knowledgeable acceptance of the physician's rationale for the order.

The significance of this example does not lie in what the nurse does or does not do in response to her discussion with the physician. Rather, the example points out how wrong questions can create confusion. Also, it demonstrates how one can mix advocacy and ethics into a simple situation that deals with only the legalities of nursing practice.

We are faced with questions of this nature every day. The human mind seems to have a penchant for creating complexity out of simplicity. The best advice that can be offered is to remove a situation completely from the questions, and even from the person asking the questions. Some call this "getting to the heart of the issue." You must be able to assess a situation objectively, with as much bias as possible removed from the facts. You must ask these questions: What does the situation involve? Does it speak to my role as nurse (or social worker, physician, and so on)? Does the law relating to my role give me guidelines or in fact tell me how to behave in that role? If it does not, then does the situation speak to my role as an advocate? Is it directly related to the informing and supporting functions? If it is not an advocacy situation, then does it involve a broader, ethical question? If it does, then how do my personal ethics relate to those of the client? If there is a conflict, what do I do? Back to advocacy. You inform and support. You do not impose. If supporting the client's decision is morally impossible for you, you remove yourself from the situation with a proper explanation—one that does not condemn but that only clarifies your position. Difficult as this may be, it is the only ethical thing you can do. You must remember that there is no consensus on which one is best. Your duty as an advocate is to inform and support—not to judge and not to rescue, both of which imply an "I know best" attitude.

The role of the advocate is clear; the laws governing practice are clear; ethical codes relating to practice serve as guidelines; personal ethical positions vary and can be much more flexible. There is no reason to mix these entities together to create unnecessary dilemmas. There are enough dilemmas in the health care system without our creating new ones. Dealing with clients who cannot make decisions— because, for example, they are unconscious or too young—can involve enough dilemmas without our making new ones by asking the wrong questions. The key to avoiding dilemmas lies in objective assessment, not only of the client but of oneself and the health care system.

•   •   •

You may feel that this chapter has added confusion to the role and process of advocacy. You may fear that there is simply too much to handle in being an advocate. That fear is unfounded. The secret to success in the role lies in recognizing its simplicity. However, the risks inherent in the role lie in acting on the simplicity only. Risk defusement lies in knowing the propensity of humans to create complexity in order to avoid dealing with the simple facts of life. In knowledge, therefore, you find a measure of safety in negotiating the man-made complexities of life. You cannot escape them. The purpose of this chapter has been to alert you to the ethical complexities that advocates encounter.

Now let us move on to the next areas of the knowledge base—the medical-industrial complex, social laws, and politics, all of which can influence the health care system and advocacy. The specifics of these areas are changeable but their influence is ever present.

NOTES ON CHAPTER 5

Since I am not an authority in the field of ethics, I hesitate to suggest definitive references in this area. I can say that I have found Kant, Mill, Fletcher, and Kohlberg, in the original as listed in the footnotes, most interesting. It is always wise to go to originals; however, there are many excellent books on the positions of ethical theorists that will do as well—for example, Frankena.

There are other articles on ethics and subjects tangential to ethics that I have found helpful. One is Yarling's two-part article "Ethical Analysis of a Nursing Problem." This consists of presentation of a case and then discussion of it in terms of the moral and legal aspects of nursing practice and in other ways. In May, 1977, a series of articles appeared in the *American Journal of Nursing* under the general title "Ethical Dilemmas in Nursing." Curtin has discussed the theories and realities of nursing ethics. She raises this question: can a nurse be legally protected if he or she practices ethically? One could, as I have done, also ask this question: can a nurse be protected if he or she practices as an advocate. Several nurses have been working with Kohlberg's writings in the area of moral development. One might be wise to look for future articles, in this area, by Ruth Bindler, Elizabeth Bridstone, the Bandmans, Catherine Murphy, and, especially, Shake Ketefian. Mila Aroskar, in an article on ethical issues in *Community Health Nursing,* provides a nice summary of the theorists and relates ethics to the larger community setting where nurses work. She is concerned with the dilemmas nurses face and with the need for policy-making to help solve these problems. Aroskar and Anne Davis are acknowledged experts and writers in the area of nursing ethics. One is well advised to keep up to date with their work.

Yarling, Roland R. "Ethical Analysis of a Nursing Problem: The Scope of Nursing Practice in Disclosing the Truth to Terminal Patients." *Supervisor Nurse* 9, May 1978, pp. 40-50, and June 1978, pp. 28-34.

"Ethical Dilemmas in Nursing—A Special AJN Supplement." *American Journal of Nursing* 77, no. 5 (May 1977):845-876.

Curtin, Leah L. "Nursing Ethics: Theories and Pragmatics." *Nursing Forum* 17, no. 1 (1978): 5-11.

Aroskar, Mila A. "Ethical Issues in Community Health Nursing." *Nursing Clinics of North America* 14, no. 1 (March 1979):35-44.

Some of the work on ethics that appears in the literature deals with specific patient conditions or problems. I will mention three such works here to give you an idea of their wide diversity. One deals with a nursing staff's efforts to maintain the autonomy of a burn patient in the decision-making process. Another deals with the ethics of giving placebos. Finally, there is a pregnant patient's bill of rights.

I have intended to provide you with only an idea of the wide range of work that touches on the subject of ethics. The above-mentioned articles are not the only ones available, nor are they necessarily the best available.

Imbus, Sharon H., and Zawacki, Bruce, E. "Autonomy for Burned Patients When Survival is Unprecedented." *The New England Journal of Medicine* 297 (August 11, 1977):308-311.

Bok, Sissela. "The Ethics of Giving Placebos." *Scientific American* 231, no. 5 (November 1974):17-23.

The Pregnant Patient's Bill of Rights and the Pregnant Patient's Responsibilities. International Childbirth Education Association, Inc. (Complimentary copy can be obtained by sending a self-addressed envelope to Box 1900, New York, N.Y. 10001; bulk order can be obtained from ICEA Publication/Distribution Center, P.O. Box 3825, Brighton Station, Rochester, N.Y. 14610.)

Chapter 6

MEDICAL-INDUSTRIAL COMPLEX, SOCIAL LAWS, POLITICS

IN CHAPTER 4 I dealt with the issues of race, age, sex, and access to education and health care and how they affect the role of the advocate. In this chapter I will examine three topics that I consider to be closely related to these issues—the medical-industrial complex, social laws, and politics. (Particular aspects of all these areas can change in importance, and other aspects may arise that are of greater importance than the ones I will discuss here. Any that arise in the future should also receive analytic scrutiny by the advocate.)

An in-depth study of these areas is not my purpose in this chapter. I will present only enough material to give you a picture of what is involved in each of the three areas. This review requires a systems analysis approach: What makes up the medical-industrial complex? How are its parts interrelated, and how do they affect the advocate? What social laws relate to the advocate? What do social laws say or allow? What aspects of the political process are related to the advocate? How are all three topics interrelated? Our purpose here is to use the knowledge we have gained thus far to see how other areas of knowledge affect the role of advocate. For example, does the social ethic affect each area? What system of ethics is operational in each? How does each of these areas affect the informing and supporting role of the advocate?

Again, for the purposes of discussion, we must deal with parts, but the parts alone will not give us a picture of the whole. A thorough understanding must be based on the resulting gestalt, since the parts are interrelated and interdependent. A change in any one can cause a change in another—or, if not a change, certainly a reaction. You must understand that when you set out to change a system either directly or by means of change in role behavior, all other systems that are in any way related to that system will also be affected. You must also understand that the very process of change itself, whether for the better or for the worse, will be resisted. Humans in general prefer to deal with the known rather than the unknown. Changes produce questions: What will happen when I . . .? What if I . . .? These are anxiety-provoking questions, and anxiety is not a desirable state for most people. The subject of change and change theory is certainly an area that an advocate might wish to explore; in fact, I advise you to do so. If you do not want to be involved in promoting change, per se, you should at least be alert to how others are making changes that will affect you. This vast subject will not be specifically discussed in this book.

MEDICAL-INDUSTRIAL COMPLEX

Who and what make up the medical-industrial complex? I will list in descending order of importance (important, that is, from the standpoint of the nurse advocate) first the members of the focal system and then the members of the ecological system. In the focal system of the medical-industrial complex are physicians, medical schools and societies, hospitals and their organizations, nurses and other health care professionals and their organizations, medical supply houses, and pharmaceutical companies. In the ecological system are insurance companies, suppliers of support services, the stockholders of these firms, unions in all types of industries, banks, and individuals.

What are the goals of the focal system? Certainly two stated goals are to provide health care to the public and to remain in business. Other goals may be stated or unstated: to make as much money as possible, to remain influential in the major decision-making centers, to keep people happy (with happiness being defined in terms of money for stockholders or workers and in terms of policy-making power for organizations), and finally to keep the peace so that the marketplace can function and money can be made. The bottom line may seem to be money, but the need for power and peace should not be underestimated. Some of us will live on less money if we think we have a say in the making of policy and if we are at least treated as if we were important.

What is the nature of the communication between the parts of the focal system, especially as it relates to goals? This question is multidimensional. The stated goal of staying in business is mixed with some unstated goals. The physicians need the hospitals to practice in; the bigger the hospital and the more prestige it has, the more prestige a physician on the staff has. Also, the better the facilities are, the better the physician's patients like the hospital and the easier the physician's work. Hospitals need nearly full occupancy to break even, so the more patients they have the better. Also, the more successful a hospital is in attracting the best physicians to its staff, the greater its prestige and the greater the number of patients that will seek its services and those of the physicians affiliated with it. The bigger and more prestigious a hospital is, the greater the prestige of the administrators and the nurses who run it. So not only is bigger better, it also pays more. We build and build and attract more and more people into a hospital to pay for the building. In the process we also attract the best people in nursing and the other health-related fields. So we can see what a stake all members of the focal system have in making a hospital bigger and better.

The goals of the various elements of the focal system are thus interrelated. It is obvious that the main parts of the focal system—physicians, hospitals, nurses, and members of other health-related professions—all have a stake in the goal of staying in business. The bigger and better the business, the more likely it is to survive. These groups strive separately and together to remain viable. They may communicate directly—as in cases of joint planning for expansion—or indirectly in terms of all wanting to have the best and moving to this goal both separately and together.

The stated goal of providing good care is common to all groups in the focal system, and again they communicate this goal to the public both as groups and as individuals. Sometimes, however, one group, by insisting on what it considers good care, may step on the toes of another group. For example, nurses may want more control of their practice to give better care, and physicians may be unwilling to give up their total control of care. Each group will claim that its stand is taken for the purpose of providing good care. The communication between these two groups may be direct or indirect, and each side may include others in order to elicit support. Another example: Nurses may claim that they need higher salaries to recruit good staff members to provide good care. The hospital may argue that if it spends more money on salaries, the quality of care will decrease because cuts in personnel will have to be made. Again, the members of each group will communicate with each other and with members of other groups to gain support for their positions. The power here generally lies with physicians and hospitals, while nurses and other professionals are in a "one-down" position. So communication between the two groups will assume a vertical, hierarchical pattern rather than a lateral, collegial one. The nurses may go outside the focal system to the public to elicit support and to put pressure on the power group. This tactic is becoming more and more of a trend; it is sometimes taking the form of strikes.

All goals show much the same patterns of communication. When a goal is of mutual benefit to all members of the focal system, it is communicated openly to the public and a united front is presented. But when the goals of different groups conflict, these goals are not communicated openly and some groups may be forced to seek outside help. It is only when infighting becomes detrimental to the goals of money and survival that unstated goals are compromised. So the way in which goals are communicated depends on the priority of the goals and the mutuality of the goals.

The unstated goals of any group can be used against that group by another to obtain, regain, or retain power. No group wants its unstated goals exposed to too much public scrutiny. Buy-offs and trade-offs are not uncommon occurrences. Despite infighting, all members of the focal system are aware that the system must survive and that if one member fails, the rest are in grave danger of following suit. So keeping the peace, if at all possible, is a major unstated goal of the focal system that is not communicated to the public.

The members of the ecological system—that is, medical supply houses, pharmaceutical companies, insurance companies, unions, other suppliers, stockholders, and banks—also have the stated goals of providing good care and staying in business and the unstated goals of money, power, and peace. As in the focal system, the communication patterns can be either direct or indirect. Pharmaceutical companies and suppliers directly support physicians, hospitals, and other professionals and their organizations by buying advertising in professional journals, therefore keeping the journals financially viable so that the professionals and others can publish their articles and views. Most of the professional journals would be out of business if these companies removed their advertisements from these journals. (Imagine what a conflict would occur if a professional wanted to publish an article that was critical of an advertiser's product.) Also, the suppliers have a direct interest in institutions becoming bigger and better. The more patients there are, the greater the amount of money that will be spent to buy new products.

In both these cases the interest is mutual and the communication direct and congenial. When the goals of two groups conflict, however, the resulting process of communication is the same as it is in the focal group. Groups with substantial power seek to use it; those with little power either give in or go to the public to seek outside pressure. Again, depending on the power each side has to threaten with, one side may win, or if the battle poses too great a threat to the whole system, a compromise will be reached and peace will result. For example, a product may be removed from the market or an author from an editor's list.

Like the focal system, the ecological system has a communication system that is indirect or hidden from outside eyes. One would think that the groups that make up the ecological system would be representative of the public's best interest. Far from it, they are tied together in making money, gaining power, and keeping the peace so that they can stay viable. These groups have money ties with each other that are almost as strong as family ties. They all invest in the supply houses. They all operate under the premise that bigger is better because the return is greater. The goal of one group is consistent with the goals of the other groups. For example, the unions attract and keep members by offering attractive health insurance plans. They also invest the members' funds in the drug and supply houses and the insurance companies. If the health of the public in general improves, there will be a cutback in the use of drugs and supplies, and union members will have to use their benefits less often. This situation will not serve the unions, because the aid the unions offer will not be needed, and therefore will not be attractive to prospective members, and the drug and supply companies will lose money and therefore pay smaller dividends on their stocks. The unions may lose in both ways at the same time.

The bottom line is that illness care is big business. There is no money, or very little, in health care. However, the unions are composed of many people, and they are also considered consumers. Although they may on the one hand benefit from the concept of bigger is better, on the other hand their members' taxes and dues pay for the implementation of this concept, so they are less reliable supporters of the illness care system than the members of the focal system. Because people in the focal system have a more direct economic stake, they can be more easily influenced by a consumer cry for lower costs. This is not to say that they will act on this demand, but they will hear it and at least verbally agree that something must be done—that is, if whatever is done does not affect them adversely. Also, most union members are not aware of the interplay between union dues and investment profits from those dues.

The groups that constitute the medical-industrial complex make strange bedfellows to say the least. Perhaps that is one reason why the average person does not clearly see the interlocking relationship between the various parts of the complex. Any major change in one part affects the whole. The communication patterns within the medical-industrial complex are quite variable, they can be very direct within and between the focal and the ecological systems, or they can be very indirect. The goals at stake at a particular moment will determine which communication pattern is the most productive. The pseudo-innocent rating of the individuals and groups that make up the complex will vary, depending on their degree of naiveté or on the extent to which they deny their own self-interest—that is, deny what is really at stake. For anyone to see and admit that his unstated goals are diametrically opposed to his stated goals is difficult. Most people have a tendency to compartmentalize goals; the greater the conflict between goals, the tighter the compartments become. This fact may, in part, explain why books that are considered "exposés" are received with such awe and with expressions like "I never would have known that." The pseudo-innocent blinders are removed for the moment, only to be replaced with the attitude "Oh well, what can I do?" or "You can't beat the system" or "People get the kind of system or government they deserve or are willing to pay for."

In general one would have to say that the *stated* ethic of the medical-industrial complex is largely egalitarian, with the libertarian mixed in, while the *unstated* ethic is mostly libertarian. Most of the groups in the complex would state that they want health care and illness care to be available to all, regardless of the ability to pay. They also would say that they believe people should be paid a fair price for their services. However, their unstated ethic, the one that rules the marketplace, is "Let the best man win." In other words, when money and power are the deciding factors, they will argue for letting the best man win. But if their own survival is at stake, their slogan becomes "Peace at any price" and they give lip service to the acceptable egalitarian view.

Thus, which ethic is most influential can be determined with certainty only when the "survival point" has been reached—that is, when power and money can no longer keep a group afloat and compromise is indeed called for. Many a government has toppled or been toppled because an analysis of whether this point had been reached was either not made or made incorrectly. One would have to question what physicians, hospitals, and professional and related groups are going to do about rising medical costs, for example. Will they continue to ignore them and therefore court the establishment of a socialized system of health care, or will they act to control these costs? The ability to control costs, however, resides not only in these groups but in all the groups that make up the medical-industrial complex. This situation is a classic example of the need to modify the extremes of the libertarian ethic in order to survive the extremes of the egalitarian ethic.

What role does ethics itself play in the medical-industrial complex? Which ethical theory is operating? Are the individuals and groups in the complex interested primarily in ends or in means to ends, or do they take the route of the situationalists?

The answer is that the various parts of the complex often take conflicting ethical positions. Another factor to consider is that the professions and the institutions are bound both by their individual codes of ethics and by the laws that govern practice. Perhaps one could safely say that no matter what ethical theory an individual or a group subscribes to, the codes and the laws will act as a check on its implementation. In addition, we are currently in a period when rigid adherence to one ethical code or another, no matter what its origin, is being seriously questioned. This places the whole question of ethics as a controlling factor in human behavior in a very precarious position. More and more one sees that what was once considered by a majority of the public to be clearly right or wrong is no longer a sure measure of public or private conduct. This fact probably accounts for much of the rise in popularity of situational ethics. The utilitarians are being attacked for the means they are using to preserve human life and for their idea that life at any price is the goal, no matter what its quality. The Kantians are being attacked as naive and even immoral in their tendency to let someone determine his own life-style, especially when the result is clearly not desirable. Of course, the question is, "Not desirable to whom?" The situationalists say, "Let's look at each situation by itself."

All three ethical positions are represented within the medical-industrial complex. Whichever position seems to serve the goals of the complex is the one that is supported at that moment. Applying Kohlberg's ideas to the medical-industrial complex seems to muddy the waters further, but does it really? Kohlberg is not so much stating a way one should behave as pointing out that if one does behave in a certain way, then this tells us something about him. He is not making a value judgment per se about behavior; rather he is saying that certain behavior indicates certain things about the development of the person who is engaging in that behavior. (One wonders if Kohlberg is not engaging in the somewhat precarious activity of revealing our unstated goals to ourselves and to others?)

How functional are the goals of the advocate in relationship to the goals of the medical-industrial complex? Are there conflicts between the goals of informing and supporting and the goals of the complex? The answer to the second question is obvious: of course there are conflicts; they are everywhere. But are the advocate's goals functional? That is the real question. Unfortunately the answer is yes and no. The practicality of an advocate's goals will depend on any number of factors. First, who is the advocate being an advocate for—self, an individual client, or a community? Has the advocate assessed the health care system? Does this assessment reveal strategies the advocate can use in the risk defusement process? Does the assessment reveal people or groups the advocate can seek out for support? Is the advocate safely within the boundaries of informing and supporting or has he or she stepped into the more precarious position of rescuer? Can the stated goals of the complex be used against the unstated goals—for example, in the area of peace at any price? Will advocacy be allowed in order to keep consumers quiet and therefore to keep the peace?

If the informing and supporting process conflicts with any of the unstated goals of those in the medical-industrial complex, then opposition to the role of advocate is guaranteed, at least from those who are directly involved with an advocate's activity. For example, if an advocate argues that a patient can receive less expensive care at home than in the hospital, and that the quality of the care will still be good, he or she knows whom to expect opposition from in imparting this information. Having fewer patients in a hospital reduces the revenue of the hospital. If an advocate argues in favor of eating good food rather than taking vitamins, those who make money from the sale of vitamins will not be her supporters. If the advocate's activities remain on an individual level, they will probably elicit attention only from those in the focal system, to whom he or she may be seen to be a direct threat. However, if these activities are expanded to a community-wide level, or perhaps even to a regional or national level, the advocate will be engaging not only the focal system but the ecological system, and the opposition will be greater. Two things are important to remember: (1) the medical-industrial complex is a formidable entity, with widespread, sometimes hidden support, and (2) its ecological system is most vulnerable to public censure and will go for peace at almost any price.

That the medical-industrial complex has an influence on the advocate's role is clear; what that influence will be depends on the scope of the role. An awareness of these facts is an important addition to the knowledge base of the advocate.

SOCIAL LAWS

I am using the term "social laws" to designate those laws that deal rather directly with the physical welfare of people. Many laws may fit into this category, but for the sake of discussion I would like to deal with three types of laws that seem to cause substantial controversy—those dealing with abortion, welfare, and food stamps. Although these three topics can be discussed separately, they are interrelated. Again, I will approach these subjects using the systems analysis method, since it may offer the easiest way to maintain some objectivity.

Abortion

What are some of the stated goals of the current federal abortion law? Abortion was legalized for perhaps two clear reasons: (1) to stop the butchery women were suffering at the hands of nonprofessional people and (2) because people believed that a woman has a right to determine whether she wants to continue a pregnancy. The unstated goals might be, for example, that unwanted children should not be born, that abortion is a method of birth control that should be used to keep the population down, that it is a legal money maker, or that it will reduce the number of unwed mothers. There are more, but these will do for a start.

When examining the communication patterns concerning abortion, one must look at who favors and who does not favor the current abortion law. Those who favor the law will certainly support its stated goals. If forced to do so, they might admit to two of the unstated goals—to avoid the birth of unwanted children and to reduce the number of unwed mothers. An anti-abortion person will use a pro-abortion person's unstated goals of promoting population control and making money as arguments against abortion. The members of each of the two opposing groups communicate directly with persons who agree with them and as directly as they can with persons they are trying to persuade to join their side. The two sides deal more indirectly with each other, except when they come into situations of confrontation. Both groups use whatever methods of communication they can—in other words, all media possibilities—and put pressure on anyone who has some measure of power either to change the law or to keep it the same.

Health professionals range between both groups in their opinions, and some do not have strong opinions. They are quite reflective of the population as a whole.

The focal system in regard to the issue of abortion consists of two groups—those who actively work to keep the present abortion law and those who actively work against it. The ecological system consists of persons who are not committed to either side but who would perhaps go along with the stated goals, without subscribing to or admitting to the unstated goals, of one group or the other. Both groups in the focal system try to win over the members of the ecological system.

Both libertarians and egalitarians can be found among members of the focal system and among members of the ecological system. In other words, abortion itself is not the issue that separates libertarians from utilitarians; rather the separating factor is the question of who should pay for abortions for the poor. Libertarians who are also ardently pro-abortion are in the most difficult position: their arguments for abortion are often in conflict with their view that people should pay for what they get, and therefore in conflict with their stated goals. The idea of free abortions for the poor through Medicaid is being attacked not only by large pro-abortion libertarian groups but also by the anti-abortion faction. The anti-abortion people are delighted that the pro-abortion libertarians are caught in this bind. The egalitarians, whether for or against abortion, do not have this problem. An egalitarian simply argues either that all who want abortions should get them with the help of Medicaid or that no one should get them at all.

Discussions of the ethical problems relating to abortion range primarily around the question "Is abortion murder?" This question can be complicated by the question "When is human life viable in utero?" "When does life begin?" There is also the question of whether the mother's life (or the quality of that life) is worth more than the child's. It would be possible to find Kantians, utilitarians, and situationalists on both sides of the issue, with each theory being used to support both views. The Kantians could say either that the mother's desires are of utmost importance or that the embryo has life and therefore must be treated as important in itself. The utilitarians could argue that the end of the mother's well-being is most important, or they could argue that the end of a living child is most important. The situational ethics people would look at each case and attempt to justify an action on the basis of the greater end of love—but love for mother or for child? The answer to that question would depend on the individual situation. So ethics is a mixed bag unless one deals with the unstated goal of any one group. A person of a firm Kantian stand who was pro-abortion would deny that there was an unstated goal of population control, or at least argue that it was not of major consideration.

The functionality of the informing and supporting role of an advocate in a situation involving abortion would depend on the group the advocate is working with, its views on the issue, and the advocate's own views. If an advocate were an anti-abortion person, it is to be hoped that she would excuse herself from situations in which she would be expected to provide information concerning abortions. In anti-abortion groups, on the other hand, she would have difficulty offering abortion as a possibility.

Anti-abortion people may take the position that the government is making them commit a crime or a sin by default by using their tax money for abortions. An advocate might be considered a party to this financial act of sin and thereby be in double trouble: not only might the advocate be accused of providing a woman with information that is considered wrong, but he or she would be upsetting libertarians by informing this poor woman that an abortion can be paid for with tax money. The issue itself is emotional enough—plus there are the normal hazards of the advocate role. When these two elements are mixed, great caution must be taken.

In all areas of social law, especially when the enactment of a law will involve taxpayers' money, an advocate must tread lightly. He or she will run into what might be called a form of irrational thinking. For example, one group may believe it is perfectly all right to spend taxpayers' money for a cause it supports, such as the past war in Vietnam, but wrong to spend tax money for a cause it does not support, such as abortion or food stamps. Such a group will contend that a taxpayer has a right to withhold his taxes from what he considers a bad cause, but it will be vehemently against persons who want to withhold tax money from a cause that it favors. The rational argument is that even though we may not like certain laws, they must receive our financial support until we can get them changed. Otherwise, arbitrary decisions concerning taxes will lead to chaos. This argument does not seem to penetrate the thinking of the radical believer. An advocate's chances of dealing with people who engage in this kind of closed-minded thinking are high when a client's case involves an area of social law. An accurate assessment, combined with the role of informing and supporting and avoidance of the rescuer role, is an advocate's best strategy. Most of the so-called dilemmas center around a conflict between a social law and what is seen as morally right or wrong. One step into the world of dilemmas and out of the advocate role can undo an advocate's effectiveness faster than anything else can. Objectivity and a clear knowledge of the nature of the role provide the safest route.

Welfare

Welfare laws were created to formalize the care of the poor. Prior to their passage such care was left to those who were moved by charity to help them. The policies governing these laws vary from place to place, and they change with time. There are perhaps two stated goals, behind such laws: (1) that it is right and good to care for the poor and (2) that it is healthy for the community to maintain at least a minimum standard of living for everyone—in other words, that poverty breeds disease. (Some might say that the second goal is an unstated one, but since it is out front in most arguments it must take its place as a stated goal.) The unstated goals of welfare laws have as much to do with the amount of help given as with the giving of help per se: "If we give the poor some money, they will be content and not turn into thieves and steal from us." (But how much is "some?" Opinions vary.) "If we help the poor, we will not feel guilty knowing that others are not at least eating and living with a roof over their heads." "What would other countries think of us if we allowed people to starve?" Finally, one unstated goal most people do not think of: "If we give the poor a reasonable amount of help, they will be content to stay in the ghetto (in other words, pay them to stay there) and not strive to move into the middle class as other poor people before them have done." One can see these unstated goals singly or in combination.

The communication patterns vary. One can perhaps say that most people are not against welfare for the poor. So the idea of welfare and the stated goals of welfare laws are easily communicated among all elements of a community. A problem arises, however, when we move to the unstated goals. The libertarians and the egalitarians are generally on opposite sides when it comes to how much service and money should be given. Egalitarians want all to share equally; they want to set up a common standard of living. Libertarians want to establish a minimum standard (usually below the common standard of the egalitarians), and then encourage the poor to rise above it through hard work and a sense of personal achievement. Again, one might say, in regard to health care, that libertarians believe the poor should be satisfied with a minimum of care and that egalitarians believe the poor should have access to the same care that the rich receive. Both groups, however, may share an unstated goal—to keep the poor in the ghetto. The egalitarians can use this unstated goal to push the libertarians into greater financial support, and it works. Most egalitarians would deny that their unstated goals are goals as such; rather they would see them as weapons that can be used to persuade the libertarians to be more generous. All egalitarians and most libertarians would vehemently deny the goal of keeping the poor in the ghetto by paying them to stay there. In fact, the views of the two groups might easily be reversed if the egalitarians frankly looked at this as a goal and if the libertarians were foolish enough to admit to it. This is not to say that this goal or idea has not been alluded to; it has, but mostly by minority groups who are wise enough to see the ultimate danger in welfare and who then push to change parts of the welfare system—for example, by encouraging better job training and urging that some persons who receive welfare payments be allowed to work without losing their benefits.

Here one sees obvious conflicts for both libertarians and egalitarians. The libertarians want people to achieve and get ahead by their own efforts, they do not want to be accused of racist policies, of keeping the poor in the ghetto. The egalitarians want to see the poor achieve, but they do not want to be accused of giving so much that they kill the very drive and initiative necessary to achievement. The solutions to these dilemmas are rarely sought by doing the obvious—asking the poor what they want and need.

It is hard to define focal and ecological systems, per se, in regard to welfare laws. One could say that the extreme egalitarians and libertarians—in other words, those strongly for or against welfare—form the focal system and that the rest of society—those in the middle ground—forms the ecological system. Each group in the focal system tries to convince those in the ecological system to support its views, and the communication patterns are like those described in regard to the abortion question.

Again, the question of the functionality of an advocate's role depends on whom the advocate is dealing with. For example, if an advocate were to tell a welfare client in an egalitarian health care system how she could receive her fair share of care and what legal options she had, the advocate would be in a safe position. If the system were libertarian, the advocate would have trouble. (This topic was discussed in fairly great detail in Chapter 4.) A more important question or problem for the advocate is centered on this question: does the client have a choice in a health care system she is not paying for, or does she take what she can get? Should the client be offered options that the system is reluctant to grant? The egalitarians would like to see the poor fight for equal care in all respects, and the libertarians would like to see the poor settle for what is offered. It must be remembered that a system (that is, a hospital) may have the stated goals of egalitarianism—equal, free care—but the unstated goals of libertarianism—pay for what you get or be satisfied with what is offered. Within such a system an advocate's efforts on behalf of a welfare client could very easily be an uphill road. The advocate's sources of support could be many or few, depending on the nature of the focal and ecological systems. If the issues of racism, sexism, and ageism enter in, the role becomes more difficult.

Again, the presence of various ethical theories can further complicate a situation. The Kantians might use their philosophical arguments for or against welfare. For example, they might say that the means—that is, the providing of money for health care—is good in itself and that the end of good health is served, and therefore argue for more welfare programs. Or they might say that the means of striving for good, by work, is good in itself, and the end of gaining it is good, and even if the end is not gained, that fact does not nullify the inherent goodness of work. The utilitarians, too, could use their philosophy to argue either way. They might argue that the end of health is good, and so provide money to gain it. Or they might reverse themselves, depending on their social ethic, and say that the end of achieving is good no matter how hard a person works or suffers to achieve. The situationalist would look at the individual situation and try to determine how love for one's fellow human beings could best be served in that situation.

The advocate is left with dilemmas if he or she tries to go beyond the informing and supporting role. To take sides in a conflict between libertarians and egalitarians or among persons of various ethical schools would only complicate the advocate's role. Such factors must be taken into account, but only to the extent that they help an advocate to assess a situation and to reduce the risks of the role.

Food stamps

The subject of food stamps generally has only a tangential relationship to an advocate's efforts to improve health care, but on occasion the relationship can be direct. The stated goal of the federal food stamp program is to provide people of marginal income, or no income, with a method of obtaining food to guarantee a minimum level of nutrition. For persons receiving welfare payments, food stamps are not charged for as such but are provided as part of the allotted welfare benefits. For persons who are not on welfare but who are still at a low income level, food stamps can be purchased at less than face value; in effect, such persons can purchase food at a large discount.

The unstated goals of the food stamp program are much the same as those of welfare laws, so I will not repeat them here. The stances of the libertarians and the egalitarians are similar to their stances in regard to welfare, and the same is true of persons of the various ethical positions.

A major controversy surrounds the situation of persons who do not qualify for welfare yet, under the law, do qualify for food stamps. In essence, the issue is whether the marginally poor should be helped to at least maintain a good level of nutrition. As a stated goal, that would hardly be questioned. And if good nutrition equals good health, then providing such nutrition meets both the unstated and the stated goals of welfare—with the added benefit that the libertarians are appeased, since the marginally poor do pay something for their food stamps. The only serious question is what the income level should be to qualify for food stamps; in other words, how poor does a person have to be?

The position of the advocate is similar to that described in connection with the welfare issue, but the problem of how to maintain good nutrition, combined with the need for eligibility requirements and the possibility of rip-offs of the system, raises different questions. For example, there is the question of whether food stamps, which are supported by taxes, should be given to people who go on strike against a company. When the coal miners were on strike a few years ago, union money ran out and they and their families qualified for food stamps. Many of the miners and their families were in such desperate straits as a result of the strike that without food stamps they could hardly have fed themselves. In such a situation the mine owners might very well argue, "Let them go back to work then. Why should our tax money be used to support them in their strike against us?" An advocate who suggests to a miner and his family that they have a right to food stamps is certainly going to come into conflict with the mine owners, who may be supplying the financial support for the hospital where the advocate works.

• • •

In dealing with any type of social law, an advocate faces two areas of potential problems. First, everyone in a community may not be in favor of a particular social law; therefore an advocate who informs and supports a client in receiving his rights under the law will come into conflict with some segments of the community. Second, the fact that a person is being given something rather than paying full value means, in the opinion of some, that he then has no right to complain about the service received or to demand better service. (In fact, when a person gets something for nothing, he tends not to complain.) So, again, the advocate who informs and supports clients by requesting that certain standards of service be maintained will come into conflict with certain groups.

Thus social laws can and do have an effect on the advocacy process. To have informed knowledgeable citizens may well be a stated goal of everyone in a community, but the unstated goal may be the opposite—that if people do not know what they have coming, they will not ask, thereby saving the taxpayers money. We live in a world of conflicts; while we want to do good, at the same time we do not want our benevolence to cost us too much, and the question of what is too much is a major variable. These conflicts must be resolved in the realm of politics, where social laws, as well as other laws related to the advocacy process, are enacted.

POLITICS

Systems analysis is not only a very handy tool for the advocate in looking at the influence of politics on the advocacy process, but it is a major tool that the successful politician uses in getting elected and staying in office. So let us approach the subject of politics from the positions of the advocate and the politician at the same time. Everyone who seeks political office has stated goals; these are the goals he elucidates for the public's benefit. Voters give these stated goals some credence, but sophisticated voters do not give them too much credence, nor should advocates. Voters, like advocates, must look at the unstated reasons why a person seeks public office and then compare them with the reasons why they, the voters, want him in office. The unstated goals of most persons who seek office are easily known. Their opponents make an effort to be sure we know these goals—at least from the opponents' points of view. But we still do not always know what the candidate will do once the office has been attained. In other words, are the unstated goals the opponents talk about the real unstated goals? In addition, history has demonstrated that once a person assumes office, the position itself can change him. Many a politician has changed his views after being elected, fooling even his strongest supporters. So in politics goals, stated and unstated, are slippery ground indeed. Perhaps the most important question is how far a politician is willing to go to maintain an office. Is there a line that his own personal sense of ethics will not allow him to cross? If there is such a line, where is it drawn? The answers to these questions represent a great unknown until the politician is actually tested under fire. Thus it is not safe to assume that a candidate will support the advocacy process, for example, just because his pre-election goals indicate that he will. His views after the election will depend on many factors.

In politics the focal system consists of persons or groups that are directly involved in the local election of a politician; therefore at election time this is the system that is most important to him. It is, of course, important to him at all times, but it receives the most attention during election campaigns. The nature of a politician's communication during a campaign will vary depending on the nature of the focal system and on what forces the politician uses to get elected. Is he using an old established political system to win an election, or is he appealing directly to the voters and thus working outside the system? Which method is used will determine how a person communicates with the politician once the office has been gained.

The ecological system is generally of tangential importance to local elections, but what persons outside the focal system think of a politician may strongly influence the opinions of persons in the focal system. For example, many a local politician has brought in holders of high offices outside the focal system to campaign for him and to add prestige to his name. Thus the person who works within the formal political system often has an advantage over the person who appeals directly to the local voter. If a politician uses this political ecological system to win an election, he will be in debt, politically, to both the focal system and the ecological system, and both systems will influence his future decisions. One could easily predict where and how pressure would be applied to him.

Likewise, the social ethic of the persons who have been most influential in getting a person elected will usually carry the most influence after the election, unless the person elected is a maverick. However, here one is dealing with a combination of who has the most power and money and who has the most influence with the voters. These can be very different groups, and they may be at odds with one another, so no general statements can be made. More often than not, a candidate whose election seems obvious, since he has power and money behind him, is defeated because the public of the focal system is not tied into the power and money group. So both egalitarians and libertarians must look to the voting public for support, regardless of the power and money that each group can bring to a campaign. How a candidate appeals to these groups for votes—that is, whether he tries for a mix of the best of both views or appeals to the extremists of one view—will certainly affect the advocacy process. For example, to press for egalitarian programs in a libertarian focal system would certainly be difficult for an advocate or a politician. In addition, if the ethic of the focal system differs from that of the ecological system, then this fact must be taken into account when an advocate or a politician assesses the influence of each ethic on the political process.

If we examine the ethical theories that the focal and ecological systems subscribe to, we again will generally find a mix-and-match situation, which will affect the nature of laws and policies. The result may be a combination of policies that while seemingly in conflict will reflect a compromise position between all elements of a community. It is only in very homogeneous communities that policies tend to be reasonably consistent. The United States is not homogeneous, especially in the large cities, and with the shift in population and the rise of the mass communications media, the rural areas are more open to change than ever before. Those who hate the necessity of compromise view this heterogeneity in a negative way, but seeking leverage through compromise can work to the benefit of the advocate in the risk defusement process. In the political arena the ethical positions run the gamut from utilitarian to Kantian to situational, as they do in the population as a whole. The functionality of an advocate's goals will depend primarily on the nature of the focal system, but also on the influence of the ecological system on the focal system.

If we then consider how the political environment may be influenced by the issues of racism, sexism, ageism, and access to education and health care, as well as by the medical-industrial complex, we will have a fairly good understanding of why certain social laws are passed. Also, we will better understand why a particular politician takes the positions he does in regard to these issues. An understanding of all these variables is necessary to an advocate. Although attaining such knowledge may seem an insurmountable task, it is not so difficult if one's advocacy is limited to a certain locale. The task becomes more complicated as one enlarges one's constituency, in much the same way that the task of decision-making is more complicated for the politician who represents a large group than it is for the politician who represents a small group.

Now let us mix the three major ethical groups together in an example to demonstrate the influence each may have on a politician and on the laws and policies he helps to formulate. Let us take a politician who assumes a libertarian stance and therefore receives financial support from the medical-industrial complex. But his constituency is a big-city mix of libertarian and egalitarian groups. Let us say that he is an advocate of situational ethics; he believes that there are many sides to any issue and that the deciding factor must be a love of humanity and, of course, individual human beings.

My prediction is that this politician will be for abortion but will not want tax money to be used to pay for abortions, except in cases in which the life of the mother is at stake. He will favor welfare but will set limits on who receives it and demand careful monitoring to see that no one cheats. He will favor the idea of food stamps but will see that only persons in dire need receive them—except in some rare situations, such as in times of strike (if he has union support in elections).

This politician will perform a very careful analysis of the political environment, and if the analysis is reasonably accurate he will be re-elected to office. He will support the advocacy process but request that an advocate try not to make waves with the powers that be. If an advocate does make waves, whether the politician supports the advocate will depend on his analysis of how the system will react to the issue under consideration. (This analysis is the same one that the advocate must make.) The politician then decides on a course of action, which will be based on the results of the analysis and on his own ethical position. This is not to say that the politician will not base the decision he makes on ethics alone, only that any individual's personal ethical position often becomes only the final deciding factor in issues that seem to be unresolvable on all other counts. It is this final, personal decision-making factor that is the most unpredictable, and the one that no manner of risk defusement strategy can guard against.

An excellent exercise is to select a social issue, pick a politician you have some knowledge of, and then examine his position on the issue to see how it may be related to the focal system or constituency that elected him. This method is used by many newswriters when they attempt to predict how a politician will act. Generally such news stories do a very superficial job; they leave out more variables than they include, which probably accounts for the errors in their predictions. The depth of an advocate's analysis will depend on the degree of risk involved in his or her actions. The greater the risk, the more time the advocate must invest in analysis to find areas of risk defusement.

•　　•　　•

Chapter 7 will deal with the topic of risk defusement itself. Although I have mentioned many ways in which the information in an advocate's knowledge base can help in this process, it may be valuable at this point to devote a chapter to the discussion of risks and hazards and how an advocate can deal with them.

NOTES ON CHAPTER 6

One of the best overall books on the health care system is:

Jonas, Steven. *Health Care Delivery in the United States*, ed. 2. New York: Springer Publishing Co., Inc., 1981.

Two other classics on the general topic of the health care system are also good reading. Although these two books are becoming outdated, I doubt that the system they describe has changed a great deal.

Ehrenreich, Barbara, and Ehrenreich, John. *The American Health Empire*. New York: Random House, Inc., 1971.
Kotelchuck, David. *Prognosis Negative*. New York: Vintage Books, 1976.

A fourth book is concerned primarily with the profession of medicine:

Illich, Ivan. *Medical Nemesis*. New York: Pantheon Books, Inc., 1976.

The first few chapters are sufficient to give the reader an idea of the author's position. This book is well documented.

The second and third books listed above were written by people who were associated with the Health Policy Advisory Center (Health PAC), located at 17 Murray St., New York, N.Y. 10007. This organization publishes a bulletin that deals with all forms of health information and all aspects of the health care system. It is my opinion that Health PAC is quite egalitarian in philosophy. Its material is generally well documented; however, I have found that the bulletin's articles in the area of nursing, can be one-sided in terms of the facts they include. But the publication has been known to print a rejoinder to an article.

One must use care in reading anything—even straightforward reporting. It is hard to find any piece of writing that does not reflect some bias on the part of the writer. This is especially true of the area of the "ism's" and the area of social laws. I am not suggesting any special readings here. Since these subjects are popular in the news, one cannot help but be exposed to all sides of the issues.

In the area of political process, I would like to recommend two books:

Redman, Eric. *The Dance of Legislation*. New York: Simon & Schuster, Inc., 1973.
Kalisch, Beatrice J., and Kalisch, Phillip A. *Politics of Nursing*. Philadelphia: J. B. Lippincott Co., 1982.

The Redman book is an excellent discussion of how legislation is enacted. It is an easy and entertaining book to read. The book by Beatrice and Phillip Kalisch is also easy and informative reading. It provides an overview of nursing involvement in the political system—past, present, and future—with emphases on the political participation of women, fiscal constraints in the health care system, and the legislative process. It is must reading for all nurses.

Chapter 7

RISKS, HAZARDS, AND COPING

ONE CAN DEAL WITH THE SUBJECT of the hazards of advocacy by presenting a list of risks and explaining how each can be handled. But that seems a rather precarious way of proceeding. One faces the possibility of omitting some risks, because this approach takes a particulate look at problems that are quite complex as a result of the number of variables involved. One is always left with the question "What if the situation were slightly different?" Furthermore, such a list may leave out a major area of risk, or one risk may suggest another, which does not appear in the list. So rather than deal with certain risks per se, by category, let us approach the subject by looking at each area of the knowledge base discussed so far and how it can be used to help an advocate cope with the risks that may be inherent in that area. In other words, once one knows how to build a house, an architect's variations on the basic theme should not pose too many problems. Once one has the principle well in hand, the details of execution come more easily.

However, before we start, one note is necessary, to still the heart of the logical reader, who has a precise memory of what has been stated in this book so far. What about the two areas of the knowledge base that have not been discussed up to now, professional practice and professional education? The information in these two areas will certainly help in defusing risks and in coping. However, up to now we have been discussing the actual role of the advocate in practice. So to maintain some continuity it seems advisable to deal next with the risks an advocate faces and how to cope with them—that is, to deal with the aspects of the knowledge base that are directly related to the advocacy process.

The key to risk defusement lies in knowing. The more a person knows about his job, the better he can do it. But the mere possession of knowledge is not enough; a person has to know how to use his knowledge to the best advantage in order to attain the goals he has set for himself. Therefore we find ourselves dealing in that commodity called wisdom. The pragmatist may consider wisdom to consist in skill in manipulation. Perhaps he is right, to an extent, but the term "manipulation" has taken on a rather negative flavor in our society, and the use of knowledge in that sense is not wisdom. Clever manipulators who use knowledge to gain their own ends get caught in their own webs sooner or later. If, however, a person uses knowledge to gain the goals of advocacy—informing and supporting *others*—then the accusation of being self-serving and the problems that go with it are almost nonexistent.

INFORMING AND SUPPORTING

Informing and supporting are at the heart of the role of advocate. The major risk defusement tools in this regard are three. The first is being sure that you have the necessary knowledge to inform accurately. We have already discussed the dangers involved in the very act of informing, so they will not be repeated here. The point here is to be sure you have accurate knowledge, that what you tell a client is in fact so. In risk defusement the main goal is to prevent a risk from developing, as well as to know how to deal with it when it does develop. You can be shot down at the very start, even in a system that tolerates advocacy, if you err in the information you give clients. So if you do not know or if you are not sure, first find out before you speak. That may seem obvious, but too often we hear people say, "Well, I'm not positive about this, but I think it is such and so." That kind of informing is foolishness. Equivocating in social conversation may be forgiven, but not in the role of advocate informer. Also, by informing accurately you establish a reputation for yourself as a knowledgeable person who must be taken seriously. This is called "gaining the respect of one's peers and co-workers." A person who has the respect of others is less likely to be attacked, at least on the basis of his professional expertise. So one major area of attack is shut off at the start. How often have we heard someone say, "Well, I wouldn't mind so much if he knew what he was talking about"? That *he would mind* is still true, but not so much. It is this *not so much* that we are after. So if you do not *know*, say so, and find out, but do not offer opinions that are not based on fact.

The second tool is knowing yourself well enough to avoid the rescuing position. The temptation to rescue is ever present. It may result from your own inclination to be a rescuer or from your wanting to have a decision over and done with because of the pressure of time. Either way, this problem is not easy to deal with. It requires a high level of awareness at all times of your own positions and all the dynamics that may be operating. It means that many times you will have to restrain yourself while you watch a client make a decision that you think, and even know, is not in his best interest. It means that no matter how rushed you are or what other priorities seem more important, you will have to restrain yourself from stepping in to hurry things. It is the difficulty, which all of us must deal with, of giving priority to long-term goals over short-term benefits. It oftentimes requires a discipline that you barely have energy enough to exert. The "gentleness of doves and the wisdom of serpents" is tested to its limits. The major restraining factor lies in your having a very clear picture of what happens to the rescuer. Not to have this picture is to run a great risk—risk not from outside forces but from yourself. Then to have to face the fact that a problem has been caused by your own impatience will make whatever penalty is involved seem even more bitter. To refuse to accept the fact you have caused your own troubles, and then to learn from the experience, leads to denial and the future repetition of the same behavior, resulting in a never-ending cycle.

So, staying within the boundaries of the role of advocate may at times be difficult, but it pays off in the end. The payoff lies in not having to accept the risk of the rescuer—and in seeing someone else grow in the ability to make decisions. An advocate will not receive any thanks at the time, but in my experience it is usually given later and much more sincerely. It is the kind of thanks that makes one smile and say to himself, "Well, it all really did pay off, didn't it? And with no lasting risk to me." If this sounds self-serving, it is; but one of the great paradoxes of life is that what may seem self-serving or selfish is often the most serving of others as well.

The third major risk-defusing tool is related to the second; it consists in knowing others well enough to recognize the games they may be playing that will involve us in confusion about our role and that may lead to our stepping out of it. For example, we may have no inclination ourselves to rescue, and our clients may not be pressuring us to do so, but any number of other people involved with us or our clients may have a stake in the decision-making process and therefore attempt to use us to gain their goals.

A careful reading of Eric Berne's book *Games People Play* will alert us to the many variations of this behavior. Berne describes people who simply like to engage in gaming as a way of life: "Let's you and him fight (so I can watch and get vicarious satisfaction)." A more serious game might involve an attempt to use someone to promote a position on an issue—for example, that a hospital's authority must be maintained even if doing so is not in a client's best interest. Such an attempt may originate in the face-saving philosophy "We professionals must stick together, even when we are wrong." The pressure on an advocate to conform to such a philosophy can be enormous, but a policy of opting for the short-term gain that comes from conforming rarely pays off over the long haul. (The situation of former President Nixon is a good example of this principle—in the extreme, of course.)

The risk factor here is threefold. First, as a result of playing a game, you will surely get caught up in its consequences later. Second, you can be sure that once you have played the game, you will be called on to play it again and again. If you refuse, you will be reminded of the fact you have played the game before—a very subtle form of blackmail. Third, by refusing to play the game you may be labeled a non–game player and perhaps be eliminated from the game altogether. On the surface this may seem to be desirable, unless non–game playing can cost you your job. However, it is at this point that one might say that the decision-making process has become personally oriented rather than client oriented. Do you want to stay in a job that requires you to play the games of the management and to run the risks involved for you as a person, or do you want to seek another job, where your dignity will be respected even if you are outside of the goals of the institution? I am not describing a utopia; there are institutions where gaming goes on but where you are respected enough so that you are not required to participate in the game.

Thus there are risks in game playing as well as in not game playing. It is not always a case of either to play or not to play. Some games are relatively harmless, a form of passing time; other games are more serious in their consequences. An analysis of a game will help one to determine what is prudent action. The ultimate purpose of such analysis is to learn how one can function in a role within a system with the least amount of risk possible.

Therefore advocates must become knowledgeable and demonstrate that they are knowledgeable, that they know themselves well enough to avoid the rescuer role, and that they either can avoid games or at least can avoid those that are the most risky. Thus, in most cases, risk defusement really amounts to preventing trouble rather than defending oneself or bailing oneself out after trouble occurs. Prior knowledge and analysis are the best weapons in the risk defusement process, as will be evident in the discussion of the remaining areas in this chapter.

SYSTEMS ANALYSIS

An advocate must look at how one part of a system influences other parts and at which areas are most important in terms of risks. An advocate must at once examine the stated goals of systems and the unstated goals, and recognize how these goals can lessen risks as well as enhance risks. The system of most immediate importance to the advocate is the focal system. What risks are inherent in the focal system in which the advocate is functioning? The answer to this question will depend on who the advocate determines is the client. For example, if the advocacy process is conducted with one hospitalized patient, then the focal system may be defined as the hospital unit and its personnel, the physician, and the family. The risks will then depend on how the unit personnel, the physician, and the family perceive the advocate's role. If an advocate is concerned with the needs of a number of patients in various units, the focal system enlarges to include the whole hospital, a number of physicians, and a number of families. If the client is a consumer outside of an institution, then the focal system enlarges further to include a number of institutions, a number of professionals in various institutions, and perhaps governmental agencies.

The larger the focal system, the greater the number of variables that will come into play and the greater the number of risks one must anticipate. However, the larger the focal system and the greater the number of variables, the greater the number of tools the advocate can use for risk defusement and the greater the amount of leeway the advocate has in the manipulating of these variables. The smaller the focal system, the fewer the risks but also the fewer the variables an advocate has to use in the defusement process. The same principle applies to goals. The smaller the system, the fewer the goals, stated or unstated, an advocate has to deal with but, by the same token, the fewer the goals the advocate has to use in the defusement process. So the size of a focal system is not an indication of the difficulty of an advocate's role.

Two important risk-defusement tools come into play here. The first, and the more important one, is the process of communication used by the advocate. The second is the advocate's knowledge of the goals of the persons directly involved in the focal system. You may at this point think that knowledge of goals is more important, but learning other people's goals can take time and the informing and supporting process cannot always wait while that knowledge is acquired. Sometimes advocates must act in spite of some incompleteness in this area while still keeping in mind the need for the information. Therefore let us deal with the communication process first.

Your greatest tool for risk defusement lies in your ability to make your position clear to everyone you work with, including physicians and clients. In other words, you open up the area of risks to discussion at the start rather than after trouble comes. It is important that everyone know where you stand so that no one is left with a feeling of shock, and the thoughtless desire for vengeance that shock produces in most people. This is most important in terms of co-workers and physicians. The shock patients feel when someone tells them the facts is more likely to be one of delight rather than anger. This reaction is not always shared by patients' families, but it is true of most patients. If co-workers and physicians are informed, they have a chance to discuss with you just what you see as your role and what you intend to do in carrying it out. If you knowledgeably maintain open communications with these two groups, about what you have told patients and especially about what you *intend* to tell them, you will do a great deal to prevent problems from developing.

In the Tuma case (see Chapter 2) the physician's point was that Tuma had not told him of the patient's fears and wishes and had not discussed with him her intention to tell the patient what alternatives she had.[1] He accused Tuma of interfering with his relationship with the patient. He based his accusation, it seems, on Tuma's lack of communication with him. One wonders whether he would not have registered the complaint anyway. But Tuma's omission gave him a basis on which to do so. This was a most telling point to many who read the case—Tuma's lack of communication with the patient's physician.

However, one can take the position that nurses, as professionals and therefore as autonomous persons, do not have to relate their actions or intended actions to other professionals, that nurses are accountable only to themselves and to their clients. That is true. But there is a difference between the autonomy of the professional's decision-making process and the communication of a decision. I am not saying that nurses need permission to be advocates, only that they should communicate to others what actions their professional behavior will entail. This is true for all professionals who deal with patients. I am not talking about the interdependency of professionals but about the need for collegial communication between professionals.

For example, in our private practice my colleagues and I on occasion needed to contact a patient's physician. Our opening statement set the tone of the relationship. We might say, "Dr. Smith, *my patient*, Mrs. Jones, told me you were *her physician*." Then we would proceed to tell the physician what our nursing care

---

[1]William Gargaro, "The Tuma Case," *Cancer Nursing* 1, no. 4 (August 1978):329-330; William Gargaro, "Update on the Tuma Case," *Cancer Nursing* 1, no. 6 (December 1978):467-468.

entailed and to request information from him concerning his care and how we could coordinate both our services to better assist the patient. We might compare what we had told the patient with what he had told the patient, so that there would be no major conflict of information. There would be no question of either physician or nurse requesting permission from the other to conduct care, only a process of coordinating our communications with the patient so that conflicting information would not be transmitted. This is the process that an advocate in any setting engages in. Communication of one's actions and intentions is necessary in establishing any role.

One approaches this process not by requesting permission to engage in the role but rather by assuming the role and proceeding to communicate whatever information is necessary in conducting that role. For example, one might approach a physician in the following way:

> While discussing with Mrs. Smith what options she might have in choosing a postoperative rehabilitation center, I told her what centers are available and how they function. I then told her to discuss the pros and cons of these with you. I pointed out that different physicians have different methods and ideas and that she should find out what your feelings are before she makes a choice.

Here, as an advocate you have done several things. You have made it clear that having such a discussion with your patient is well within your role, that you will provide your patient with information, and that the patient has a choice but that before she decides it would be wise and prudent to seek out the professional opinion of her physician. I would follow up this statement by asking the physician what his ideas are, thus opening the situation to a collegial discussion of how one matches centers to patients' needs. It is entirely possible that the physician may object to a nurse's having such a discussion with Mrs. Smith, stepping on what he sees as his exclusive right to communicate with his patient. In any case, it is best to have both professionals' positions out in the open rather than to have the physician go to Mrs. Smith and get hit with "What the nurse told me, doctor, is . . ." and then to have him retaliate in front of the patient with "The nurse had no right to say those things." Most of us would like to avoid confrontations. But this is not always possible; even if we say nothing, we can be accused of saying nothing. In most cases the preceding method will lead to a collegial discussion between the physician and the nurse and will improve all their future working relationships.

When you approach another professional from a well-stated professional position of your own, the fact that you are doing so is usually recognized and reacted to accordingly. You do not ask permission to engage in a professional act that you have a right to engage in. If you do, then you are assuming that you do not have the right. If permission is asked and it is denied, then the asker will retort with "What right do you have to say I can't engage in my own professional activities?" The obvious answer will be "If you had a right, why did you have to ask permission?" You see the ball of twine you can create. Instead, if you are asked what right you have to give a patient certain information, you can proceed to educate the asker on the proper role and activities of the professional nurse and advocate. In nursing this situation might occur quite often, until others are made aware of the role and the activities involved in it. Open communication among the many professionals that are involved in the care of any one patient is essential to avoid confusion and the risks that result from confusion.

Communication thus is an essential tool in the risk defusement process. Communication should be open, straightforward, and factual—not the pseudo-innocent type that leads to game playing. Communication is related directly to knowing the goals of others in the focal system.

When you communicate your role as an advocate, you are also communicating your goals. The reactions of other people to your goals and intended behavior will go far in telling you what their own goals, both stated and unstated, are. Here is a simple example: A co-worker may respond to you by saying, "Yes, advocacy is good; we all should do it" (stated goal). "But it takes time, and the doctors may object" (unstated goals of "I'm too busy" and "Keep the peace"). You automatically can assume that two things may happen in this situation. First, if the co-worker is pressured to function as an advocate, you will not get support from the co-worker and he or she may even speak against the advocacy role. Second, if another person, say a physician or a member of a patient's family, objects to your actions and then proceeds to cause trouble, you will receive little support from this co-worker, who wants to keep the peace.

A second example can be hypothesized from the Tuma case. The son may have said, "Yes, we know how mother feels about chemotherapy and how she hates all medication, and we sympathize with these feelings" (stated goal). "But we want her to live no matter what, and chemotherapy may give her a chance" (unstated goal). The son's reactions to any suggestions that may cause the mother to refuse chemotherapy would therefore be predictable. Had the son made those statements (I do not know if he did), then the advocate would have been both prudent and wise in discussing the situation with the physician, instead of getting caught in the son's game of "Let's you and him fight."

In the example of Mrs. Smith and the rehabilitation centers, Mrs. Smith might say, "My physician has suggested a center, but I don't like it and would hate to go there" (stated goal). "But I like the doctor, and he knows best, and I wouldn't want to make him mad" (unstated goal). Then the nurse would indeed be both prudent and wise in having a discussion with Mrs. Smith's physician. Can't you just see Mrs. Smith saying to her physician, "Oh, doctor, the nurse tole me center XYZ is just grand, but I know you prefer center ABC, and I do so want to do what you know is best, but what do you think?" In effect, Mrs. Smith would be saying, "Let's you and the nurse fight, and maybe I'll get center XYZ."

Knowing a person's stated and unstated goals allows you to plan a communication strategy that can remove much of the risk posed by the pseudo-innocent communications and game playing of others. This is not to imply that others are bent on getting you into trouble but rather that, to avoid trouble themselves, they may act in ways that place you in a difficult position. So know the goals of the focal system, and keep your communications with others open and factual. Remember that gaming is a normal activity but that it takes two or more to play. Of course, there is a risk in not being a game player, especially when you are involved with a consummate game player. If you do not play, he will either stop or go find another player. If he stops, fine; if he goes to find another player, you could be out of a job, if he is your boss.

SOCIAL ETHIC

Since we have discussed the social ethic in detail in Chapter 4, as well as in Chapter 6, we can be rather brief here. What is most important to the advocate in terms of risk defusement is to know what the unstated social ethic of the focal system is and how it is related to the stated ethic, as well as how both relate to the stated ethic and the unstated ethic of the ecological system. When these ethics are all congruent with each other—that is, the unstated goals and the stated goals are the same and both systems have the same ethic—then the ability to predict risk is high. The communication process is usually open and aboveboard about who gets what and who pays for it. Therefore the advocate knows rather precisely where he or she stands in relation to each system and how advocacy on any issue will be received. Also, the advocate's patients are more knowledgeable about what they can expect to receive.

However, when stated goals of egalitarianism, for public consumption, are overridden by unstated goals of libertarianism, the issues get sticky. If you tell a patient what he can expect from a health care system based on the stated goals of egalitarianism, when you in fact know that the libertarian ethic is what is practiced, then you must plan a strategy that will reduce the obvious risk involved in this kind of advocacy. As dangerous as it may seem on the surface, using people's stated goals to get them to compromise their unstated goals is a not uncommon practice. For example, if the stated goals of an institution are egalitarian and the unstated goals are libertarian, and you offer a patient a charity option that will cost the system money, you could use as a strategy an appeal to the stated goals. The institution may let this practice go once or twice, but then it will find some means to stop it from developing further. The institution would prefer to get rid of you rather than to have its libertarian unstated goals revealed. You must remember that all or most unstated goals are meant to remain just that—unstated, *hidden*. It is only when you go too far in the use of the kind of strategy just described that others will resort to attempts to eliminate you to get you off their backs. Use of stated goals to win a point is often called "appealing to someone's higher instincts." But you do not want to make this appeal too frequently; you must not forget that the unstated goals are the ones that have the most influence on a person or an institution.

The reverse of the above situation can occur. It may be strategically wise to use the unstated goals as a lever against the stated goals. This strategy may sit better with an individual or a system, but the reverse danger exists. No one will want to admit that you have appealed to what he may think others will consider his baser instincts. He may agree with you inside, but he will not want others to know what he holds dear as unstated goals. For example, take a libertarian administrator who makes an exception for a non–fee-paying person because he has hidden egalitarian goals. He will consider one or two cases as just that—exceptions. But if an advocate persists, the danger that the administrator's egalitarian values will be exposed may be more than he can tolerate. Such exposure could mean that he would have to leave that health care system. If his first priority is financial survival in that system, he will compromise his unstated goals to keep his job. You may say, "Well, that's unusual. What kind of person would compromise his unstated goals just for financial security?" You must remember that all of a person's goals are ranked—that a belief in egalitarianism may be subordinate to the need to survive financially. In addition, even if a person's unstated goals are the most influential in his decision-making process, if two sets of unstated goals come into conflict one will win out over the other. It is not unusual for stated goals to conflict with unstated goals, but conflict between two or more unstated goals occurs with equal frequency.

For an advocate to use the strategy of playing stated goals against unstated goals as a means of risk defusement, without taking into account that all goals have a priority ranking, could be a serious miscalculation. What may look like a simple strategy on the surface can easily boomerang without warning. This is not to say that for risk defusement the use of stated goals against unstated goals is not a good strategy; it is, and it is one that is used a good deal. But when using this strategy one must remember that every goal has a priority ranking and that it is this ranking that is the most difficult to analyze. It is not hard to find out what others hold dear, but it is hard to discover what they hold *most dear*. This kind of information is obtained most easily if the advocate engages in direct, open communication at the start. Communicating openly encourages others to communicate openly in turn.

Let me say at this point that compromise is not a bad thing. It has received bad publicity in recent years, and a negative connotation has been cast upon it. Is it better to lose a battle than to lose the war, to humbly give a bit of ground today in order to gain the whole field tomorrow? If you believe that it is, then you will suffer today's criticism for tomorrow's praise. Never forget that short-term goals are more manipulable and flexible than long-term goals, which you invest with your deepest principle. As an advocate you must examine your goals and the priorities you assign to them and how far you can go without letting your basic principles be undermined. In other words, you must know the priority ranking of your own goals as well as try to discern the ranking of the goals of others. This kind of thoughtful application of knowledge goes a long way in the risk defusement strategies you develop in the advocacy process.

Finally, remember that you analyze the goals of a system in terms of what you want to accomplish at a particular time. If your goal or request changes, you must reanalyze the system in terms of your new goal. If, for example, your goal is to get nurses' salaries improved, your analysis will be concerned primarily with financial matters. However, if your goal is to institute a new practice model, your analysis will focus on how professionals relate to each other within the system. Systems analysis is an ongoing process, not an isolated phenomenon.

ETHICS AND LEGALITIES

At this point someone may accuse me of using the sacrosanct area of ethics as a means to manipulate a system—in other words, using ethics as a means to gain the end of advocacy. Let me still the heart of the purist scholar of ethics: using ethics in that way is not my purpose. Instead, I would like to raise this question: how can advocates cope with myriad ethical positions and still fulfill their role? They will need to understand various ethical stands and how each can or cannot be of help to them. Remember, we will be mixing ethics and legalities together in discussing coping strategies. The two are closely aligned, with ethics being of broader scope than the laws since many laws arise out of ethics.

One of the best tools for an advocate is the informed consent form. The law requires that a patient give informed consent; in most cases a written consent form must be signed by the patient prior to surgery or other treatment. This permit describes the nature of the surgery or treatment, but the description generally consists of little more than the name of the intended procedure—for example, mastectomy, appendectomy, chemotherapy, or radiation. The form does not address the question of postoperative or post-treatment effects on the patient. It is wise, ethical, and prudent for a surgeon to discuss these things with a patient, since the law does require such a discussion. Thus an advocate can use the law as a support in the informing and supporting role. But the advocate cannot always know to what extent the surgeon has informed the patient.

A surgeon who has fulfilled the letter of the law is generally safe and can always fall back on the reasoning that it is not wise to tell a patient too much, since it may unnecessarily scare him. Surgeons may find a great deal of support for this position among members of patients' families, other professionals, and members of the general public, many of whom are of the opinion that a physician "knows best" because of past experience with patients. In addition, a rescuer may believe that patients must be protected from what he thinks are unnecessary fears. A rescuer may say, "Leave these decisions to your doctor, honey. He will take care of you." This is a commonly heard statement.

The advocate's experience—that well-informed patients are more cooperative—and her belief that people have a right to be fully informed may be given little credence—even in the face of research evidence demonstrating the good effects of exposing patients to complete preoperative teaching in preparation for the postoperative period. The philosophies "Ignorance is bliss" and "What you don't know can't hurt you," though blatantly false, still may be adhered to. In the short term they work for the protection of the professional's time, the time required to inform patients and to answer their questions. The long-range problems that occur because of these attitudes are ignored or brushed aside: "Well, we will cross that bridge when we come to it" or "Don't look for trouble." It is amazing to see denial of the obvious— bordering on ignorance—so rampant among professionals, who have more education than the average members of the public.

In the face of this the advocate must use all the tools available; the tool an advocate must most often fall back on is a plea for ethical behavior. No professional wants to be accused of unethical practice, and it is neither wise nor prudent for an advocate to make this accusation in an open and forthright way. For example, it is probably better to suggest that there may be more to a case than meets the eye than to begin by accusing a person of deliberately covering up facts. For example, the suggestion that a patient or a family member may sue if he finds out that some facts have been kept from him goes a long way in aiding the full disclosure process. In this day and age the slightest hint of a malpractice suit overrides much of the denial and secrecy engaged in by professionals. If an advocate is asked on what basis a patient could sue, he or she can always fall back on the statement "The lack of fully informed consent can be considered illegal and unethical behavior." Whether a lawsuit of this nature can actually be won is not the point; the risk defusement tool consists of placing the thought of the possibility of a lawsuit in a professional's mind. This tactic may open the door to more information being given the client. This tactic can be used as a risk defusement strategy before an advocate informs a patient, or it can be used after a patient has been informed, to handle the accusation that the advocate had no right to inform the patient.

I may be accused, and rightly so, of encouraging advocates to engage in subtle manipulation through the use of veiled threats. But when you are working in an environment in which the level of denial is high, and in which arguments based on what is right and logical fall on deaf ears, you may have to fall back to a reward-and-punishment strategy. Refer back to Kohlberg's stages. When the people you are dealing with are operating at the stage in which only the fear of punishment from others deters actions, or at the stage in which the opinions of others are the only basis for proper actions, then veiled threats may be all that people will listen to. The appeal to sweet reason and logic and what is right or wrong may be outside their stage of moral development. However, the veiled threat of an accusation of unethical behavior is a tool that the advocate uses only when he or she is forced to deal with an immediate and unexpected danger. In addition, remember that a threat is no good if you do not intend to carry it out, and the other person must know that you intend to do so. Do not threaten if you have no intention of acting on the threat. The veiled threat is a short-term tool and has very little effect on long-term behavior, so other, more lasting tools must be developed.

One of the most effective tools is to assist in the setting up of seminars on ethics for the professionals in a focal system. It is best if these seminars are interdisciplinary, since the views of all can then be heard and each professional group will know what information the other groups have been exposed to. In these seminars the role of the advocate must be explained and explored. The nature of the times makes the establishment of these seminars much easier than in the past, since the members of the health professions are being pressured by consumer and government bodies to be more accountable to the public. Also, the increase in the number of malpractice suits has made these kinds of activities more attractive to professionals. All activities of this nature aid advocates in the risk defusement area. Advocates must make use of such seminars and attend them themselves, so that they can make the case for advocacy effectively and clearly and gain support for the advocacy process.

Again, lest I be accused of being too pragmatic and of viewing ethics as a tool and not as a good in itself, let me put your mind to rest. Advocacy embodies the highest sense of ethical behavior. Moreover, advocacy is action oriented; it is more than a philosophy it is only good to have. In other words, to act ethically is better than simply to believe that ethical behavior is good. My position is like that of the mother who must either disguise a medicine in sweets to get her children to take it or threaten them with dire consequences if they do not take it. We humans do not always do what we know is good; in fact, some of us seem to go out of our way to do the reverse. The same is true for the advocate. Although many people may agree that advocacy is good, they often must be bribed or threatened into being advocates or at least not obstructing the advocacy of others. Tactics of this kind are not necessary when one is dealing with people who are in Kohlberg's third level. But as Kohlberg said himself, most Americans are not at that level; rather they are at the conventional level or lower, where factors outside themselves force them to act in an ethical way.

I will not go into an examination of the laws that affect the advocate, since they vary from place to place. It suffices to say that as an advocate you must become familiar with the laws of your state that reflect on the advocacy process. Those that govern informed consent are the first you should know; the next, of course, are the laws that govern your license to practice. I suggest that you become familiar with articles on informed consent, the law, and dilemmas, and then keep up-to-date on new articles and laws as they appear. Also, as an advocate you would be remiss indeed if you did not keep informed about what legislation concerning advocacy is before your state legislature and if you did not write and speak about how it may affect your role.

Anyone working in the area of advocacy needs all the help he can get in the risk defusement process, and knowledge about the law is a valuable help in this process. Moreover, I am suggesting that advocates assume an activist's role, that they participate in the formation of laws that will protect them while they are attempting to fulfill their function of doing what is ethically right for clients.

So we have a careful mix of pragmatism and ethics, which is really the theme of this chapter on risk defusement. The last thing one wants to be accused of is an idealism that does not have a basis for realization in the working world. That is the final accusation that will be thrown at all advocates: "My dear, you just don't understand how it is. I know you mean well, but life isn't the way you see it, so just be a good nurse and keep your mouth shut." Only a demonstration of knowledge about the real world and the consequences of a non-advocacy position will serve as a meaningful rebuttal.

As I said in Chapter 2, knowledge is a valuable commodity. We tend to hoard it, to keep it from others, for to share knowledge is to share power—in this case, the power patients need to control the decision-making process, to become adults and not remain the children that health professionals have been able to manipulate so easily. Therefore advocates must use all the tools at their command, and ethics is a valuable one. Knowledge about the law is even more valuable. So I urge you to read the articles listed at the end of this chapter; they all provide valuable risk defusement activities.

There are two other topics relating to ethics that the advocate should become familiar with—the ethical codes of the professions and the documents known as "patients' bills of rights," which are published by professional organizations. Neither the codes nor the bills of rights are totally incorporated into the law; rather they are statements that are supposed to govern conduct. The professions and the organizations that draw up these codes and bills of rights can hold an individual or a group accountable for proper behavior under them. But unless the codes or bills of rights are written into the law, no one can truly be bound by them. They can bring down moral censure, but they cannot produce legal action. Generally, moral censure is enough to make most professionals fall into line, but when push comes to shove it is the law that carries the most weight.

The codes and bills tend to deal broadly with what is considered good behavior rather than with what is considered legal behavior. In other words, one may be able to behave in what some would consider an unethical manner without being called to formal justice for it. This situation is not wrong on all counts; one must remember that even though laws tend to act against unethical behavior, they also act against freedom. So it is only when there is a consensus on what is clearly wrong and harmful to others that a law is enacted. We have only to go back to our discussions of libertarianism and egalitarianism and of Kantian, utilitarian, and situational ethics to see that there are many positions and supports for those positions. Therefore the parts of the codes and bills of rights that are made into law are done so only by a consensus of all the parties that they affect. This does not make them totally ineffectual as a tool for the advocate. For the advocate who invokes them as a risk defusement strategy is also calling on the moral pressure of the group that wrote them in the first place.

It is obvious that legal pressure carries more weight, but moral pressure has an effect as well, especially for those who place value on the opinions of their fellow professionals. And many do place value on what other professionals think of them, since one's fellow professionals produce referrals (and thus money), bestow honors, and serve as an audience for articles. So moral pressure and sanctions, although they work more indirectly than the law, can have important repercussions in the life of the professional.

In discussing codes, I would like to use the code of the American Nurses' Association as an example. It consists of 11 statements:

1. The nurse provides services with respect for human dignity and the uniqueness of the client unrestricted by considerations of social or economic status, personal attributes, or the nature of health problems.
2. The nurse safeguards the client's right to privacy by judiciously protecting information of a confidential nature.
3. The nurse acts to safeguard the client and the public when health care and safety are affected by the incompetent, unethical, or illegal practice of any person.
4. The nurse assumes responsibility and accountability for individual nursing judgments and actions.
5. The nurse maintains competence in nursing.
6. The nurse exercises informed judgment and uses individual competence and qualifications as criteria in seeking consultation, accepting responsibilities, and delegating nursing activities to others.
7. The nurse participates in activities that contribute to the ongoing development of the profession's body of knowledge.
8. The nurse participates in the profession's efforts to implement and improve standards of nursing.
9. The nurse participates in the profession's efforts to establish and maintain conditions of employment conducive to high quality nursing care.
10. The nurse participates in the profession's effort to protect the public from misinformation and misrepresentation and to maintain the integrity of nursing.
11. The nurse collaborates with members of the health professions and other citizens in promoting community and national efforts to meet the health needs of the public.[2]

[2]American Nurses' Association, *Code for Nurses With Interpretive Statements* (Kansas City, Mo.: The Association, 1976). Reprinted with the permission of the American Nurses' Association.

Some of these statements are explicit and unequivocal; others are more open to interpretation. Consider statement 4: "The nurse assumes responsibility and accountability for individual nursing judgments and actions." That is quite explicit, and it is written into the nursing practice laws of most states. In other words, a nurse is held legally responsible for what he or she does. But statement 11 says, "The nurse collaborates with members of the health professions and other citizens in promoting community and national efforts to meet the health needs of the public." How can such a provision be enforced? The fact is that it cannot be enforced; that is why such statements in professional codes cannot be written into law. Statement 4 deals with what one *must* do and with what can be enforced under the laws concerning licensure of nurses, while statement 11 deals with what one *should* do but is not legally bound to do.

This same general pattern exists in all the codes as well as in the various bills of rights. The advocate should know what these documents contain, as well as which stipulations are enforceable under the law and which are more or less amenable to moral pressure. Some are not even that; they simply are idealized goals that we hope to aim for, such as statement 11 in the code just discussed. The codes and bills of rights should be scrutinized for provisions that can be directly used to exert legal as well as moral pressure in the risk defusement process.

ISSUES AND SOCIAL LAWS

We have discussed the issues of race, sex, age, and access to health care and education, as well as social laws—that is, laws relating to such subjects as abortion, welfare, and food stamps. We know that an advocate who becomes involved in any of these areas faces risks—risks over and above those connected with the simple informing and supporting functions of advocacy. These risks will result from some very strong prejudices on the part of some of the people with whom the advocate must deal. These feelings may be openly stated, or they may be covered up and thus not apparent unless something or someone causes them to be revealed. So the first area of risk defusement for the advocate is having some knowledge of the existence of these feelings. Thus we return once again to systems analysis. Since the advocate knows that there are mixed opinions on social issues, if it looks as though he or she will get involved in any of them he or she must discover what the stated and unstated feelings of the members of the focal group are concerning them.

The old cliché "Forewarned is forearmed" holds true here. To be caught unaware leaves one little time for thought and none for planning strategies to cope. Furthermore, it is not enough to know what the feelings or opinions of others are; it is also necessary to know to what extent or extreme these feelings or opinions are held. Also, are these feelings true of everyone in the focal system? Are they true of everyone in the ecological system? If opinions are held in various degrees, how much power do persons with extreme views have? What you are looking for is some kind of leverage to use to dilute the risk posed by an extremist, who may object to your advocacy. This may sound like a lot of work, but it isn't; it doesn't take much effort to find out what most people's feelings are on social issues. In fact, some people tell you even when you don't want to know.

Sometimes, using the leverage of one person or group against another is not necessary. Often a simple statement such as "Well, you know if we don't inform this patient of his rights, we could be accused of being prejudiced" will work. Again, we are dealing with a very subtle form of threat, not a direct threat from us but from the sanctions of others. Direct threats from advocates, as you know, can be very danger-ous to the advocates themselves. One must be very sure of himself or must be in a position of power to make a direct threat. If an advocate is dealing with a clear breach of ethics or the law that is causing a clear violation of the rights of others, then the advocate has no choice but to speak out, no matter what is at stake. But in such cases the advocate will not have to look far to find support. Most people are too prudent or ethical to stand for that kind of behavior. Violations of the rights of others usually result from the absence of what might be called decent behavior—behavior that is not explicitly required by law or that is only tangentially mentioned by ethical codes. It is this type of subtle violation that is best met with the subtle threat of sanctions by others.

Many of us have prejudices and even exercise them, but we do not want others to find out about them. The advocate is not out to reform the world and rid it or a focal system of all prejudice. That would be a good idea, but it is not very realistic. An advocate's best hope is to keep prejudice under some control, especially when it concerns the rights of patients. But there is little an advocate can do in a system that is in full accord, for example, with a racist policy. An advocate's best bet is to get out of it and then try to obtain support from persons on the outside who can bring community or organizational pressure on that system to reform. An advocate who attempts such a reform from the inside will soon be on the outside anyway. It is better to leave with an intact reputation and *good written* references, and then spill the beans. Too often people try to bring about reform from within and find that the system retaliates by discrediting them. Outsiders then do not know whom to believe.

However, you should realize that we have been talking only about systems that are so unified on an issue that no amount of work from the inside would do any good. Systems of this kind are not very common any more, but some do still exist. One of the classic examples I have seen involved a nurse who took a job in what she later found out was a "Medicaid mill" of the worst sort. Not only was the city being ripped off, but the clients were being ripped off as well. There was no chance for the nurse to reform this system, since its purpose was to make money in this manner.

She left the situation with the excuse of returning to school full time and received a good reference for her nursing work. She then went to the local nursing organization and with its full support and help notified the local city officials of the situation. The result was that the system was put out of business. It had no comeback, such as calling the nurse a poor worker or a disgruntled worker who caused trouble on the job, since it had put in writing what a great nurse she was. Because of her good references, the nursing organization and the city officials gave her complaints much more serious consideration than they would have if she had left under a cloud. The nurse made it clear to the people she sought support from how she had left and why she had left. In other words, everything was out in the open; she established herself as a good nurse, as an honest person, and as someone who would not tolerate unethical and illegal behavior in a so-called health facility. One could say that she analyzed the situation, took risk defusement precautions, and acted. By the way, she did return to school as a full-time student and has since become a rather outspoken consumer advocate for the poor. With a reputation as a knowledgeable nurse and with good credentials, she has become very effective.

This leads us to the area of politics as a source of risk defusement. The advocate who ventures into the realm of politics does so for several reasons, not the least of these being to help establish laws to protect the advocacy process. One area of major focus here must be to get the laws on informed consent more clearly and firmly established. Three changes would help this process immensely. First, what informed consent means should be more clearly spelled out in the law and on the consent forms that patients sign. This alone would help the advocate, since patients would be better informed at the start. It also would help the advocate to make better use of the law in the risk defusement process—for example, when she is questioned about informing patients.

Second, patients should be granted free access to all their hospital and other professional records. This would pose a form of after-the-fact threat to many professionals but would act as a major deterrant to the kind of secrecy that is prevalent now, a secrecy under which many patients' rights are denied them without their even knowing it. Many physicians and others say that such disclosure would increase the number of questionable (their term) malpractice suits. In fact, what decreases the number of malpractice suits is a decrease in the amount of malpractice. And providing patients with detailed and clearly written consent forms would be the best defense a professional could have against false accusations.

The third change that would benefit the nurse advocate, or any advocate who has a professional license, would be to have the laws governing the license more clearly spell out the duties involved. Ideally, the laws should in fact state that one of a nurse's responsibilities is to be a patient's advocate, that a nurse is bound to inform and support patients. A nurse then could not be accused of overstepping his or her professional role, or of interfering in the relationship between a patient and another professional, just because the nurse informed the patient of his rights and options. Such a change would have saved Tuma a lot of problems. If the advocate role were written into the licensure laws of all the professions, anyone who did not inform and support patients could be held liable for failing to do so.

The law is a great help not only in assisting someone to do what is right but also in supporting someone who refuses to do what is wrong. For example, a nurse is held legally liable for the medications he or she gives to patients. Therefore if a nurse suspects that a drug order is improper, he or she is legally bound to refuse to give the medication. Many a nurse who has been threatened with retribution if he or she does not give a drug has used the law to support the right to refuse, and that has usually been the end of the matter. If such threats continue, all the nurse has to do is appeal or threaten to appeal to the state licensure bureau. This works like magic, since no institution wants a state licensing group investigating its practices.

These are just three possible changes in the law that could help the advocate in the risk defusement process. There are many more. The advocate's role in creating and changing laws lies in appealing to politicians to get laws passed or changed. This is not easy, since numerous special interest groups do not want certain types of laws. The advocate's task then becomes to find out who has the most influence with the politicians. Who is a politician most dependent on for election and re-election? One sure bet is the consumers in his area who go to the polls to vote. If an advocate can get these consumers sufficiently educated, active, and vocal, then even the special interest groups often must stand aside. Again, knowledge and political astuteness on the part of the advocate are called for.

Oddly enough, one major factor that advocates have on their side when they work for patient and consumer rights is that they can be accused of representing a special interest—themselves. People like good causes that they can see also promise gain for them. In addition, the average American today is tired of being ripped off by special interest groups who have the money and power to influence politicians. Since nurses are not seen as having such power, and since advocacy offers no financial gain for nurses, but a great deal of gain for the consumer in terms of self-determination and disclosure of information that should have been his in the first place, the issue of patient rights has a great deal of appeal. But it will also encounter a great deal of opposition. That is why it is so necessary for advocates to have as much consumer support as possible and, if possible, to have consumers out in front verbally pushing the issue. Keep in mind that it is not necessary that an advocate receive credit for passage of a good law; getting the good law is reward enough.

• • •

A final note before we leave the subject of coping with risk: the advocate should avoid whenever possible the whole area of dilemmas. When dealing with conscious, alert patients who are informable and who can make decisions, dilemmas will not concern the advocate. If an advocate believes that a bad decision made by a patient has led to a dilemma, then one would have to ask, a dilemma for whom? Certainly not for the patient—he made the decision. And how can the advocate be considered to be facing a dilemma, since the advocate has nothing to do with the decision-making process? It is not a dilemma for the advocate if he or she does not like a patient's decision, since the advocate has nothing to say about it. In other words, the advocate has no choice; there is no dilemma when there are no choices.

In my life I have made many decisions that I now consider wrong and that others probably thought wrong at the time. But I would not have the pain of any of them removed, if the removal of pain also meant the removal of my right to make my own decisions. That's what freedom of choice is; you either have it, for better or for worse, or you do not have it. So do not feel bad about the seemingly bad decisions of others; rather be glad that you live in a country where people have the right to make decisions at all. Remember, what you deprive others of, even if for a good reason, you yourself can be deprived of in the future, and perhaps not for a good reason.

True dilemmas can occur when you are dealing with unconscious patients or with infants, who cannot make decisions for themselves. Rescuing in the true sense, not the gaming sense, then comes into play. In such a situation, the victim is truly a victim; he cannot change roles and make you the victim. In other words, here the term "victim" means one who is totally without defense. Your advocacy will consist in using all your skills to guarantee ethical conduct on the part of everyone who is engaged in the care of such a person. In such a situation you are moving from informing someone of his rights, so that he can act on the information, to actually having to defend those rights yourself. This can be hazardous, but the knowledge and skills you gain as an advocate in the informing and supporting role are the same ones you use here. Some unnecessary dilemmas may occur in these cases because so many people are engaged in the decision-making process; the more people that are involved, the greater the number of possible choices that will be fought out. The safest stance for the advocate is to try to guarantee that the decisions are ethical and that they are made with the best interests of the patient in mind. Even then there will be variables you will just have to live with and pray for the best.

Now let us move on to the area of professional education. Although the discussion in the next chapter will be geared to the nursing profession, much of it will be applicable to professional education in general. Even if you are not a health care professional, it will be informative for you to become familiar with the subject, especially if you are an advocate in any of the health-related fields. Knowing how nursing education is conducted and how nursing is practiced will help you in the advocacy process; it will help you to understand how the health care system functions and how it needs to be and can be changed. The public and even many professionals are ignorant about the educational process and the reasons behind many of the twists and turns it takes. This is not to say that a conspiracy of silence reigns but rather that the average person does not read the books and journals that deal with issues concerning the health professions and neither do many practicing professionals. Nonprofessionals may be excused, but there is no excuse for professionals who do not keep up-to-date about the forces that determine the future of their practice and education. We have a habit of speaking of faceless "they" who influence our practice, deriding their power but forgetting that we gave it up. Again, knowledge is power. If we want to effect change in a system, we must know and understand that system.

NOTES ON CHAPTER 7

The types of knowledge needed for risk defusement have already been discussed in Chapters 1 through 6. However, I cannot emphasize enough the need to know the law or laws governing the practice of nursing in the state in which you are working. You must also be alert to the kinds of laws that govern the availability of information to consumers. One of the best sources of knowledge in this regard is a state nurses' association. Its legislative committee usually keeps track of all laws that could in any way be related to nursing or the health care system. It is also important to follow legislative developments on a national level. Since laws are constantly changing, it is absolutely necessary to keep up to date.

Aside from keeping up to date in your reading and in the law, it is of help to be involved in an association or at least in some formal aspect of one's profession—that is, to be a part of a professional network of peers. This can be accomplished on a local, state, or even national basis. Remember that other people are involved in the same activities you are and that people who are in similar positions and who have similar concerns, problems, and needs can be very supportive of each other.

I would like to recommend a book that deals with the broad subject of the rights of professional health workers:

Annas, George J., Glanty, Leonard H., and Katz, Barbara F. *The Rights of Doctors, Nurses, and Allied Health Professionals.* New York: Avon Books, 1981.

This is one in a long series of books by these authors that deal with the rights of various groups. The book is easy and informative reading, and the discussions are documented by references to actual court cases. There is also a section on how to find court cases in a law library.

Finally, the saying "He who hesitates is lost" is not always true. To act on instinct, without facts or information, can be a very dangerous thing. However, to hesitate or procrastinate in getting the facts or information, or in seeking out knowledgeable advice, can be equally dangerous. The keys to risk defusement are knowledge and its thoughtful application.

Chapter 8

PROFESSIONAL EDUCATION IN HEALTH SERVICES

ONE CAN EXAMINE PROFESSIONAL EDUCATION in any number of ways. I suppose the most unbiased way is to proceed in a strictly historical manner, but that tends to be a bit boring, especially to the reader who has some knowledge of professional education. Therefore, since we have used the knowledge base set forth in Chapter 1 to describe advocacy in general and the systems method set forth in Chapter 3 to look at parts of advocacy, it seems appropriate at this point to combine the two approaches to look at professional education. First, we will use the four major areas of the knowledge base—informing and supporting, systems analysis, social ethic, and ethics—to obtain an overall view of the health care professions. Second, we will move to systems analysis to examine one profession in more detail—nursing. Third, we will deal with the professions as they relate to issues, the medical-industrial complex, social laws, and politics. Finally, we will look at how an understanding of professional education can aid the advocate, no matter what his or her profession, in the risk defusement area, and at the role of the advocate in professional education.

OVERVIEW OF EDUCATION IN THE HEALTH CARE PROFESSIONS

At this point let me make it clear that I am talking about professional education, not about professional practice. The two do not necessarily go hand in hand. Sometimes the educators are ahead of the field, and sometimes the reverse is true. More often than not, the goals of the two groups are at variance with each other. So, with this in mind, let us look only at education while remembering that both the practice field and education do influence each other, more often for the good of the consumer than not. Friction within a profession, or what might be called disunity, is not always a bad thing. Remember, no one takes readily to change, and change is not necessarily good. People who work for change only for the sake of change forget that innovations are often only reinventions of the wheel.

Informing and supporting

What role do educators in the health care professions play in informing and supporting? Whom do they inform, and whom do they support?

First, as a given, we know that people talk most to people they consider to be of their own kind. Physicians talk most often to physicians, social workers to social workers, lawyers to lawyers, and nurses to nurses. Educators in the professions talk first to other educators, then to their students, then to their colleagues in the practice field, and finally, if at all, to consumers. It seems safe to say that the educators within a profession inform each other of what they are doing and that, to a lesser degree, depending on the congruence of their goals, they support each other. One need only look at the kinds of conferences that are scheduled within professional groups to see this process in action. It is a natural thing, and a good thing, that fellow professionals have an opportunity to share with each other the roles they have chosen to play in their profession—that is, the strategies of teaching, practice, or administration. These strategies have an important place in the successful enacting of the professional role and in the attainment of the goals of that role.

A person's role in a profession may vary widely depending on how he views his place in that profession. It stands to reason that a physician educator will have more in common with another physician educator than with a physician practitioner. The same is true in other professions. We tend to inform and support first those we are closest to and to inform and support others later.

Students are a captive audience that we educators talk to every day; they listen to us, at least for the time we have them. That this informing process tends to be a one-way street is true and sometimes unfortunate. Students support their instructors more often than instructors support their students. As long as students hew to the teacher's line, they are supported. But let them go off on a tangent or even, God forbid, go beyond the teacher, and more often than not the support is removed. (But that process is the title of another, as yet hypothetical book, to be called *Student Abuse; or, We Eat Our Children.*) This problem is not limited to the health care professions; it occurs in all areas of academia. It also occurs in the practice arena in all the professions. As long as the young, be they students, educators, or practitioners, understand that informing comes from the elders—in other words, those who "know best"—and as long as they stay in line until they win their spurs and become elders themselves, they will be supported. If they step out of line, act as though they may know as much as their elders do (or more) and as though they can inform also, the support will be removed, at the least, and lessons to bring them back into line will be taught. And if those measures do not work, they will be ostracized. This pattern is not peculiar to education and the professions; it exists in all walks of life. The novel *Dress Gray*, by Lucian K. Truscott IV, about West Point, describes an extreme example of this process.

The third group that educators in the health care professions inform and support consists of practitioners in the field. The informing and supporting process here runs more smoothly in some professions than in others. In general, there is an ongoing dialogue between the practice field and the professional schools. When new knowledge is gained in the schools, it is fed into the practice arena. There it is used, and the results—including any new discoveries made in actual practice—are returned to the schools.

For a long while, most research emanated from the centers of education, and the findings were then transferred to the practice arenas. This trend is changing; we are now seeing more and more research being conducted in the practice arena and the findings being fed to the colleges.

The process of informing and supporting runs quite smoothly between education and practice until one of the two starts making demands for change that the other cannot accept. For example, 20 years ago most of the research in nursing came out of the colleges and the bulk of the best-educated nurses were teaching in the colleges. So information traveled primarily from the colleges to the practice field. But as more and more nurses educated at the baccalaureate and higher levels entered the practice field and began conducting research and exerting leadership comparable to that of the educators, the informing process started to become a two-way street.

Then nurses in the field began to question whether all the changes that the educators wanted made in nursing practice were good for the practice. No longer would they simply accept everything that was dictated to them by the educators. Their non-acceptance sometimes took the form of accusations: "You in the ivory towers of academia don't know what reality is" or "Well, it might look good theoretically and on paper, but this is the real world and it won't work here." So although the informing by the educators continued, the support from practicing nurses was not total. One could say that it had become situational: if information was found valuable and workable, it was supported; if it was not found so, it was rejected. The hold on knowledge and leadership was shifting. Since knowledge and leadership are power, one can say that educators were losing power and being forced to share it with nurses in the field. This process never sits well, no matter what the group, and it did not sit well with the educators.

The result was some disunity within the profession, demonstrated by a constant call for professional unity. One saw and heard this call in all professional meetings and in the journals where nurses publish. Nurses were divided and at war with themselves at the same time that they were trying to unite and fend off the attack of their traditional enemies, hospital associations and physicians, who wanted to dominate and control what they saw as a profession of women whom they believed were there for the sole purpose of serving them. It was like trying to fight off an invasion while at the same time trying to control a revolution in your own land. This division of attention made it difficult to bring either the war with outsiders or the revolution from within to a satisfactory conclusion. Needless to say, the outsiders used the revolution to divide nurses further and to weaken the profession.

Nurses see themselves as an autonomous health profession—a profession that is independent of all other professions, especially medicine. Nurses have always been in the forefront of informing consumers about their health and reaching out into the community to provide information and health care. Therefore, in dealing with the attack on them from hospitals and physicians, they counterattacked by informing consumers about what these two groups were doing, not only to the nursing profession but to the consumers themselves. In other words, they sought allies, and they supported consumer movements that would make hospitals and physicians more accountable to consumers, thus helping to divert the attention of physicians and hospitals away from their destructive attacks on the nursing profession. Meanwhile, nurses continued to try to cope with their internal revolution. This dual struggle is still an ongoing process.

This type of situation has perhaps been more visible in nursing than in other professions. However, the same process has occurred in other professions. Practitioners and educators in law, medicine, and social work are suffering the same problems for many of the same reasons. Their problems are not as visible because their educational systems are not as fragmented as nursing's. But they are all undergoing revolutions and at the same time having to face attacks from consumers and from members of other professions.

This brings us to the topic of how educators in the professions inform consumers about education in the professions and then obtain support from them. The professions with the most prestige (that is, rewards in terms of money and power), such as law and medicine, have an easier job than other professions. The reward for professionals in these fields are great, and consumers know this. These professions therefore do not have to recruit students by informing the public of the virtues of the professions. In fact, they can keep a low profile, since they have more applicants than they can admit to their professional schools. But the question of support presents the opposite problem. The education of professionals is expensive and thus requires consumer support in the form of taxes and grants. So the informing process consists of stating the consumers' needs for doctors and lawyers and pleading for support so that these needs can be met. In other words, support becomes a two-way street. The educators of professionals argue that they are supporting the consumers' needs for lawyers and doctors and that it is therefore in the consumers' own best interest to help them in this endeavor by furnishing money. This appeal is otherwise known as "I'm only trying to help you," mixed with a bit of "We know what is best for you." All the professions are doing the same thing, but the public is more cognizant of what a lawyer or a doctor does than it is of what a nurse or a social worker does. In addition, the practice field is more lucrative for a lawyer or a doctor, and everyone wants his son or daughter to be one. (However this last phenomenon can backfire and has backfired. The consumer movement is much more critical of persons or groups it sees as making the most money and therefore is quicker to attack them than it is to attack the less well paid professionals. Being a member of one of the lucrative professions can indeed be a double-edged sword.)

The problem with informing the public about the nursing profession and gaining and giving support is that the profession has not gotten its educational house in order. The educators do not speak with one voice. For example, we have three systems of educational preparation, each of which allows graduates to sit for a state board examination in order to receive a license as a registered nurse: the two-year associate degree program, the three-year diploma program, and the four-year baccalaureate degree program. Although the three systems do not prepare students for the same kind of practice, their graduates all have the same license. (Now try to explain *that* to the consumer—and to prospective nursing students.) Efforts over the past 15 to 20 years to rectify this situation have helped cause great divisions in nursing, not only between the various educators in the three programs but also between the educators and the nurses in the practice fields. Practicing nurses have been saying, "This is what we need to carry on," and educators have been saying, "This is what you are going to get, because we know better." Whatever solutions are offered to correct this problem are going to have dissenters. Any change in the educational system is going to be resisted by the group that sees that change as putting it out of business.

Intelligent compromise that will benefit both the profession and the consumers is made even more difficult by outside forces who do not want to see the profession united and who will use those nurses who have the most to lose as a result of change as weapons to keep the various factions fighting. Therefore the nursing profession is made more vulnerable to attack and takeover by persons who stand to gain by controlling nurses.

The nurse educator who advocates excellence in nursing education in order to promote excellence in nursing practice has a difficult job indeed. In the informing and supporting role, such an educator faces resistance from those outside nursing and even more resistance from within, from those who do not like what he or she is informing about. One has only to look at what is going on in education in the other professions to see that advocates for excellence in professional education, which may demand changes in programs to meet changes in society, are not going to be welcomed by those who want a system to stay the same. Whenever systems change, power shifts, and those it shifts away from will resist the change the most. The advocate who demands excellence in the educational process for any profession can expect to be attacked by all groups in which changes have to be made to achieve that excellence.

In the worlds of business and politics the process of bringing about change is not unlike that in education, but it is made somewhat easier by the fact that results come faster and nothing succeeds in gaining acceptance so much as success—that is, making money and gaining power. A businessman who steps outside the common practice, but thereby becomes a billionaire, is difficult to criticize. The same is true of a politician who gets elected outside the confines of an established political system. The very speed of results aids this process, but excellence in education takes longer to produce results, and in a society that is geared to instant gratification, the concept of long-term gain often has little value. It's "Eat, drink, and be merry, for tomorrow we may die." We forget that we may not die, but only be hungry, thirsty, and sad. The advocate must not forget that his or her "cry in the wilderness" may be heard and acted on by others who have not been yet able to find their voices. So those who have soft voices must support those who have loud voices, and those who act must hope that silence on the part of others only hides their quiet support. The absence of supporting voices does not necessarily mean the absence of support; support may be quiet yet powerful.

Systems analysis

Since I will be using systems analysis later to provide an in-depth look into education in one profession, nursing, I will simply present here a brief discussion of the ways in which systems analysis can help you to divide fact from fiction in professional education in general and to understand what the educational system in the health care professions is all about.

One could say that the stated goals of the institutions that offer professional education are to turn out the best prepared practitioners possible by providing the best education possible, in the context of today's needs. The unstated goals are to attract enough students and financial help to stay solvent, to gain a good reputation (if not the best) among professional schools, and to be in a position to attract and hire the best in the field as professors. The stated goals and the unstated goals are somewhat supportive of each other. It is only when the attracting and keeping of good faculty members and the financial needs of the institution become problems that the stated goals suffer. For example, faculty members may want to do more research than teaching, or they may be resistant to innovations that may require them to take more time with students. Or if an institution must increase enrollment and income to stay viable, even at the price of dilution of teaching and research, then it also has a problem. In times of plenty, when the public is willing and able to pay for well-prepared professionals, the stated goals and the unstated can mesh fairly easily. But when the economy is weak or when the consumer does not prize professionals or their services, then hard choices must be made.

The stated goals of a professional school are communicated frequently and effectively to consumers of the practice and to possible students for recruitment. The unstated goals are also communicated, but mainly to persons already in the profession, to attract them to a certain school. The unstated goals are also communicated to persons who hold the financial purse strings, so that they will know that a school is worthy and the best and therefore should be funded, and to prospective students, so that they also will know that a school is the best. However, there is a mix of communications here. The public may well know the stated goals as well as the unstated goals. This is okay, since the public wants the best, too. The dilution of the quality of teaching is certainly not a goal of an institution, but it can happen as a consequence of attempts to achieve unstated goals. Professionals and current students will see this happen long before the general public even suspects it. Also, because of the ebb-and-flow nature of the economy, by the time a reduction in the quality of teaching caused by a shortage of funds is detected, the flow of money may have changed, allowing the school to say, "That is all behind us now and won't happen again." The stated and unstated goals of the professional schools are probably much more out in the open than those of many other organizations, since colleges—both public and private—are much more visible than most other groups in the medical-industrial complex, such as hospitals.

I have stated that professional educators communicate first with each other, then with students, then with fellow professionals in practice, and then with the public. Under the heading of "public," the groups they communicate with the most are the ones that control the money—legislators, alumni, foundations, other persons who have or control money, and finally the public at large.

The communications are not terribly pseudo-innocent, unless the unstated goals strongly override the stated goals and thus are played down, or unless educators are appealing to a special interest group and therefore gear their communications to that group, ignoring other realities. The stances educators assume range from expert ("We know best") to supplicant ("We need your help"). One is most likely to see pseudo-innocent communication emanating from professional educators, or even practicing professionals, who plead with others to save them from being dominated by outside forces while at the same time do little for themselves to strengthen their profession or school. Whenever the denial of reality is present, one will also see a measure of pseudo-innocent communication.

The focal group and the ecological group can be defined in one of two ways, depending on the purpose of an analysis. If one is looking at an issue that concerns more than education, one must include in the focal group all aspects of a profession—that is, education, practice, and professional organizations. Then the ecological group becomes anyone else who is connected with the issue. If the issue is concerned primarily with education, then the college or colleges themselves become the focal system, and everything else, even the practice field, becomes the ecological system. The communication patterns will vary accordingly.

Social ethic

The social ethic of professional education is a mix of libertarianism and egalitarianism. All professional schools say they do not discriminate in terms of race, creed, financial ability, and so on. However, they do want to attract the very best students they can—those able to excel intellectually—and they do need students who are able to pay. While they do offer scholarships and loans, most schools have an academic cutoff point that a recruit must meet in order to be accepted. Thus the schools' egalitarianism does not extend to those who cannot pay their own way or qualify for scholarships or loans or to those whose past academic records are poor. This situation does tend to keep the students in the professional schools mostly white and mostly from the middle and upper classes.

Ethics

Every professional school teaches its profession's code of ethics as part of the process of preparing students for their future practice. The ethical stances of particular schools, as indicated by curriculum and by the emphasis placed on various aspects of practice, vary a great deal. One can perhaps best classify professional schools as situational. They do have their Kantians and their utilitarians, and it is perhaps the balance these two maintain that prevents one from becoming predominant and that leads to the prevalence of the situational position. Rarely does a purist ethical stance survive the multiple forces that help determine the future of the practice, and therefore the focus of the curriculum. Because a school must win, lose, or compromise, and since one of its unstated goals is to remain solvent, compromise of a situational type is not unusual.

For example, over the past 10 years or so, many professional schools have changed the lengths of their programs, more often shortening them than lengthening them, as well as changing their entrance requirements. Some medical schools now require three years of college rather than four, and look at the overall potential of students rather than at test scores or grades only. Also, changes in curriculum have been made in response to pressure from funding groups, the public, and persons in the practice fields. Some of these changes are good and needed, but some are not. These latter changes are sometimes made as compromises, to allow an institution to stay viable.

So no matter what educators may profess, their track record seems to place them in the situational ethics school. This is not to say that when we grow and change because we have learned more and better, we automatically become situational ethics people. One must examine the reasons behind a change—the motivation—to be able to identify a person or institution's ethical position.

In general, professional education is reflective of the society it serves. One could hardly expect it to be otherwise. If it varied too much from the norms of the society that supports it, it would cease to exist. It has been said that human beings get the kind of government they deserve. That may not always be true, but to the extent that it is true we can also say that society gets the kind of professional education it deserves. Page says this in a more scholarly and definitive way:

> A profession acquires recognition, relevance, and even meaning in terms of its relationship to [a] society, its culture and institutions, and its other members. Professions acquire recognition and relevance primarily in terms of needs, conditions, and traditions of particular societies and their members. It is societies (and often vested interest within them) that determine, in accord with their different technological and economic levels of development and their socioeconomic, political and cultural conditions, and values, what professional skills and knowledge they most need and desire. By various financial means, institutions will then emerge to train interested individuals to supply those needs.
>
> Logically, then, the professions open to individuals in any particular society are

the property not of the individuals but of society. What individuals acquire through training is professional knowledge and skill, not a profession or even part ownership of one.[1]

SYSTEMS ANALYSIS OF NURSING EDUCATION

In order not to be repetitious, let us say that the overall goals of nursing education, their methods of communication, their social ethics, and their ethical positions do not vary greatly from those of other professional groups. Nursing educators may be more egalitarian in some respects, but the social ethic will differ from program to program. (The practice of nursing is more egalitarian, but we will leave that topic to the next chapter.)

What distinguishes the nursing profession from other professions is the diversity and division that exist within its educational programs. By diversity I mean in the kinds of practice a program prepares its graduates for. For example, graduate schools prepare nurses not only to practice nursing at the specialist or consultant level but also to teach nursing, to administer nursing education programs, and to do research at the master's and Ph.D. levels. Many other types of professional schools prepare students only to practice a profession. Few people in law, medicine, or dentistry have Ph.D.'s. Lawyers, physicians, and dentists can earn academic doctorates in fields related to their work, but not in law, medicine, or dentistry per se. That is, a J.D., an M.D., or a D.D.S. is not the academic equivalent of a Ph.D. The diversity in the nursing profession also results from the fact that nurses are prepared in the basic practice in diploma programs, associate degree programs, and baccalaureate programs. Many in nursing education would argue that the diploma and associate degree programs do not prepare professional nurses, only nursing technicians, and that professional education exists only at the baccalaureate level. But others in the health fields and the public consider all nurses equal, no matter what their education.

Many professionals have technical support groups; dentists have dental technicians, for example. In 1965 the American Nurses' Association produced a position paper saying that the associate degree graduate and the diploma graduate should constitute such a support group. But taking this position and then acting in a manner that makes it a reality are not the same thing. For example, according to this plan the diploma and licensed practical nurse schools would be phased out, leaving the associate degree programs and baccalaureate programs to produce the technicians and the professionals, respectively. The reality is that although the number of diploma programs has decreased, they are still with us, and the number of licensed practical nurse programs has actually increased.

[1]B.B. Page, "Who Owns the Professions?" *Hastings Center Report* 5, no. 5 (October 1975):7-8.

Diploma and associate degree graduates have always taken the same licensing examinations as baccalaureate graduates. And despite the fact that the three types of education do differ, the three types of graduates have always been hired for, and expected to do, the same job. There has been little effort to differentiate in practice according to what the graduates have been educated to do. Thus it is no wonder that people think that all nurses are alike.

The divisions among the educators of the three types of programs really became verbal in the mid-1970s, when efforts were finally made to solve the problem. A plan was proposed that would require all registered nurses to have baccalaureate-level training. This plan was to be implemented by 1985. Had the problem been corrected in the 1960s, when most nurses went on record favoring the proposed change, such a move may have been easier. But that is hindsight.

This kind of problem does not exist in any of the other professions. Therefore one sees a greater measure of unity among the educators in those professions and a less complex system of goals and communication patterns than one sees in nursing.

Goals

An unstated goal of any educator is to prevent the closing of the school in which he or she teaches. Educators in the diploma programs thus have fought to stay in business and have enlisted help to do so—even the help of those who could be classified as the natural enemies of the nursing profession. By enemies I mean those who want the profession of nursing to be subservient and dependent on them—in other words, hospital associations and physicians. Educators in diploma programs in effect called the fox into the hen house to defend them; he will do so and then eat you at his leisure. This has occurred, and is still occurring, in nursing.

While educators in the associate degree programs generally have agreed in principle that their graduates should assume the role of technician, their unstated goals of being prestigious and being seen as powerful would not be met if the instruction they provide were considered to be limited to a technical level or if it ever came about that this instruction prepared a student for a different license. One wonders if such faculty members do not then see themselves as downgraded, because they are not teaching at the baccalaureate level? Educators in the baccalaureate programs say that such an attitude is foolishness, that associate degree nurses perform a service that is just as needed as that performed by baccalaureate nurses but different in kind. This is true, but let us not be pseudo-innocent and deny the unspoken reality that to teach baccalaureate, master's, and doctoral students in major colleges is not seen by some to be the same in terms of public prestige as teaching in community colleges. The need for prestige is a common disease of the human race; it infects all of us, not just nurses. It is not something to be proud of, but its existence should not be denied.

I have no doubt that the nursing profession will solve this problem and get on with the business of educating nurses to provide the service the public needs, but the process of doing so will be painful for the profession, for the educators, and for the nursing schools. While, in general, the goals are the same for all educators of nurses, these goals take on different hues when division occurs that threatens the viability of some of the nursing schools. We try to speak with a united voice to persons outside the nursing profession about our goals in education. But within we are at war, a revolutionary war, while at the same time we are trying to survive an attack from without.

Communications

The communication patterns of nursing educators are indeed complex. Educators in nursing talk to other educators in nursing first, mainly to those of similar programs, and then to other people, whether in nursing or not, who will help their programs remain viable. There is also a tendency toward "one-up" or "one-down" communications. Because of the unspoken hierarchy that ranges from doctoral education down to the associate degree level, the associate degree educators can develop a sense of being spoken down to. This does not help them to feel wanted, needed, accepted, or supported.

Many in nursing do not view nursing education in terms of a hierarchy. They are the ones who will bring solutions to the problem of division, but only when they and others are able to face all the ramifications of the human condition that exist on the unstated-goal level. Everyone must realize that the means required to reach unity are as important as the goal of unity. One cannot simply say that all types of nursing programs are needed and necessary. One must act as if he really believed this.

Focal and ecological systems

The focal and ecological systems in nursing education are obvious but changeable. The focal system will change depending on the issue involved. If an issue threatens all of nursing education, the focal system will consist of everyone in nursing education. But if an issue threatens only one part, the focal system will be smaller and the goals different.

At this point it might help to remember that when one assesses a system, one does so for a reason; that reason will determine how one defines a focal system, and the goals of that system. Such an assessment is not as complex as it seems. We are dealing with generalities here to demonstrate a method and a pattern, but when the process is put into play and the issue or reason behind an analysis is clearly defined, then the seeming complexity at the general level becomes simple and clear. This approach makes possible a great deal of objectivity on the part of the assessor; it allows a person to glean fact from fiction, or shall we say fact from rhetoric.

Social ethic

The social ethic in nursing education is a combination of egalitarianism and libertarianism, much as it is in all types of professional education. But in nursing it might be safe to say that the emphasis of one over the other varies according to a hierarchical grading. That is, nursing education is more egalitarian at the basic or early stages of the educational process—for example, at the associate degree level—than at the upper levels of graduate study. The principal reasons for this are the financial expense that is involved in continuing one's education and the intellectual ability that is necessary to be able to achieve in advanced education. Educators at all levels want the best students who can achieve the academic hurdles—and who can either pay for their education or qualify for scholarships or loans.

The reality is that it takes more intellectual ability at the higher levels of scholarship and that it costs more money. So, as in other fields of professional education, the students in the graduate schools are primarily white and from the middle and upper classes, because nonwhite students and lower-class students often have poorer educational backgrounds. However, nursing, through a push for federal grants, has done more than other professional groups to equalize this situation. Although it, like the other professions, has the stated goal of giving the best in education to meet current needs, it is also more service oriented and more egalitarian than most of the other professions. Perhaps this is because nurses have never gained the position of money, power, and prestige enjoyed by members of some of the other professions and therefore have generally maintained a democratic attitude toward all of mankind, rich and poor alike. Some might argue that because nursing has been mainly a woman's profession, nurses care more and better. Or one could say that since nurses never have had a lot of money and do not expect to get a lot of money, they can identify better with the poor. Or one could argue that the egalitarian stance of the profession is related to its orientation to prevention rather than to treatment. Or a combination of any or all of these factors could be at work, with other reasons thrown in. Whatever its causes, egalitarianism does exist in the practice and in the educative process. It is admirable and needed, and it also provides nurses with a neat weapon to fight off the encroachment of other professions who wish to dominate them. Nurses can with cleaner hands appeal directly to consumers in an effort to maintain their autonomy. Nursing-education admission policies are a nice example of libertarianism and egalitarianism working together for the benefit of educators and consumers.

Ethics

Little needs to be said here beyond what has already been said about ethics in general for all those in professional education. Nursing, like other professions, has a code of ethics. Ethical positions within the profession vary greatly, but in general the ethical stance could be classified as situational, as could the ethical positions of other professions.

One point here has not been touched on before. In nursing education there is, as in other types of professional education, a group of people who have moved into the field of ethics—or should we say combined their professional education with the study of ethics. Often the members of this group have more in common with other ethical theorists than with professional educators in their own fields. However, they maintain their identities within the professional fields of their basic education. For example, they are experts in medical ethics, nursing ethics, or theological ethics. The study of ethics comes first, but the professional school is what employs and pays them. So although they write and speak about medical ethics or nursing ethics, they are somehow removed from the nitty-gritty, everyday conflicts in professional education. I do not mean to say that these conflicts are not of deep concern to them, nor do I mean to imply that they are not concerned with professional education per se. But because of their interest in and care about ethics, they have been able to remove themselves from the forefront of the more common battles of other educators.

All of us in nursing education are indeed lucky to have these specialists in ethics; they serve as a conscience that stands out from us and says, "But what are the ethical consequences of your behavior—not only for students but also in terms of the practice arena?" I am not sure that we particularly like these people, or prize them very highly. Who needs a conscience that says, "Hey, isn't that one drink too many?" or "Are you really sure that's the right thing to do?" We tell them, "Enough already," but we do not want them to go too far away.

It is hard to classify this group of professional educators who are also experts in ethics as Kantians, utilitarians, or situationalists. It may not be necessary to do so; in their diversity of ethical position, they are very similar to other subgroups of educators—for example, those who have become experts in law or administration. Each of these experts provides professional education in his or her field with another dimension—a dimension that is important to the educative process and therefore to the practice process. In nursing, experts in ethics keep us in touch with the fact that a professional group must be aware of the ethical problems involved in the educative and practice process. These people serve as our own in-house "devil's advocates." Like them or not, we have them, and that is a blessing for the consumers of education, our students, and for the consumers of service, our clients.

Some of the best-known ethical theorists in nursing seem to be Kantians, caring about both means and ends. They are verbal beyond the walls of their employing universities. However, in their writings they have thus far devoted their attention more to the practice arena than to the educational process. One can only hope that they will correct this oversight. This oversight exists among all the ethical theorists of all the professions. They, like consumers, must realize that practice stems from education, and that although practice is then modified in the field, education leaves its indelible mark. So although nursing education may prize its caring aspects, that caring must be framed in an ethically knowledgeable stance, to provide nursing practitioners with a firm base upon which they can then go forth to be in fact the advocates that nursing educators say they want to produce.

FOUR AREAS OF SOCIETAL INFLUENCE ON PROFESSIONAL EDUCATION
Issues

It might be safe to say that how persons in professional education react to issues will affect in some degree what their students learn and believe about these issues and how they will react to them in the practice arena. This is not true for all students, but it would be hard for anyone to go to a school and engage in an educative process that was in actuality, if not by policy, racist, sexist, or ageist, without some of such an attitude rubbing off. The age, sex, and race of one's fellow students will tell a person a great deal about a professional school's attitudes toward access to professional education and, to a lesser degree, access to health care.

RACISM Most students in professional schools are white—somewhere around 85%, although this figure rises as high as 95%. Most schools fall somewhere in between these two percentages. One sees this tendency more in medicine and dentistry than in social work or nursing. The high cost and the small number of openings may have a lot to do with making medical and dental schools more competitive and with making admission to them more difficult for persons who come from backgrounds in which they have been victims of discrimination. Nursing and social work schools are more open, and the education they provide is less expensive. The faculties of professional schools are also mostly white—but, again, less so in nursing and social work.

Although many believe we live in a racist society, it is not my purpose here to declare that our professional schools are racist by intent, but rather that they reflect the general educational and social trends of the society they are a part of.

Without a blend of students and teachers from various ethnic backgrounds, it is hard to see how a professional curriculum can give students a proper education in how to meet the needs of everyone in society. All groups should be represented, and their needs should be clarified by their input into curriculums and by their representation in faculties and student bodies. Secondhand knowledge of the "we know best" type has never been effective. It is hard to "know best" when you have never been there—when you have never associated with persons of backgrounds different from your own. The professional schools and curriculums do not always reflect the realities of the health care needs of various groups. Therefore the health care system itself does not always meet the needs of these groups. Many attempts are being made, on several fronts, to correct this situation, but at least for the present it remains a problem in the professional educative process.

SEXISM   Like racism, sexism constitutes a problem in professional education. Discrimination against women is more true for medicine and dentistry than for social work; almost the opposite exists in nursing. Medicine and dentistry are male dominated, social work has a more even mix of men and women, with women outnumbering men, and nursing is female dominated. What has been said about professional education not meeting the needs of those not represented in the schools in terms of race is true for sex as well. The movement for women's liberation has brought forth a rash of books on the subject of medicine's failings in the practice area of women's needs. Perhaps less sexism is seen in the practice of dentistry. (It is difficult to be sexist about teeth.) In social work little sexism is apparent in the practice field; in nursing it is hard to tell. One the one hand, at least in my experience, female nurses have a tendency to be more tolerant of their male patients than their female patients. That is, their patience is more durable, the forgiving quality women have is greater in measure for men than for women. But, on the other hand, is their understanding of male patients greater than male physicians' understanding of female patients? I doubt it. For how can it be? In a society that tends to separate men and women and to prevent the common activity that could lead to a true understanding of each other's trials, one cannot hope for magical means to bridge artificially created barriers.

These barriers affect the educational process as well as the practice arena. They tend to prevent the establishment of a collegial relationship among professionals that would work for the benefit of both the educational and the practice fields.

AGEISM   The average age of students in professional schools of all kinds is still in the range of 20 to 30. We Americans prize youth. This fact is demonstrated throughout our society—in movies, television programs, other forms of entertainment, advertisements, clothing styles, and so on. The concept of an older person going back to school to seek a second career is new on the scene. The appearance of an older person in our professional schools as a beginner is a phenomenon we treat as an aberration.

We view older teachers in our professional schools in a somewhat better light. We accept that they have not only knowledge but experience to impart to the young. This attitude also exists, but to a lesser degree, in the practice field. By "lesser degree" I mean that there is a trend to retire our professionals younger and younger, to make room for the up and coming. But one must question how this movement to youth affects the availability of the knowledge needed to treat elderly patients.

It seems we are moving more and more toward an isolation philosophy in regard to older people. We design homes and villages to house the elderly, because they will be "happier among their own kind." One cannot help but wonder whether the admission criteria to our professional schools, which seem to be balanced in favor of the young, do not contribute to this process. We deplore in print the treatment of the aged in nursing homes, but no one in the professions does much about it.

• • •

These three factors—racism, sexism, and ageism—are all seen in the realm of professional education. They are all operative, in an unstated way, in the admission criteria of the educational programs. They are also reflected in the curriculums of the educational programs, which often fail to emphasize the treatment certain groups of patients may need that is special and different in kind from the so-called average. These factors are reflected further in the practice arena. So, despite the many established programs we have for minority groups, plus affirmative action, and programs for the aging, we see in reality little that could be called positive in effecting real change. The consciousness of the need is there, but its translation into measures that will *in fact* make a difference may not be.

ACCESS TO EDUCATION The issues of racism, sexism, and ageism are central to the issue of access to education. The professional schools are only a small part of the whole of higher education. The problems exist in all areas. Professional education alone cannot bear the brunt of the criticism for these problems; like higher education in general, it only reflects the society it serves. True, educators in the professions could be more flexible and forward thinking, but we all resist change. Even when society does shift its views, the professional schools sometimes have to be brought kicking and screaming into line.

That change is occurring in small measure is true. That it is seen to be happening faster in social work and nursing than in other fields is true. But is this because nurses and social workers are more humane, or is it because they are less prestige oriented and therefore less guarded about who enters their arenas? The greater the power and the glory and the more lucrative the venture, the more it is guarded from persons who seek to share it. The greater the number of people who share it, the less there is for those who already have it. Hence the age-old story of monopoly. This tendency is human and understandable, but it destroys the very fabric of the society that it depends on to survive. We put our short-term desires above our long-term needs and say, like Scarlett O'Hara, "Tomorrow is another day."

We must face the fact that our tomorrows will quickly become our todays and that we may be unprepared to deal with problems that will no longer wait.

Many short-term solutions in the form of crash programs in professional curriculums have been devised in an attempt to meet various needs in the practice arena. These programs, such as family practice medicine, nurse practitioners, technicians in all areas, and outreach clinics, have often been poorly staffed, administered, and financed. There are affirmative action programs that admit unprepared people—people who cannot, for whatever reason, cope with the rigors of the professional education curriculums and who therefore need expensive remedial work, which the taxpayers object to. The American solution has been to pour money into an immediate problem area without having a proper regard for the deep-seated cause of the problem. When money fails, we say, "See, I told you so." Such failures have often led to radical swings from right to left in society, which are reflected in the area of education. There are some who keep their heads and ride with the tide, trying to maintain a middle ground and a balance. They make changes in the most pressing areas and experiment with innovations just enough to satisfy the short-term goals of radical activists, while seeking the slower pace of long-term goals. But there are too few of these people.

●   ●   ●

Professional education reflects about the same attitudes and positions concerning these issues that the society it serves does. The more powerful the profession and the more entrenched it is, the slower it will be to make change, especially change that it sees as affecting its power. It will not resist change to the point of being totally discredited by society, for fear of losing the support it needs to function. However, it will use all the power at its command to delay and dilute the changes demanded.

Some in professional education will strongly resist changes demanded by persons in the same profession who are in the practice arena. The "we know best" argument of "your elders and your teachers" never fails to be heard. When all else fails, changes are made, but they are likely to be called "experimental," to be done on a small scale, and to be thought of as needing careful evaluation. There is much good in this approach, but it is also a classic delaying tactic. The sad paradox is that once an innovation catches on and is highly praised by all and financial rewards are bestowed in the form of grants, people cannot wait to get on the band wagon, and careful evaluation often goes out the window while money pours in the door.

It is the same in all facets of society, not just in professional education. The intellect rarely has total governance over the body and the emotions. Sometimes this is good, sometimes bad, but always it is the reality—a reality that advocates must understand and not necessarily beat their heads against. Time and patience are on the side of what is good and what functions in a durable way. The survival of man as a species demonstrates this fact.

Medical-industrial complex

The medical-industrial complex, you will remember, is made up of all health care professionals, their organizations, hospitals, industries that supply these groups and institutions, businesses that have a financial stake in them, unions, and so on. We have already discussed the goals, both stated and unstated, of the members of this complex. They all say they work for good health care and illness care, and they all want to remain in business, make profits, or at least stay solvent. One can then view their pressures on professional education by a process of simple logic.

If the professional schools are the training ground of future professionals and if these professionals aid in determining the future viability and profits of the medical-industrial complex, then the complex will have a vested interest in what these professionals are taught and how they are educated. For example, if bigger is better (that is, more profitable and powerful), then the students should be taught this fact, and what better way to do so than to locate the professional schools in large medical centers. If specialization demands more advanced technology and more expensively equipped centers and rewards professionals with more money and prestige, then students must be exposed to this fact so that they will desire specialization also and pressure the schools to orient their curriculum toward specialization. If the leaders and spokesmen for the professions come out of the large, expensively equipped centers, then students will emulate these powerful people by gravitating to these centers themselves.

An interesting pattern can be noticed. If a professional school, particularly a medical school, is not located at the start in or near a large hospital medical center, either one will grow up around the school or the school will establish a close affiliation with one, even if it is miles away. Cornell Medical School is an excellent example, with the university located in upstate New York and the medical college in New York City. Certainly there are practical reasons for this. The professional schools do need the hospital facilities for the clinical aspects of the educational program. But do not lose sight of the rewards for both institutions. The hospital gains prestige from having a medical school affiliate with it; the medical school gains prestige by affiliating with a large hospital center. And as each grows bigger and more prestigious, so do all the groups in the medical-industrial complex that serve both institutions. Both institutions then can attract the best professional practitioners and the best students. It is the same with all professional schools in the health care services. However, there are only so many large medical centers, and therefore the smaller schools or those that either have less influence or are located too far from large hospitals affiliate with smaller, less prestigious hospitals. But such an affiliation does not remove the desire from the students and even the educators to be better associated, and it does not eliminate the tendency to emulate the professionals in the larger institutions.

If society finds that it has a need for more family practitioners in rural areas or in poor areas of cities, then it will find ways of making such practice a desirable idea and goal for the professional schools. Grants will pour in to the professional schools to educate students who will gear themselves toward this goal. Ten years or so ago, we saw medical schools set up tracks for both family practice medicine and what was called community medicine. But no matter how attractive the schools tried to make these programs to students, we did not see hoards of physicians rushing to the country and into community service. You see, we did too good a job of selling the money, prestige, and power of the large medical centers, mixed with the glories of specialization, to suddenly turn young heads in the opposite direction. This same phenomenon was and still is true for the other health care professions as well, but to a lesser extent. One learns young in this society to go where the power and the money are.

Society thus was still left with the question of how to meet the needs of the inner cities and the outlying communities. I can only speculate on what the thinking was then, but it may have gone something like this: "Well, if the physicians won't go, is there someone else who will be *almost* as good? Ah ha! Remember the medics who did such a good job in the wars? So why not create physicians' assistants?" But, alas, this was easier said than done. To create a new class of medical workers was no simple task. The need to start from scratch in the educative process meant that even filling immediate needs was a difficult, long-range proposition. Furthermore, like physicians themselves, many of these new physician's assistants liked to stay near the seats of power and money, and physicians found them useful in taking care of the more "mundane" aspects of medical practice.

Before we go on, let us identify the people whose thinking we are talking about. They included social-minded professionals, politicians, and lay people who saw that many people were in need of health care but were not receiving it. They then pressured the medical profession to meet this need and joined with it in determining how to do so and whose aid to enlist. Those enlisted included physicians, other professionals, other members of the medical-industrial complex, and additional politicians. But the group was physician dominated and oriented, since that was seen to be the problem—a lack of physicians.

The members of this group saw that a large body of professionals was already there in the field—nurses. They thought to themselves: "Nurses are well educated and have been, at least in the past, subservient to physicians. So let's use them." Well, a direct attempt to turn nurses into physicians' assistants did not go far. The nursing profession rose up in arms and said, "Hey, don't raid our profession to do what you refuse to do." However, at this time—the late 1960s and the early 1970s—there were many in nursing who were not content with the traditional role of the nurse, and they were reaching out more and more into the community to fulfill the nursing role in the independent manner of a true professional. Some called this change "expanding the role of the nurse"; others saw it as simply fulfilling the same role in an independent, professional manner. In any case, a professional group was available to meet the new needs and new demands of society. These professionals had already been doing so in small numbers, but now more were moving into this area. So what could be more logical than to push the idea of using nurses to meet the societal cry for help? Now, leaving aside a footnoted history of what happened next, and the motivations on the part of the movers, let's just see what the results were and speculate on what they may become.

Despite the excellent education that nurses had, they lacked one thing the physician's assistants had—skill in the physical assessment of patients, the kind of detailed assessment a physician performs to determine the presence or absence of disease and the diagnosis, if a disease is present. Programs to rectify this situation were started, and they grew all over the country with the full cooperation of some nursing educators and physicians. These professionals worked together to correct what they saw as a deficiency in the education of nurses—a deficiency that would have to be removed if they were to move into the new role of "nurse practitioner." (Note that the term "physician's assistant" was not used. Nurses would have had none of that. Instead they coined a new term, "nurse practitioner," to designate what they saw as a new position in the practice realm.)

Did the development of nurse practitioners expand the practice of some nurses? Yes. Did it bring a broader range of nursing practice to the public? Yes and no. Where it was added to the already excellent practice of nursing, as just another tool, the answer is yes. Where it became the most important, and sometimes the only, tool, the answer is no. Then one must ask this question: did persons in the rural and inner-city areas, who needed the care the most, benefit from this movement? Well, yes and no. They benefited to the same small extent that the family and community practice movement in medicine benefited. Although nurses have worked in rural and inner-city areas to a greater extent than physicians, there is no reason to think that nurses will go out now in greater numbers just because we expanded the scope of the practice. You see they, too, are only human. Nurses have also been educated by the medical-industrial complex to know that bigger is better, more profitable, and more prestigious. They, too, want to be where the action is and where the money is and to receive the rewards of the system.

So society says that we have a need, the medical-industrial complex then says that to survive we had better help meet that need, and it pressures the professional schools to alter their curriculums to meet the need. But none of these three groups—society, the complex, or the professional schools—can make students live by such a stated goal when everyone is operating with unstated goals of power, prestige, money, and reward. "Practice what I preach" is not nearly as influential an admonition as "Practice what I practice."

The influence of the medical-industrial complex on professional education is as great as that of society, but since the complex is a part of society, we could expect little else. One final note here: If it seems I have made the nursing profession look like a puppet of the medical-industrial complex, let me immediately correct that impression. The people who pressured for the move to the so-called expanded role—that is, the adding of additional skills to the education of the nurse—may have reaped more than they bargained for. Some nurses have become the subservient substitutes for physicians' assistants that were wished for by medicine, but many others have used this expanded-role movement to emphasize the independent nature of professional practice. Although many nurses *have* replaced the interns and residents in the hospital emergency and outpatient departments and taken on the same subservient role to attending physicians that young interns have assumed, others have moved out and claimed the role of independent care-giver to clients, acting as equal colleagues of physicians in their particular fields of medicine. Many physicians are now feeling threatened by these nurse practitioners.

Many who sow seeds are surprised when they turn into flowers. Seeds are only tiny bits in our hands that later can become flowers, weeds, or trees, which then share our territory. Advocates must be aware of this reality. Short-term goals and means can become the ends themselves.

Social laws

In this book I have dealt with three areas of social law—abortion, welfare, and food stamps. Rather than go into a further discussion of these topics per se, let us just look at how social laws in general can influence professional education and how professional education can respond to them. How the law can influence an educational system has been touched on in terms of affirmative action programs for admission to professional programs. We have seen how laws that mandate better health care in rural and inner-city areas can add to or change the direction of some professional curriculums. The movement toward, and federal financing for, the improvement of mental health has led to the creation of more and better graduate programs in this area. Thus, if society has needs that are not being met, it will pass laws that will dictate a certain practice that will meet those needs. The nature of that practice, the role that professionals will have in it, and how well equipped they currently are to fill that role will determine the way in which professional education will have to change in order to meet the demands of those laws.

So a social law can dictate professional practice, and the needs of the practice will dictate the role the professional schools have in preparing people to meet the requirements of the law. Many think that persons in the professional schools are indeed autonomous and that they will do as they please in the educative process. The reality is far from this. Although the process of change may seem slow to an activist, who wants professional education to change quickly to become more accountable to the society it serves, this process is indeed effected. But the mere passage of a law can be relatively ineffectual without the financial teeth needed for implementation built into it. Professional schools can stall a long time in meeting legal requirements, but the lure of money rarely fails to speed up the process.

For example, mental health workers have always been sorely needed in this country, and this need never has been met by the classic professional groups of psychologists and psychiatrists. But in the 1960s, when laws were passed that provided money for the preparation of nurses, social workers, and others who would specialize in the mental health field, and money for mental health clinics and patient fees, the professional schools of nursing and social work began turning out these specialists in large numbers. The psychologists and the psychiatrists were left back at the ranch saying, "Hey, what's going on?" The psychiatrists, especially, who constitute a specialty group in medicine, are still fighting the licensure of these other professionals and constantly criticizing the education they receive, even when it is superior to their own education in the mental health field.

Consumer groups all over the country are turning more and more to the passage of consumer laws to get the changes they desire. They are, in essence, saying that if the people who can make a difference refuse to, then they will force them to under the law. What this means for professional education is that professional schools can no longer be complacent and feel that they are above the society they serve and therefore that society will take what they choose to give it. If educators in the professions want to be the knowledgeable leaders they purport to be, they are going to have to be out in the forefront of change; otherwise they will be in the position of being led by that change. One could say that society has invaded that ivory tower and is shaking it to be heard. But it seems it is not only words that consumer groups want now but action.

Politics

Years ago politicians tended to feel they had much leeway in making promises while campaigning that they had no intention of fulfilling once in office. But with the advent of a more knowledgeable consumer and voting body, politicians have become much more careful about what they promise and more serious about attempting to deliver on their promises. For example, if politicians promise that professional educators will be more accountable to the needs of the electorate, you can bet they will try to find ways to make this a reality. If they cannot convince the educators to go along, they will then force the issue by passing laws and providing financial incentives to make educators accountable.

The professionals know this situation; one only has to look at one group, physicians, to see the extent of this knowledge. Physicians contribute more money to the political process than any other professional group and more than most other industrial and special interest groups. All the professional groups have lobbies in Washington, and the educators of professionals do as well. There is not a profession or a professional school in this country that is not alert to the legislative process and to the financial ramifications of that process. Professionals are well aware of how legislation can affect professional education. They strive to be appointed to consultive bodies that will have a say in the drafting of legislation, and they court their local and national politicians.

Furthermore, professionals are alert to consumer and societal pressure on politicians, and so they go directly to consumers with their positions. We see them more and more, professionals of all fields, on television, in newspapers, in magazines, pushing their views on consumers. One reason why educators become involved in this practice is the tendency of people to blame the educational process for many of the woes of society. We see the best example of this in the blame being heaped on primary and secondary schools for the functional illiteracy of our children. Even when we know that many factors other than the schools have played a part in this problem, we focus first on the schools. So, too, it is with the higher levels of the educational process. If our health needs are not met, it is the professionals who are at fault and then in turn the schools that produce them. Therefore, the professionals go to the public to plead for money and means to meet social needs—that is, to have the consumers pressure the politicians to provide more financing.

We, as a society, do not do a good job of seeing a gestalt—all the factors that go into a situation. We not only want instant action, we want instant scapegoats. We look for short-term, easy answers to long-term, difficult problems. We have created a society that thrives on instant gratification; in the face of the reality of complex problems, we demand the impossible.

• • •

One can easily see that many factors divide various areas of professional education and the professions from each other but that equally as many factors unite them. All professional schools attempt to perform a balancing act in order to survive as independent entities, to educate their students to meet society's needs, and to remain financially viable parts of society. Issues, the medical-industrial complex, social laws, and politics are all as influential in the educative process as they are in setting the future directions of society. It is the interplay of these entities that the advocate must see and understand. Professional education, if it wants to produce advocates, must provide this understanding.

ADVOCATE'S ROLE IN PROFESSIONAL EDUCATION

Here we can see the advocate in any number of roles: as educator to improve the professional schools, as advocate for students in the schools, as professional who advocates that the schools do more for the practice area, as advocate for clients who would benefit from changes in emphasis in the education of professionals. One could write a book on this subject, or even on one of these particular types of advocacy. However, for our purposes let us generalize and see how four areas of the knowledge base—issues, medical-industrial complex, social laws, and politics—are related to, or helpful in, risk defusement for the advocate in any role. In other words, how do we use these areas of the knowledge base, in whatever our capacity as advocate for professional education, to defuse or lessen risks, and what risks are inherent in these areas as they relate to professional education?

Issues

Whenever you are working, for example, for access to professional education regardless of race, sex, or age and based on competence alone, you are going to run into opposition. If an individual is competent and still denied access, you can be reasonably sure that you are dealing with some kind of prejudice. However, accusing someone or an institution of being prejudiced, especially if prejudice is seen as morally reprehensible, is sure to be risky. Furthermore, you can be reasonably sure that such an accusation will be met with denial and an attitude of injured pride that you could have said such a thing. One of the first arguments you will hear as a defense goes as follows: "We are only looking out for the welfare of the public." This statement will be accompanied by all kinds of reasons why a person was not admitted. These reasons will be phrased in a way that makes you, the accuser, look as though you do not care at all about the welfare of the public, thereby placing you in the time-wasting position of having to defend yourself—a very clever tactic that is used every day in one form or another. It causes delay in dealing with the main issue, and it may discredit you as a justifiable accuser who should be listened to. Therefore, accusing someone of prejudice is not a good first tactic to use when trying to bring about change. It labels you as the enemy and someone to be suspicious of and eliminated, through discrediting if possible.

There are, however, several excellent and positive positions an advocate can take in approaching educators. These positions all tend to fall under the heading "What admitting this group or person can do for you." First you point out that if they admit a certain person or group, they cannot be accused of being prejudiced. This argument is simple and quite effective in a society that says one of its stated goals is to "stamp out prejudice." Second, you tell educators that admitting certain groups will demonstrate that they are making attempts to meet the affirmative action goals that many federal funds—and many private foundation funds—are tied to. Here you are appealing to the unstated goal of remaining financially viable. Third, you point out that minority students may bring with them ideas that can be used in the curriculum to aid professionals in dealing with minorities in the delivery area. Thus the school will look innovative and appear to be truly accountable to all in society; it will be an

institution that other schools will emulate, that students will want to go to, and that
the public will fund. Several unstated goals—fame, power, and prestige—thus will
be met. The point here is to know the goals, stated and unstated, of the professional
schools and to direct your arguments to these goals in a very positive manner. The
slang question or expression "What's in it for me?" is what you should address
yourself to. The list of answers to this question can become quite long, depending on
your knowledge and creativity.

The advocate must be prepared to deal with all the reasons why professional
schools may not want to admit a certain person or group. (If possible, these should be
integrated into the positive approaches just discussed. If that is not possible, then do
not mention them, but be prepared to deal with them. You may think of reasons that
the educators have not thought of yet, and you do not want to add to their negativ-
ism.) For example, educators may say that if women find out that a school is admitting women, it will be swamped with female applicants—a point that has some basis
in reality. One possible answer (tongue in cheek): "Do you really think that female
applicants will outscore many male applicants on their entrance examinations?" (Now
there's an interesting thought.)

Some statements or reasons will be so inane that they do not warrant an
answer. They may be said only to get you to lose your temper. For these remarks it is
best to be properly schooled in the technique of "crossing communications." For
example, to the remark "They have a funny odor," reply, "That's a lovely picture on
your wall; I'll bet it's a collector's item." The strategy is to act as though you did not
hear the remark and to remain very friendly. The message gets through without your
showing the disdain that you feel. This is very hard to do sometimes, but to honor the
shamefulness of another person by responding to it often only makes it worse. Of
course if the remark is repeated or screamed at you, it is hard not to respond. One
effective technique is to revert to a first-name basis, or to use the person's formal
title, and to ask a question such as this: "Jeff (or Dr. Smith), is that what is really
bothering you? Is that the core of the question?" This technique is called putting the
ball back into the other person's court and hoping for a more playable shot next time.
The point of all this is to avoid making veiled, and not-so-veiled, threats. Some
people will rise to such challenges every time, to defend their honor or their positions, without thought to the consequences for themselves or the institutions they
represent.

If a positive, reasonable approach fails or if communication with the powers
who make decisions is not possible, then the best approach is to arm oneself with all
the pressures that society and the law offer you and to use either the veiled-threat or
the open-threat method. Threats are not ineffectual, but if they bring about change in
a person or a system, that change will be granted begrudgingly, and it stands a good
chance of being reversed at the first opportunity. For a new policy to be truly
effective, the people most responsible for the policy must be committed to making it
successful.

Risk defusement entails first an approach that will not create an unnecessary amount of threat and sense of attack. Second, the approach must demonstrate that the advocate is armed with societal support and the law, if possible. Whether a compromise is appropriate will depend on a realistic estimate of how much gain the advocate can reasonably hope to make and how the compromise fits with his or her ethical standards. However, some things can never be compromised. Advocates must live with the reality of their world and their society but also with themselves.

Medical-industrial complex

One's tactics will depend in many ways on the nature of what one is advocating, which is true in all advocacy situations. So first one must examine the nature of what it is one wants to do. Then one must look at the people who are involved and what their special interest is and what their goals are, mainly their unstated goals. One can usually be sure that these goals will include financial viability, if not profit, and staying viable as a system.

In terms of professional education, you will be dealing with the medical-industrial complex in two main ways: (1) experiencing pressure from it to change an educational system to better meet the needs of the complex and (2) bringing pressure to bear on it to support, financially or otherwise, an educational system you favor. No matter which is the case, the approach is similar to the one we discussed in dealing with issues—that is, a positive approach that is designed either to deter an action or to promote one. This approach generally involves appealing to someone's own best interests. Since we are using the term "complex" to include all groups in the health field and groups that benefit financially from the activities of those in the field, you have a broad area of societal pressure to use. Institutions that are heavily reliant on public support or regulation to remain viable are much more susceptible to societal pressure than those that are privately funded. However, even privately funded institutions are vulnerable to societal pressure. Few institutions are without some form of public support. And even if they are, they still rely on private funding from members of society.

To keep from looking like the consummate utilitarian, who is interested in ends and not in the means required to gain them, is the reason why one should use the positive approach. One not only must find some satisfaction in having gained a good end but also must be able to live with the actions one used to gain that end. Thus I am not advocating utilitarianism, but rather a careful weighing of goals against what one has to do to gain them. Gaining a good end by questionable means will backfire, either by exposure of the means at a later date or by one's being unable to live with oneself. To reduce oneself to the level of one's opponents may provide a short-term gain but will rarely provide any long-term benefit. To win at any price is *not* the name of the game; one must win or lose while still maintaining one's ethical standards.

In dealing with the medical-industrial complex, an advocate will find that having a knowledge of Kohlberg's developmental stages of ethics is very helpful. Kohlberg provides a good guideline to what one can expect from a marketplace psychology and how one can combat this attitude while still maintaining one's standards of ethical behavior.

One risk for the advocate for excellence in professional education lies in the necessity to forgo at times the short-term gains, in the form of funding, that can result from the acceptance of an innovation. The problem is to tell the difference between an innovation that is a stopgap measure and one that has lasting benefit—a distinction that often is not apparent until after the latest innovation has run its course. Bandwagons that do not have the underpinnings of sound principles of professional and educational practice should be avoided. If innovators have not thought out the consequences of an innovation, then an advocate must insist that they do. Advocates will hear the argument that time and timing are essential to success, but they should never fail to ask, "For the success of whom and what?"

Advocacy, especially consumer advocacy, is on the rise, and many are tempted to join in the role. It is the "in" thing to do. But remember that any change you are urged to make is a change *from* something else. So while you are examining what someone wants to change to, you are obligated to examine what it is you would be changing from. In other words, do not get caught in the trap of those who argue for change for the sake of change. Too often we are accused of throwing babies out with the bathwater and of having to go back and create new babies.

Some persons or groups in the medical-industrial complex may press either for additions to current professional school curriculums or for deletions from them. For example, some in the medical-industrial complex might want educators to promote new drugs or technology, while others in the complex might want such information withheld from the general public. Or some groups in the complex might want to fund educational programs that will benefit them. Likewise, educators might want the complex to fund programs for their own reasons.

The medical-industrial complex can indeed offer many possibilities for advocacy that relates to professional education. Such advocacy will usually involve either supporting interference by the complex in the educational process or discouraging such interference. In this type of advocacy one needs to be very careful to perform thorough assessments of situations. This type of advocacy is risky, while at the same time it offers many good risk-defusement tactics. It is an exciting area of advocacy, but it requires knowledge on a broad base.

Social laws

The areas of social law we have dealt with—abortion, welfare, and food stamps—have little direct effect on professional education, unless one is soliciting the support of the professional schools in one or more of these areas. It might be said that, in general, while professional schools state egalitarian principles, they more likely practice libertarian ones. Likewise, they will probably support egalitarian goals of new social laws, but mostly in principle. If a social law, however, affects the libertarian policy of a school, there might be less of this support. In general, one could say that professional education is torn between its stated goals and its unstated goals when it comes to the enactment of egalitarian social laws.

An advocate must examine each social law in and of itself and assess how it will affect professional education. He or she will find active support for some, a divided house for some, and limited support, if any, for others. If a social law will adversely affect the financing and viability of a professional school, then to hope for the school's support of the law is indeed not realistic. However, one must remember that all the professions and their educational components will not react the same way to a particular law. For example, many in the profession of medicine or dentistry may see a move toward the socialization of health care as a threat, while many in nursing and social work may not see such a move as harming them very much. The more one has to lose in money and power, the more threatened he will tend to be. The stated goals of the good of society and service to all often have been demonstrated to be a dubious cover for what really counts—money, power, and control. This is not true only of professionals in the health fields. Lawyers fought fiercely to maintain a fee-fixing system that did not allow for competition in the marketplace. Advocates cannot work against this situation simply by making accusations of greed. Money, power, and control are interwoven concepts, one aiding and abetting the other. A social law that may reduce the financial gain of the professional practice area and that may remove some of the control or monopoly of service cannot expect to gain the support of the educational component of that profession.

An advocate would be well advised, after an assessment, to proceed, if possible, with the positive approach described in the section on issues, and then to move into the area of consumer or societal support. However, a word of caution here: not all social legislation is in fact as good as it looks on the surface. What may seem to be noble goals for the betterment of society may, in fact, be the very thing that will lock disadvantaged people into expecting the government to take care of them with no return or effort on their part. They may benefit from some short-term improvement in health care and the quality and availability of food but end up still in the ghetto, with the ghetto getting worse and worse and their chances of getting out of it or changing it becoming smaller and smaller, because of a reduction in the incentive to do so. We are almost back to the informing and supporting aspect of advocacy, which involves helping people to make their own decisions and to avoid a dependency state, in which decisions are made for them. Power and self-determination lie in the decision-making process. When we give this up, we give up freedom. For example, we can decide to be pregnant or not, and then enjoy or not enjoy the consequences of the decision. Or we can give up this right of decision to others—perhaps by means of a government-mandated sterilization law. This is not fiction; it happened in India in the 1970s.

Whenever you accept anything you have not earned, you also accept the conditions of the gift. The advocate must look very closely at those conditions. Also, the advocate must look at who will gain by a social law. Who other than the recipient of the proposed service will gain? How could the law be manipulated for the financial gain of persons that the law is not intended to serve? (Witness the large number of "Medicaid mills" in this country.) On the other hand, the advocate must be careful that the safeguards or regulations built into a law to prevent fraud are not so restrictive as to prevent the law from serving the function it was designed for. Formulating an effective social law is a very complicated process, and perfection is a fool's dream. It is unrealistic to assume that humans will act in a reasonable manner in regard to matters that concern money.

There are risks involved in working for a social law that may lessen the power of a professional group, and there are risks involved in advocating a law that will in the long run not dilute the benefits it is designed to give. It seems redundant to say so, but here again we are faced with the necessary component of knowledge, and the need to weigh the glory of short-term gain against the chances for long-term gain, or loss. In a society that is geared to instant gratification, any advocacy that seems to interfere with this tendency will not be totally welcome. Change occurs in the realm of professional education at a much slower rate than in the practice arena. So time taken in assessment to determine long-term goals is on the advocate's side. Also, in professional education, professionals are more often exposed to the thinking of persons outside the profession—other educators—than they are in the practice arena. This exposure is by nature a broadening experience. It is this breadth of thinking that the advocate must draw on in the risk defusement process. However, the world of academia can become as insular as the practice field, if not more so. Reality sometimes has a hard time being heard when it knocks on *that* door.

Politics

Leaving aside everything we have said about the role of politics in the advocacy process, its risks and the tactics used to defuse the risks, let us simply ask these questions: how can the political process affect professional education, and what can the advocate do to enhance the positive effects and to lessen the negative effects?

Politicians can pass laws that have direct effects on licensure, on the financing of education, and thus on the curriculums of the professional schools. For example, politicians can pass licensure laws that can broaden the practice field of a profession, narrow it, or bring other groups into it that may infringe on it or enhance it. Politicians can provide special funding to promote the training of more people in special areas of education. Such funding can shift the emphasis of a professional school and lead to the creation of new programs. So one can say that politicians have two weapons (if one does not mind calling them that): manipulation of the licensure laws and the use of money. Both can be employed to make professional educators more amenable to the needs and changes in society.

However, two can play at this game. The educators in a profession can sponsor legislation themselves to bring about the changes they want. Or other professional groups, or society in general, can pressure legislators to sponsor legislation to bring about certain changes. All proponents of change tend to use the same tactics, which have been discussed earlier. The advocate's attitude toward legislation that would affect professional education is similar to that discussed in connection with other areas—particularly social laws. Advocates must look closely at the legislation being proposed by any group, to compare the short-term gains with the long-term gains. Also, they must look at individual legislators themselves in terms of what special interests they have as human beings and what special interests they may be inclined to represent.

It can't help but occur to a person inclined toward gaming and intrigue that politics could be a very satisfying field for him. This is not to be construed as a negative judgment, only as a statement of fact. It is not anti-educational, anti-professional, or anti-ethical to be attracted to this arena. In fact, one would hope that people who have high ethical, professional, and educational standards would be inclined to enter it. Advocates for excellence in professional education would be well advised to educate themselves in the intricacies of politics. The books mentioned in the notes to Chapter 6 are an excellent place to start.

•   •   •

Advocacy in the area of professional education cannot be totally separated from advocacy in the professional practice area, or from advocacy in the consumer area. The intertwining, or perhaps one can say the holistic nature of society, causes each area to interact with the others. The time we have spent in looking at professional education and its overlap with practice will enable us to spend less time in the area of professional practice. One could say that the practice stems from the educational process, but that would be too simplistic. Rather, one sees an interchange between the two that can be smooth and forward thinking or filled with conflict. Advocates must be aware that what they strive for in terms of professional education will affect the practice field, and the reverse, of course, is equally true. To be truly effective, they must take both areas into consideration in the advocacy process. They must have clear definitions of their own personal goals in regard to excellence in education and excellence in practice. They must be aware of possible personal conflicts in connection with these areas, and they must decide where they are willing to compromise in order to create a balance between long-term gain or short-term gain. Finally, they must be aware of the nature of the society of which they are a part. It indeed takes the "gentleness of doves and the wisdom of serpents" to walk this path safely.

Now let us take a look at the practice arena of the health care professions and see what lies ahead for the advocate in this area. We will use an integrated approach and deal only with areas not yet discussed.

NOTES ON CHAPTER 8

The literature on professional education is vast, and the literature on the profession of nursing and its various programs is very large in itself. So rather than inundating you with a reading list of great length, which might reflect my personal biases, let me suggest that you read at random in many areas, from a position of seeking knowledge or information. While you read, you should keep a few questions, or premises, in mind:

1. It is said that the work of a professional differs from that of a technician or from that of a person who works at a job for a set length of time each day and can then leave it until the next day. If this is true, what does this mean in terms of the education necessary to socialize a person into the role of professional?
2. What does the public need in terms of nursing, and who can provide for this need in the cheapest and safest way possible? How do we best organize our educational sytem to provide these needed people? Are there needed tasks or services that nursing technicians can do? What do nurses trained at the baccalaureate level offer that is needed? What do we need that a master's education can provide, and, finally, what do we want our doctorally prepared people to do? If we start with the needs of the client and then move to the needs of the people who work in the profession, these questions can be answered more easily and curriculums can be more circumspectly designed to meet these needs. Innovations that are only reinventions of the wheel will be easily identified and then incorporated more inexpensively into a current system, if they are incorporated at all.

With these questions answered, you will be in a better position to examine all the special interests that will impinge upon the educational system. This process is known as keeping up to date with new technology, new needs of people, and new preventive or curative treatments, and then redesigning current curriculums to meet these needs.

If you have your facts at hand and operate on the basis of sound principles, you will be in a better position to listen to the experts, politicians, or special interest groups who are pushing for expensive new programs that may be needed and effective or that may simply be new variations on old themes. I am not suggesting that curriculum changes will not be needed in the future, or that new programs will not be necessary. Rather I am recommending that you approach proposed innovations from a position of some objectivity—objectivity that is based on knowledge and on the needs of society.

Chapter 9

PROFESSIONAL
PRACTICE

Professional practice is the tenth and last area of the knowledge base. The advocate in the health care system must have a good understanding of all ten areas in order to be effective and to survive in the advocate role. Since the main work of an advocate is done in the practice arena, much that would normally be discussed in this chapter has already been integrated into the discussions of the other areas. There are, however, some important aspects of the practice arena that have not been discussed specifically; these topics have a direct bearing on advocacy and on risk defusement.

In this chapter, I have identified three such topics; there are, of course, others. These three topics have not been explored directly, but in some chapters they have been touched on tangentially. They are as follows: (1) how professionals are organized in the real world to work, a topic I will discuss under the heading "Professional Practice Designs"; (2) how professionals are paid (does the person paying the piper really call the tune?), to be discussed, under "Pay versus Accountability"; and (3) the effectiveness of licensing, certifying, and accrediting procedures, to be dealt with under "Regulatory Mechanisms." These three areas have much in common. They tend to be interdependent and interrelated. One could say that the regulatory mechanisms will determine the organizational design, as well as pay and accountability. If one wanted to make definitive changes in organizational design or accountability, one could use regulatory mechanisms to do so. One could also say that organization will determine pay and accountability.

We are dealing in this chapter with the advocate's role as he or she confronts the practice field as it exists today. What an advocate will be aware of first is the organization or practice design, then pay and accountability, and finally how the regulatory systems work. So let us proceed to discuss these topics in that sequence.

PROFESSIONAL PRACTICE DESIGNS

Let us deal with four of the health professions—medicine, dentistry, social work, and nursing; because of the complexity of nursing, we will spend more time with it. The main organizational pattern of medicine and dentistry is private practice. This is perhaps more true today of dentistry than of medicine. Medicine, because of the many specialities within it and the close association it has with hospitals, is more complex in its organizational patterns than dentistry. Most dentists work in private practice. Some are associated with dental schools, and some are attached to large medical centers, but private practice is their prevailing organizational design. Medicine, on the other hand, has moved into a more complex pattern, but the concept of private practice is still maintained as much as possible. In its purest form, private practice is characterized by a single physician working alone. However, it is common for a physician to join one or more other physicians to form a partnership. The partners share the same offices but still maintain their own patients, although they cover for each other when they are on vacation or otherwise absent. Some partners form corporations; these function as partnerships, but the finances are handled in a more profitable manner for tax purposes. In general, all three of these types of private practice are still located in the community.

When a physician works in a larger organizational framework, some eroding of the private practice modality may occur. For example, a physician can be employed by a medical school but still maintain a private practice. Or a physician may have a private practice, teaching responsibilities, and service responsibilities at a large medical complex. There are many variations of such arrangements, but in general many physicians maintain private practices, in which they receive direct payments from patients and in which they are responsible for the total management of patients' cases, while also having part of their practice under the control of an institution, at least in terms of fees. However, a few physicians work only for a salary from an institution; these physicians still make independent decisions concerning the treatment of patients. Most physicians who are paid in this manner work in large medical institutions, health maintenance organizations (HMOs), foundation or company hospitals, or small institutions that hire physicians to cover emergency rooms or to supervise resident programs. The physician's decision-making process remains independent, but he or she can be dismissed from the payroll of the institution. Some dentists also work in this type of situation.

An important aspect of medical practice is the system of internship and residency that exists for the training of newly licensed physicians. Similar systems exist in other professions, but they are not nearly as prominent as the system in medicine, and the learning period is much shorter. Newly licensed physicians are employed by institutions, and they work under the supervision of attending physicians in those institutions. They are there to learn and to become proficient in speciality areas of medicine. The length of time involved depends on the requirements for certification in a particular area. Interns and residents are salaried to help them maintain themselves and to compensate them for the services they render while they are learning. The independence of their practice ranges from very little in the first years to a great deal in the senior years of residency, but they primarily treat "service" patients, not the private patients of attending physicians. Even with service patients the final authority is in the hands of the attending physicians in charge of the various services. So decision-making authority in terms of patient treatment increases with time, but in all cases an attending physician has the final say. The extent of independence a senior resident has varies from institution to institution. In some a senior resident can be almost totally independent in treating service patients.

What concerns the advocate at this point is the degree of control that an intern or a resident has over the advocacy process. The answer is simple: the degree of control will depend on the degree of the intern or resident's independence in determining the treatment process. In private practice the control of treatment is in one physician's hands. However, when intern and residents, as well as a private physician, are involved in a case, the control is decentralized and an advocate thus has more tools to use in risk defusement. An advocate must be aware of who has the final word and how final that word is. Is it subject to pressure, and, if so, pressure from where?

It is not unusual to see an attending physician or an institution covering for or supporting an intern or a resident even when the intern or resident has clearly made an error. Often it is only when a malpractice suit is imminent that support is withdrawn in a public way. This is not to imply that the errors of interns and residents go unnoticed or uncorrected or that the interns and residents go undisciplined, but rather that such errors are kept within the family, so to speak. If an advocate is not a member of that family, he or she will have a problem. Corrective and disciplinary measures are indeed taken, but they are not generally on public display and thus rarely can help an advocate at the time when he or she may need that help the most. Outside interference in this disciplinary system is not allowed, not because it would undermine the discipline but rather because of the built-up fallacy of "the doctor knows best" and the fear that if anyone should expose this idea as a fallacy, the structure of medicine would be weakened.

There is nothing wrong with the idea of private practice or the independence of decision making, but there is something wrong with the added concept of "we alone will monitor our own, because we know best." This attitude has no relationship to private practice or to independence in professional practice. So it is not the organizational structure of medicine that is being questioned, but rather the need of those within it always to be right and their fear of admitting error. The bottom line is to protect your own, even when they err. This is what consumers and members of other professions are blaming the profession of medicine for. One fears that instead of correcting this situation, physicians are closing ranks to arm against criticism while complaining about "unwarranted" attacks from outside—a dangerous position for medicine but one that advocates would best be advised to keep in mind in the risk defusement process.

The professions of social work and nursing resemble each other in the general nature of their organizational patterns. That is, most nurses and social workers are employed by institutions or by public or private agencies. In recent years some social workers and a few nurses have gone into private practice, but this is only a budding trend. Because social workers and nurses work for institutions, they are in a position that is similar to that of the interns and residents of medicine—that is, they can be relieved of their jobs. But this is where the similarity stops. Neither nurses nor social workers have the independence in the decision-making aspects of practice that physicians have. They are both much more dependent on institutions and on the pressures of the medical profession. This is less true of social work, since physicians and hospitals are not very interested in that aspect of a patient's welfare. Social workers are concerned primarily with the financial problems of patients and with their social needs. The extent to which a social worker's interest in a patient conflicts with the desires of a physician or an institution will determine the amount of pressure that is placed on him or her to come into line with those desires. Since nurses are more involved than social workers are in the day-to-day activities of patients, physicians, and institutions, they are more likely to be subjected to such pressure.

An advocate in either social work or nursing has a poor support system, primarily because the organizational design under which these professionals operate does not provide social workers and nurses with a power base. Also, nurses and social workers do not have a history of independence in the decision-making process as it relates to their practice. The public has not seen them in the realm of private practice, a realm that helps to establish decision-making authority of a kind that the public is used to paying for directly. Instead, nurses and social workers are seen as servants of an organization. They are there to provide a service that others have determined the public is entitled to receive. I hesitate to say this, but I fear that most social workers and nurses see themselves in this manner. Until these two professions change their own images and then communicate this change to the public, the advocate within either will have a hard time. For it is not only the internal support of the medical profession itself that helps physicians control their practice; it is also the support of those outside the profession. Social work and nursing are terribly lacking in both types of support.

Most nurses work within institutions as salaried employees. Within a hospital the nursing administration is answerable to the hospital administration. There is generally a board of trustees at the top, and it has only been in the last 10 or 15 years that some, not all, directors of nurses have even sat in on the meetings of this board. In addition, there is a medical board that has a great deal of influence with the board of trustees—as much as, if not more than, the hospital administrator. Within the nursing department there exists a hierarchy of authority—authority over all the practices of the nursing staff. This hierarchy runs from the director to the assistant directors to supervisors to head nurses and finally to the staff nurses, who are the direct deliverers of nursing care. Many of these positions have changed titles over the last few years. One sees such titles as "team leader" and "coordinator"; nevertheless, the hierarchy remains. The names may change, but the game is the same. Although the staff nurses, by virtue of their license, should have authority over their practice if they are to be held responsible and accountable for it, they do not have such authority in reality. Someone else determines when they will work, whom they will care for each day, and, many times, what that care will be. Even physicians will still write what are called "orders" that actually prescribe nursing care. One must question the legality of this, since physicians are not licensed to practice nursing.

So the practice of a staff nurse is supervised not only by a head nurse and a supervisor but even by other professionals, such as physicians. Professional practice, by definition, means independent activity. We see very little of this among nurses in our hospitals, because of the very nature of the nursing organizational pattern. Contributing to this situation is the fact that since all nurses have the same license, even if they have different levels of education, they often are all employed to do the same thing. One might expect to see the nursing technicians—the diploma and associate degree nurses—working under some kind of professional supervision, but one should not see nurses with baccalaureate degrees or master's degrees doing the same thing as the nursing technicians. But one does. The profession itself allows this situation, and the organization of the nursing service requires it, so the baccalaureate nurse has no support from within nursing to practice as a professional with authority over that practice.

Members of the public see this situation when they are patients and therefore do not have an image of nurses as independent practicing professionals. This is the picture that is also projected in television programs, movies, and novels. Nurses who are involved in higher education or in some of the profession's organizations generally are the ones who talk about the independent and autonomous nature of professional practice. Some nurses in hospitals give lip service to this view, but talk is not action.

Within individual nursing units there have been and still are three main delivery designs: functional, team, and primary care. These designs are not differentiated according to educational preparation, and all still carry many aspects of supervision. In functional nursing the work of the unit is divided up by the head nurse. One nurse gives all the medications, another gives all the treatments, and the rest are assigned patients for baths and similar duties. The assignments change on a rotating basis. In team nursing there is still a head nurse, but there are also team leaders. The team leaders divide up the work among the members of the team in much the same fashion as the head nurse does in the functional system. The role of team leader is often a rotating one, with baccalaureate nurses often serving as members of teams and not as leaders. In primary care nursing, each nurse is assigned a number of patients for whom he or she provides total care during their hospital stays. It is said that under this system a nurse has 24-hour responsibility and determines the care on that basis. But a nurse has no authority over the nurses on other shifts to guarantee that care is, in fact, given. Also, nurses of all educational levels can be primary care nurses. The primary care design may be a move in the right direction, but it still solves none of the basic problems. The one thing it does do is to provide a patient with some continuity of care, since he has the same nurse over a period of time. That in itself is no small thing, at least from the point of view of patients.

In my book *The Case for Consultation*, I suggested what I termed a "professional model" for the organizational design of care in nursing situations of all kinds. It placed authority directly into the hands of the professionally prepared (baccalaureate) nurse. Supervision was removed, and support was provided that would allow this nurse to have authority over care on a 24-hour basis. Removing supervision placed nursing administrators in the position of having to find other ways to hold this nurse accountable for the care he or she was responsible for. When you remove authority from a group, you remove some of its feeling of power. So how well this model would be accepted by nursing administrators is questionable. It is one thing to talk about nurses having authority over their practice; it is another thing to act in a manner that makes that philosophy a reality.

One of the interesting facts about the poor organizational designs that exist in nursing services is that they are all of nurses' own making. In reality no outside group stands in the way of nurses determining how care will be delivered on the unit level. Nurses have already experimented with three delivery designs and some variations of them. To go further and devise a truly professional design would not involve much additional difficulty. So nurses themselves are the primary obstacle to the practice being organized in a manner that allows them to have the authority over their practice that other professionals have.

Since professional authority is denied to nurses, mainly by other nurses, they will indeed have difficulty when they try to exercise their authority to be patients' advocates. They know where authority lies when they are dealing with other professionals, but in nursing determining where authority lies is like playing Russian roulette. You know there is authority somewhere, just as you know there is a bullet somewhere in the gun. A director of nurses can say that authority rests with the nurse giving the care, or perhaps with the head nurse, who can say it is with the supervisor, who can say it lies with the director, who then can say, "No, I delegated it to you people." This process is called gaming. It is engaged in throughout a hospital by members of all the professions. When things go right with a patient, everyone is willing to take the credit; when something goes wrong, the buck-passing begins. This is one of the main reasons why patients who sue for malpractice name physicians, nurses, and hospitals. By including them all, they assume that they are bound to find out who was responsible.

When you choose to be an advocate, you are also choosing not to play the game, because you are placing the responsibility for decision making where it belongs, in the patient's hands. It is a strange paradox to see a group of people who want to pass the responsibility around but who refuse to include the one group that it really belongs to, the patients. An advocate needs all the knowledge he or she can get to defuse the risk that an organizational structure of this nature obviously can produce. One of the best moves a nurse advocate can make is to do everything possible to change a nursing organizational design so that it allows for professional practice, places authority over practice where it belongs, in the professional nurse's hands, and places in the patient's hands the authority over whether that practice is acceptable.

Such a change will not be easy, for whenever a change shifts power from one group to another, those who see themselves as losing will resist. The best strategy is to demonstrate how the change will benefit those at the top—that it will remove them from the position of being responsible for every error made by every nurse in the hospital. The more you control everyone, the more responsible you are for errors; the more responsible you are, the more grief you get. The people at the top may well buy an idea that offers them less grief. There are other selling points; for example, they will look innovative and professional, they will gain prestige, and they may even attract more and better nurses because of a design that will let nurses really practice nursing. *When suggesting a design change, an advocate must demonstrate how it will help the leadership.*

It is easy to see that any organizational structure in which authority, responsibility, and accountability are not clearly placed is dangerous for an advocate. Now let us look at how health care professionals are paid and what this means in terms of accountability. This topic overlaps with the topic of practice designs in that much of what we have said about authority is also relevant here. So we can be brief and discuss only those areas we have not mentioned.

PAY VERSUS ACCOUNTABILITY

Let's go back to a question I asked at the beginning of this chapter. Does the person paying the piper really call the tune? In the health services, from the patient's point of view, the answer is generally no, but sometimes yes. From the point of view of a professional or an institution, the answer is generally yes, but sometimes no. This situation is not as strange as it may seem; it has to do both with power and with the peculiar nature of the health services. First, the professional has more power than the consumer, so although the consumer is paying for a service, he is not in a powerful—that is, knowledgeable—enough position to truly determine what that service should be. Second, usually a consumer can go from store to store and shop for a television set, for example, with no questions being asked and with a feeling of being welcomed and courted by all until he settles on a particular set. This nice capitalistic pastime is not encouraged by health care professionals, nor is much free choice possible in regard to health care. A person may pick his physician, but he will go to the hospital that the physician has permission to admit to. Or a person can pick his own hospital, but then he must pick a physician who practices there. He has no choice, or very little choice, of nurses or social workers.

Why can't the consumer always call the tune he pays for? Well, aside from the reasons already mentioned, he may not know the name of the tune—that is, the service needed—or he may not get the band that plays that tune—in other words, the hospital he wants. The health care system's inner workings and structure stand in his way. For example, take professionals who are in private practice and need customers. They are not like other people who sell services or products; they do not like people who shop around, although for public consumption they suggest that they encourage shopping around. There are several reasons for this situation. First, there is the syndrome I have discussed before in this book: "We know best, so you should trust us. Therefore why shop around? We are all qualified." Also, people who shop around are acting as though they know what they want and therefore can be demanding, and who wants a demanding patient? "Compliance is what we prize." Furthermore, people who change professionals because they are dissatisfied, especially if they do so more than once, are frowned upon. Of course, you do not have to tell a professional that you have seen someone else, but when he or she asks for your records of past illnesses, the truth will come out. If your new professional calls the other professional and is told that you were not a "good" patient, whatever that may mean, you will then be seen in an even more negative light (in other words, labeled a difficult patient). God help you if you want to change physicians while you are in a hospital; that process has complications that we have neither time nor space to go into. It is almost a book in itself.

Let me give a personal example to illustrate part of what I have been saying. One time I changed physicians and told the new physician why I changed. I also needed to be admitted to the hospital on the very day that I changed, and I needed a surgeon. Now, the new medical man was sympathetic with the reason why I changed physicians. I did not know a surgeon at that hospital, so I told my new physician to pick the best. As I walked out of his office to go to the hospital, he gave me these parting words: "Now, Mary, I don't want you causing trouble for Dr. so-and-so, nor do I want you raising hell in the hospital." I grinned and said, "Not unnecessarily so." Obviously my reputation as an advocate has preceded me, as had my ability to pick, choose, and change.

Most of what we have said so far is true of all professionals in private practice, not only physicians. They all have the same disease. But when you run into professionals who are paid by an institution and not by you directly, you have even more problems. If you find that the service you are receiving is poor, you can fire a professional you directly pay for and change to another, but you cannot fire one in an institution who is salaried and therefore paid indirectly by you. You are then left with only two choices: you can complain loudly to the person's superiors, and perhaps threaten a malpractice suit, in the hope that the service will improve or that a different person will be assigned to you, or you can discharge yourself from that institution. Either way you are laying yourself open to gaining the reputation of being a difficult patient and then being treated as such. Either the care will improve, if you are powerful enough, or you will be avoided, despite the fact you are paying for proper service. The bottom line is that personal power, prestige, or connections will go farther in determining the tune than the mere fact that you have paid for the tune.

So the answer to the question "Can the patient call the tune if he pays the piper?" is generally no, but sometimes yes, depending on *who the patient is*. Also, how a professional is paid will determine how much a patient can hold him or her accountable in a direct fashion. The shorter the route between the payer and payee, the greater the accountability. That is, the greater the extent to which authority is fixed at the level of the person providing the care directly, the greater the extent to which responsibility and accountability can be placed at that level. Advocates must know this when they are giving information to consumers. They must tell consumers how this system works, describe both the good aspects and the bad aspects, and let the consumers then decide what risks and chances they want to take within that system. An advocate should not tell a patient that he can change professionals or hospitals without telling him the consequences of that action and how he can combat those consequences.

It is hard to be honest about how a profession that you are a member of works, especially if it does not work in the consumer's best interest. Also, you will not be winning friends among your professional colleagues with this kind of honesty— especially if your patients tell your colleagues how honest you are. The best policy for an advocate is to make information public on a wide range for consumers. Educate consumers so that they can educate others and can bring group pressure for change, and use all the knowledge at your command. Always remember that you can use the stated goals of professions to weaken their unstated goals and to discourage certain practices. No one wants to have his unstated goals revealed, especially if they are not professionally or service oriented.

Now let us look at the question of pay and accountability from the point of view of professionals and institutions. Yes, the one who pays the piper generally calls the tune, but not always. Professionals in private practice who provide revenue to other professionals or to institutions, through high referral or admission rates, can indeed call tunes. They can turn a month's delay into a two-day delay to see a specialist if they are sending many patients to that specialist. Or they can get new equipment for their practice in an institution if they provide that institution with many patients. In fact, they can have whole new units and operating rooms built just for them.

The reverse of this situation is true when an institution pays a profession's salary. This is especially true for the professions of social work and nursing, more so for nursing. An institution can dictate, within the limits of the licensure laws, what the practice of a nurse or a social worker will entail and what its limits will be in terms of authority. (This is also true, but to a lesser extent, for physicians when an institution pays a physician's salary.) The institution calls the tune, within limits, and the only recourse for the professional is to quit or to organize others in the institution to bring pressure on the institution to change its ways. There has indeed been an increase in the number of unions among nurses. So recourse through unions is possible, but you pay the price of allowing a union to limit or dictate your practice.

Unions are not known for their toleration of independence in their members. It seems that if the essence of professional practice is its independence, then there is a large area of potential conflict with a union. The interns and residents who have unionized to combat what they see as the oppression of hospitals that employ them also face this problem.

In dealing with unions, an advocate, again, must know where the power lies and must be familiar with the stated and unstated goals. A positive approach is preferable in all situations—an appeal to what is best for a union. Since unions can pressure institutions to be more receptive to the wishes of consumers as well to those of their members, an advocate's appeal should match both aims. Unions love to get consumer support on the one hand, but they also do not want to lose members. The advocate walks a very narrow path. It is balance, based on knowledge, that counts.

So although it seems that the payer should call the tune, whether he actually does will depend on the market. The fact that a supplier has a monopoly on a product or service makes it difficult for the buyer to call the tune. But the very existence of a monopoly also makes the holder of it vulnerable to pressure to be accountable or risk losing that monopoly. Which brings us to the subject of licensure, certification, and accreditation. Are there regulatory mechanisms that will help the advocate?

REGULATORY MECHANISMS

Individual professionals are subject to two regulatory mechanisms—state licensure and association certification. An individual takes a state board examination, which, if passed, grants him or her a license to practice a profession. The licensure laws of the states dictate the scope of the practice and describe, in a broad way, what is legal practice and what is not. The individual is then held directly accountable to maintain his or her practice within the boundaries of the law or risk the loss of the license. Among the health professions, nursing, medicine, dentistry, pharmacy, and a few others have such a licensing procedure. (Social work has a certification policy, but not a state licensing procedure.) The license establishes the basic level of practice in a profession. Beyond this a professional can be certified by a professional association to practice a specialty. The standards for certification are established by the association, which also gives the examinations for certification.

Requirements for certification vary from profession to profession and even within a profession from specialty to specialty. The requirements for maintaining one's certification once it has been received also vary. In the case of licensure, however, once a license has been received and a person has been registered, he or she generally keeps that license for life without any further requirements, except for maintaining the registration on an annual or biennial basis. In the past several years, though, some states have passed laws requiring that professionals take a certain number of hours of continuing education each year or registration period. So although the license cannot be lost, a professional must have the additional education in order to renew his registration, which he or she must do in order to practice. This process is called mandatory continuing education. It is not true of all professions or in all states, but it is becoming more common every day.

Professional schools are subject to the regulatory mechanism known as accreditation. Most professional schools are parts of colleges or universities. Colleges and universities are accredited in and of themselves by regional accrediting groups. However, the professional schools within a college or university are further accredited by specialized accrediting bodies of the professions. In some professions this specialized accreditation is necessary for a school to remain open; in others it is not. Specialized accreditation does help in attracting students and in gaining prestige, and in many cases it is needed to qualify for federal funding.

The subject of licensure, certification, and accreditation is involved and in a constant state of change. The level of advocacy one is engaged in will determine the depth of knowledge one will find useful. On the client level, knowledge about licensure is a must, and some knowledge of certification is important as well. In the educational arena, knowledge of accreditation becomes very important. Many professions say they are tightening up in all three areas so as to provide greater accountability to the consumer. However, some of this so-called tightening up may be nothing more than an attempt to create a greater monopoly on a service. One can probably surmise that a bit of both is true. The advocate must keep this in mind.

Advocates must recognize how they can use regulatory processes to help in risk defusement, while at the same time being aware that their advocacy may take a turn that will threaten these very mechanisms and the viability of a professional or a profession. A threatening posture is not a good one for an advocate. As I have stated before, it is always best to appeal to someone's best interests first; only when this fails does one resort to the defense of an attack through the regulatory mechanisms. For example, if you are asked to participate in an act that is questionable under the law, you can best approach a refusal by pointing out to the person who suggests this activity the fact that he may be risking his or her license. If this fails, you can point out how you may be risking your own license. If this fails and the pressure still is on you to cooperate, you have the final choice of threatening to reveal the person's intentions to others.

Generally, the possibility that an action could cause a professional to lose a license or a school to have its accreditation called into question or lost is enough to persuade the person to pause. It is hoped that a rethinking of the problem—whatever it may be—will result and that another approach will be devised. Oftentimes all one needs to say is "I wonder what the law is?" or "I wonder if there are any legal ramifications to this?" The recent increase in the number of malpractice suits, the rise of the consumer movement, and the increasingly close scrutiny of government agencies have helped bring about more careful thought on the part of professionals in the health care field, which was once almost a law unto itself. Although professionals still live in fairly closed systems in comparison to other groups, these systems are being penetrated more and more each day. From the advocate's point of view, the more open a system is, the safer he or she is, because the basis of advocacy is informing and supporting.

• • •

These three areas—how professions are organized, how professionals are paid, and how professionals are regulated—are intertwined. A change in one will generally bring about change in one or both of the others. For example, the advocate must be aware of what a seemingly small change in billing practices, such as the institution of a system whereby third-party payments would go directly to all professionals rather than be channeled through and controlled by physicians and/or hospitals, may mean to the way in which professionals are organized in the work situation, especially in institutions. The advocate must be aware that a change in a licensure law, to give greater autonomy to a profession, also may result in a change in the way that profession organizes itself in the work situation. So while an advocate may seem to be working in only one of the three areas, it would be naive to deny the effect of that advocacy on the other areas. Opposition to one's advocacy may not be directed to the immediate situation but rather to what other people may see as the future results in other areas.

There are very few isolated phenomenon in the practice field, and there will be even fewer in the future. The growth and acceptance of advocacy itself will effect change. Advocacy will open the health care system, but those who do not want it opened will resist this process. It is necessary for advocates to understand this fact, to be able to predict areas of risk, and to be familiar with the tools needed to defuse these risks.

NOTES ON CHAPTER 9

What I said in the notes for Chapter 8 is true here as well, if not more so. It is a difficult task to keep up with all the changes and innovations that appear in the practice field. They occur much more rapidly than changes in the educational field. In addition, they are based, for the most part, on much more flimsy ground than those in education. The hidden agendas of special interest groups are much more extensive and even harder to identify. Special interest groups in the practice field have the special advantage, in terms of persuasion, of making use of "pilot" projects to support their positions. In general, these positions are presented to the public only because the special interest groups need public money to reach their goals. If they did not need public money, or at least public moral support, the public would not hear from them directly; rather they would do their thing and let public support grow from the grass roots level. This may sound a bit harsh; it is always possible a good idea has come up that is not only innovative but needed. However, in the practice field the ability of special interest groups to institute innovations without sound public support is much greater than in the educational field. Therefore, greater scrutiny on the part of advocates is called for.

People are easily seduced by the new and by the bandwagon phenomenon (or call it "keeping up with the Joneses"). If your neighbor has something, you want it too.

The many variables that go into changes suggested in the practice field are more vast and harder to identify then those in education. However, never forget that changes in the two fields frequently go hand-in-hand, even though a change in one usually precedes the corresponding change in the other. The interchange between education and practice and the effects of one on the other must never be forgotten. So, if you approve of a change in one, do not forget that it will have an effect on the other. Look at this effect even if it is not featured at the time. Be alert to the seductiveness of appeals to short-term goals. Remember that imposing a short-term solution on a long-term problem may mean that the problem will be more difficult to solve in the future.

Chapter 10

KNOWLEDGE—
PLEASURE?
PAIN?
SURVIVAL?
. . . A GESTALT

WHAT THE NINE PRECEDING CHAPTERS mean in terms of a gestalt will vary from reader to reader. I would like to share with you what they mean to me—the me that is composed of many parts, or shall we say the many roles I have played in life. These roles include student, practicing professional nurse, educator of nurses, member of several nursing organizations, advocate, consumer of health care, and member of the society we have been discussing. Furthermore, this is the me that has listened to and discussed the opinions of the people whom I asked to criticize these chapters for me. In this last chapter I would like to address two questions: What thoughts do I have about what I have written and about what others have said about what I have written? Have I left out anything? So first let's talk a bit about what I have written and what it seems to mean to me and to the people who have given me their opinions about it, and then let me discuss two or three final topics that did not seem to fit into the preceding chapters.

MEANING OF THE GESTALT

I would like to focus on three areas here. First, one of my colleagues seems to think I have written a professional survival manual that applies to any job or position and only used advocacy as a vehicle for that purpose. This was not my intent—that is, not a stated goal. Perhaps is was an unstated goal? More likely it was a combination of both. I stated near the beginning of this book that one must be an advocate for oneself first, that if one could not do this, one would be rather ineffective as an advocate for others. That is true. If you cannot survive as an effective professional, you cannot be an advocate for clients. Therefore, if I have been teaching you how to survive, perhaps that is only as it should be. I have had to learn how to survive in each of the many roles I have played, or give it up. One reader told me, "You know, in my job I have to expend so much energy just making it from day to day and from crisis to crisis that I sometimes have little left over for others, or even for doing my job well." Yes, isn't it true, and isn't that a sorry thing to have to say? I have heard people outside the health professions—in insurance, law, teaching, construction— say much the same thing. They say that simply fighting day to day to be able to do their jobs is almost a full-time task, that the actual work of the job sometimes becomes secondary.

In thinking about these comments I realize that my colleague was right—a grasp of the knowledge base of survival is indeed essential to an advocate. The ability to survive must be second nature to an advocate; he or she must be able to act and to react without having to take too much time in analysis of each troublesome occurrence, studying or psyching out a system. If we truly want to be effective in a job, we need to be able to handle with ease and speed all the matters that will come up to interfere with the actual work of that job. Surviving must become as automatic with us as driving a car, riding a bike, or swimming. We need to be able to plan our actions and reactions with speed and accuracy. We do not have enough time or energy in a day to analyze each problem that arises because we did not do our homework. If we do not take time to do something right the first time, we will not have time later to do it over. To develop this attitude and to act on the basis of it, we must have a realistic view of life, because a pseudo-innocent position will defeat us.

This is not to say that one is required to be cynical, only realistic about the human condition, and forgiving of self and others, while still learning how not to err twice in the same manner. To get caught up in a paranoiac attitude about life or about a health care system, which can then lead to a desire for vengeance, is the most self-defeating thing that can happen to a person. To develop an attitude of cynicism and mistrust of one's fellow human beings is just as self-defeating and as blinding to the good in life and in other people. Extremism and gluttony seem to be somewhat alike. Some people say that extremists are only adhering with excessive tenacity to principles that may otherwise be admirable. It seems to me that they adhere more to an overindulgence in self-righteousness and rigidity, which represents a poor view of self and others and little ability to forgive either. This is pseudo-innocence at its worst.

Knowing is a key to reality and to effective coping with reality. It is, as I have said many times, the key to effective advocacy as well as the key to professional survival. Each of us has a role or roles to play, a job or several jobs to do in this life. Ignorance about how to do them need not be self-imposed, and we cannot expect others always to lead us by the hand in acquiring the knowledge needed to be reasonably successful. In our society all that is required is the self-discipline to go out and acquire the necessary knowledge.

A second meaning of the gestalt of the preceding nine chapters is the manner in which the various areas of knowledge were approached and presented. I was told by a second colleague that I had written a book not on advocacy but on systems analysis—that is, a new approach to systems analysis—and used advocacy as a vehicle to do so. Again, this was not my intent, not my "stated goal." But, again, was it an unstated goal? I'm not sure. You see, unstated goals can be unstated even to the person who holds them. I can say that my approach to life does take on a rather logical bent. The illogical or the unexplainable does not leave me with a comfortable feeling. Dealing with life and problems in less than a logical style seems inadequate in terms of gaining knowledge about one's role and job. Furthermore, a systematic approach to analysis is about the only method we have to approximate objectivity—to perceive the current reality of the world in which we function. I am not claiming that the reality is sane, only stating that we need an adequate reflection of that reality, sane or insane.

The illogical or the unexplainable leaves most people uncomfortable. We like to know where we stand, even if we may not like what we discover. If we know where we stand, we can at least make a decision about whether we want to remain in that position. If we choose to remain, we can then determine what we can or cannot do in that position. Thus a systematic approach to the gaining of knowledge seems not only logical but realistic. It combines the need to know with the need to see reality in order to combat the dangers of pseudo-innocence.

There are many methods of analyzing systems, but the end result must always be an accurate reporting of the facts as they exist in that system. How one then uses these facts to determine how one will behave is another matter entirely. Whenever one moves outside the framework of logic in the collection of data, one runs the risk of skipping over material that may be important to a successful assessment of a system. The overlooking of some important data is always a factor; we cannot think of everything. But if we at least set up a systematic and logical approach, we can hope to glean the most data in the most objective way possible. To set a goal of learning everything, in a society that is as ever-changing as ours, is unrealistic. Therefore it is equally unrealistic to blame ourselves too much if we miss a detail or two. We learn and go on from there. The processes of learning and knowing, instead of discouraging us, make us aware of the necessity of the continuing search for knowledge.

A third meaning of the gestalt is the multiplicity of factors that affect the advocate role. By factors I mean all those things the advocate must take into account in the process of being an advocate—not only the human being an advocate is dealing with but the society that person is a member of and the system in which he is at that moment involved. This wide range of required knowledge almost boggles the mind. It is not surprising that one might ask, "How can anyone be expected to be knowledgeable in all these areas?"

We are dealing with knowledge on two levels: the knowledge of the expert and the knowledge of awareness. The expert's knowledge is not totally required. But the advocate at least must be aware that many factors are involved and that these factors vary from situation to situation. The advocate also must know that he or she will have to seek out further knowledge as the need arises. If an advocate does not know something, he or she at least must be able to seek out knowledgeable consultation in that area. The risk defusement process does not leave room for a defense of "I didn't know."

The assessment process will quickly point out to you what you do not know; then you must go and find out. This process is similar to the learning process of a student. A student knows what he will be tested on. So he masters the areas he is lacking in, or he fails. What seems complex as a process is in fact very simple. Whenever you embark on a new venture, the success of that venture will depend on how well you have prepared for it and on what you will do when you run into areas of trouble.

The three areas I have just discussed will certainly be part of the gestalt arrived at by anyone who has read the first nine chapters of this book. The order of importance will vary from reader to reader. The importance of advocacy for self (or call it professional survival) a knowledge of systems assessment, and an awareness of the many factors involved in advocacy are all essential tools I hope you have acquired from reading these chapters. My approach has been more one of synthesis than one of fact gathering and in-depth analysis. I have chosen to synthesize from facts and my experience and to provide you with resources that you can go to glean your own facts and to arrive at the same synthesis I did or to arrive at your own.

• • •

While writing about advocacy and the many variables associated with it, two thoughts kept recurring to me. They do not fit into the organization of this book but in a way are very much parts of this book—almost as underlying themes. The first theme is the almost base ignorance on the part of consumers about health care systems and about their right to basic care. The second theme is the extent to which we professionals abuse our "children"—that is, our young, up-and-coming professionals. These two areas make up the rest of my gestalt, and I would like to reflect on them a bit.

THE IMPOSED IGNORANCE OF CONSUMERS

I call the ignorance of the consumer "imposed" because I see it as being forced on him both by the health care system, a system that maintains an attitude of "We know best," and by the consumer himself, who subscribes to the belief "What you don't know can't hurt you" and who puts the care of his automobile or television set before the care of his body. These two factors work together to maintain a very high level of ignorance. It is only when tragedy occurs and we find out how little we know and how little we are told that we experience the pain of this ignorance. This pain has been well documented by people who write about their own experiences— wives who write about the horror of their husbands' heart attacks and deaths, parents who write about the inadequate care and treatment their children have received. These people all say that if they had only known more, their situations would have been different. A good percentage of these books become best-sellers, and all sing a "ain't it awful" theme.

But no matter how painful or heartbreaking these stories are, little is changed. The consumer continues, by choice, to remain ignorant, and the system chooses to keep him that way. This is not to say that no efforts are being made to educate the public or that all consumers want to remain ignorant. Efforts to provide knowledge and to gain knowledge are being made, but not by the vast majority of health care professionals and consumers. I believe that an individual has the personal responsibility to get the facts that he needs to care for himself, but I believe that the health care system is even more responsible to provide these facts, whether or not anyone chooses to use them. If a person knows something and then chooses not to act on that knowledge, that is his choice, but the health care professionals must fulfill their responsibility in the informing process.

Many consumer advocates have insisted that either the health care professions police themselves better or more severe regulations will be imposed on them. I have no argument with better internal discipline, or call it "peer review." However, increased regulation will do little but increase the bureaucratic red tape, the paper work, and the cost of health care without measurably improving the quality of care. Barbara Gordon, in her recent book *I'm Dancing as Fast as I Can*, which concerns her experience with psychotherapy, cries out for something to be done to prevent incompetent therapists from practicing. But even she admits to not knowing how this could be done. She criticizes not only psychiatrists but everyone else who practices psychotherapy—nurses, social workers, psychologists, and lay therapists. Gordon says that all have been found wanting to one degree or another by one group or another.[1]

A tightening of regulations will not make health professionals care more or better or differently. The greatest protection a consumer has is to be informed and to demand the treatment he knows he has a right to expect, or shop elsewhere. It is only when consumers begin to make demands on a system, and threaten to remove their support from it, that changes will be made. Professionals are as much victims of the philosophy of the health care marketplace as consumers are. We must get professionals off their pedestals, pedestals we put them on, and realize that they are only people who sell a service. All the advocacy in the world will be of little avail unless consumers themselves are willing to make decisions and to take some responsibility for the situation that currently exists.

Thus, although professionals are responsible for informing clients, they are not responsible for making their decisions. In this age of mass communications the cry of "I didn't know" is no longer acceptable. It has never been acceptable from a professional, and it is becoming less acceptable from consumers. The advocate cannot afford to be caught between a system that wants to maintain secrecy and consumers who do not care enough to know. This is why I speak so strongly against the rescuer role and in favor of professional survival and systems analysis. The advocate walks a narrow, hazardous path, and knowledge is the only guide he or she has to avoid the majority of the hazards.

Although my heart aches when I hear horror stories from patients and families about their experiences with hospitals and health care professionals, I cannot help but want to cry out (sometimes I actually do), "But why didn't you ask questions and insist on knowing, or threaten a lawsuit if you were not told?" You see, I do not

[1]Barbara Gordon, *I'm Dancing as Fast as I Can* (New York: Harper and Row, Publishers, Inc., 1979).

believe consumers are to be treated as poor innocents who are totally at the mercy of the health care system. Nor do I believe that professionals should be viewed as all-caring. However, if one were to place blame, more would fall on the professionals' side. Professionals have the power and the control to change the system but have refused to do so. A simple act such as providing patients with full copies of all their health records, including hospital charts, would go a long way toward removing the veil of secrecy that shrouds the system. The necessity of seeking a court order or a lawyer to gain access to one's own records in a supposedly free country leaves one asking, "What is freedom?" The system can change this policy—overnight, if it chooses—or consumers can go to the politicians and have laws made to change it.

In order to prevent others from knowing, we must work hard to maintain their complacency. We seem to be quite successful at this. "We know best" and "I'll take care of you" from professionals, combined with "You decide" and "You know best" from patients, along with a lowering of a sense of individual responsibility, go far in maintaining the status quo. To the consumer I can only say, "If it is ignorance you want, it is ignorance you will get." To the professional I say, "If you continue to maintain ignorance as a policy of the system, you risk having that system destroyed, and if you maintain the all-knowing, rescuer attitude, you will soon find that you have become a victim yourself." Dissatisfied clients (victims of questionable practices) are already becoming the persecutors (initiators of malpractice suits) of professional rescuers; this can only continue as a very dangerous and expensive game for all players.

I would like to end this section by saying that the greatest disservice we do our young students is to allow them to go out into the professional world with the admonition to be advocates without teaching them the reality of that world and that role. Better they should be a little less idealistic and a little more realistic—and survive. Also, we do a disservice to consumers by allowing the fairyland of a Dr. Welby or a Dr. Kildare to sell them on the all-caring and all-knowing world of the health system. A little reality in our television programs would go far to educate the public; at present they tend to perpetuate the current ignorance.

WINNING YOUR SPURS

Throughout this book has been the theme of the risk an advocate faces from his or her fellow professionals. In many cases the very people who tell you what your job is also stand in the way of your doing it. This is true not only of members of the health professions but of all humankind. Our species seems unable to tolerate the success of its young unless that success is achieved with pain and deference. We humans are a very hypocritical lot. We want our children to do as we say, not as we do. But then we cannot stand it when they do better than we do, since that fact may reflect on our own shortcomings. This phenomenon is called double-binding, which some claim is a major cause of mental illness.

Angry consumers have written books about the health care system. Books have also been written about the pain of learning how to be a member of an established professional system. Why don't young professionals band together and make the system change? Perhaps young professionals, like consumers, do not want to believe that change is needed. They seem to want to live in an idealized world, in ignorance and complacency, rather than to make the effort required to learn what lies in store for them, and to change it.

Why don't the established professionals in the system, who "know best," make these changes? They could do so easier than the young could. Perhaps we are dealing with a hoarding-of-knowledge problem. In knowledge lies power—the power to make decisions. To share knowledge would seem to reduce this power. So the attitude becomes "Don't share this precious knowledge with consumers, or let young professionals exercise their knowledge too much, or they will threaten the power we have gained through our longevity. We had to suffer—why should they have it so easy?" To break what seems to be a behavioral pattern of long standing in the health delivery system will not be easy; it may not even be possible. For to do so will require a major change in the way we regard the security that power gives us. Being top man, whether we are right or wrong, seems more important than the end result of that behavior.

I could tell several stories of accomplished professionals who have allowed the young not only to achieve but to go beyond them. Later they have been rewarded with the respect and friendship of these young successful people. Thus their rewards seem to lie not only in their own success but in the reflected glory of the success of the people they have helped. This situation keeps these older, experienced professionals young and in touch with the changes and progress of their younger colleagues. They are called on even in their retirement years to give advice—indeed an honor to the respect they have gained through their behavior. Was this a long-term, calculated goal? I don't believe so. Rather it was a way of perceiving the world and other people in it, a respect for knowledge and ability that superseded their own need for praise and power, an ability to share combined with the awareness of the need to do so. We cannot know it all and we cannot make decisions for others. Leadership does not mean accepting and insisting on the responsibility for all decision making. Rather it means knowing when we are responsible and when we can delegate authority, hold others responsible, and reward them accordingly.

Many books and theories about the growth and development of children are concerned with the gaining of independence necessary to the life process. However, we seem to stop thinking of growth and development as a process when a child reaches the age of consent. What about nurturing the growth and development of young professionals? They need to gain independence and a respect for what they have learned and can contribute. I am not claiming that this is overlooked but rather that the nurturing of independence is not common enough. Too often we see students being taught to adhere to the party line of their elders. We say, "When you have proven yourself, we will let you share in the power and the decision-making process." What it often boils down to is that when we can no longer prevent them from having power, we acquiesce and say, "Now you can have power, because you have proven yourself." We do not give in until they either have taken power from us or are about to do so.

I call this process abusive—as evidenced by the large number of students we lose because they will not or cannot endure it. This process is also abusive in terms of what we have taught those students who do succeed. By our role modeling we have set a pattern for them that they may very well emulate in dealing with future young professionals. Many of the books on child abuse have a similar theme—that abused children turn into abusive parents, a perpetuation of a pattern. One of the many treatments for abusive parents is to teach them how not to be abusive by loving them—in other words, providing them with the love they did not have as children in hopes that they will be able to translate this into the way they treat their own children.

I am prescribing a similar treatment for professionals who have "arrived" to use with young professionals. In other words, if we want young professionals to be advocates, we must be the ones who help them defuse the risks in the role and not the ones who add to those risks. We must be willing to share the power of the decision-making process not only with consumers but with our young professionals— not only for the survival of both these groups but for our own survival as well. For we will surely become victims and fail if we do not share the power, and we will be teaching others this same victim-and-failure role.

In the final analysis we must understand that we are all consumers of health care, either now or later. How we can expect to be treated when we need that care will depend on how we teach others to behave now. The only insurance we have of the quality of this future treatment is our willingness to invest ourselves now. We get out of something only what we put into it. Ignorance begets ignorance, abuse abuse, and love love. We must admit to our humanness, both the failings of it and the blessings of it; we must try to rise above the failings and enhance the blessings. I hope I have expressed the need to do so, as well as provided a guide of sorts to how to do so. The answer to the question "Are we our brothers' keepers?" is that we *are* our brothers and that we are to love others as we do ourselves. Love of others is not devoid of a sense of healthy selfishness, or call it respect for self. This is the essence of freedom; it is "the wisdom of serpents and the gentleness of doves."

BIBLIOGRAPHY

This bibliography is composed of the works that have appeared in the footnotes or in the end-of-chapter notes, as well as other works that may be helpful. Because of the breadth of knowledge that is necessary for the enactment of the role of advocate in the safest way possible, no bibliography could be sufficient. The small quantity of material from 1979 to the present results, in part, from the nature of the book publishing business. It also results from the fact that new, in terms of publication date, is not necessarily new in terms of ideas and knowledge.

What is good about reading the new and up to date, in terms of publication date, is that someone may come up with a truly new idea. More important, a new variation on an old theme may be very meaningful to you; it may help you to reexamine the old theme and to use it in a way that an earlier author had not thought of.

I have found that an extensive bibliography is good for the vastly curious but that a shorter list is more practical in terms of actual use by students. The most important things for students of advocacy to remember are to include many views in their reading and to be aware of their own personal views.

Allport, Gordon. *The Nature of Prejudice*. New York: Anchor Books, 1958.

Annas, George J., Glanty, Leonard H., and Katz, Barbara F. *The Rights of Doctors, Nurses, and Allied Health Professionals*. New York: Avon Books, 1981.

Aroskar, Mila A. "Ethical Issues in Community Health Nursing." *Nursing Clinics of North America* 14, no. 1 (March 1979):35-44.

Ashley, J.A. *Hospitals, Paternalism and the Role of the Nurse*. New York: Teachers College Press, 1976.

Ashley, Jo Ann. "Nursing and Early Feminism," *American Journal of Nursing* 75, no. 9 (September 1976):1465-1467.

Bender, Marilyn. "When the Boss is a Woman." *Esquire* 89, no. 5 (March 28, 1978):35-41.

Bennis, Warren, et al., eds. *The Planning of Change*. New York: Holt, Rinehart & Winston, 1962.

Bindler, Ruth. "Moral Development in Nursing Education." *Image* 9, no. 1 (February, 1977).

Bok, Sissela. "The Ethics of Giving Placebos." *Scientific American* 231, no. 5 (November 1974):17-23.

Bondman, Bertran, and Bondman, Elsie. "Do Nurses Have Rights?" *American Journal of Nursing* 78, no. 1 (January 1976):84-86.

Brink, Pamela J. "Patientology: Just Another Ology." *Nursing Outlook* September 1978, pp. 574-575.

Brooks, Patricia. "Plugging into the Old Girl Network." *Working Women* 2, no. 7 (July 1977):26-29.

Buchanan, James M. *The Limits of Liberty*. Chicago: University of Chicago Press, 1975.

Bullough, Bonnie, "Influences on Role Expansion." *American Journal of Nursing*, September 1976, pp. 1476-1481.

Bullough, Bonnie, and Bullough, Vern. *Poverty, Ethnic Identity and Health Care*. New York: Appleton-Century-Crofts, 1972.

Chesler, P., and Goodman, E.J. *Women, Money and Power*. New York: William Morrow & Co., Inc., 1976.

Colt, Avery, et al. "Home Health Care is Good Economics." *Nursing Outlook* 25, no. 10 (October 1977):632-636.

Cobbs, John. "Egalitarianism: Threat To a Free Market." *Business Week*, Dec. 1, 1975, pp. 62-65.

Curtin, Leah L. "Nursing Ethics: Theories and Pragmatics." *Nursing Forum* 17, no. 1 (1978): 5-11.

Davis, Ann J., and Aroskar, Mila A. *Ethical Dilemmas and Nursing Practice.* New York: Appleton-Century-Crofts, 1978.

Dean, Patricia Geary. "Toward Androgeny." *Image* 10, no. 1 (February 1978):10-14.

De Beauvoir, S. *The Second Sex,* New York: Vintage Books, 1974.

Dyer, Wayne W. *Your Erroneous Zones,* Funk and Wagnalls, New York: 1976.

Ehrenreich, Barbara, and Ehrenreich, John. *The American Health Empire.* New York: Random House, Inc., 1971.

"Equality: American Dream or Nightmare?" *U.S. News and World Report* 79 (Aug. 4, 1975) pp. 26-36.

"Ethical Dilemmas in Nursing—A Special AJN Supplement" (a 14-article series). *American Journal of Nursing* 77, no. 5 (May 1977):845-876.

Etizioni, Amitai. *Complex Organizations.* New York: Holt, Rinehart & Winston, 1962.

Fagin, Claire, McClure, Margaret, and Schlotfeldt, Rozella. "Can We Bring Order Out of the Chaos of Nursing Education?," *American Journal of Nursing,* January 1976, pp. 98-107.

Fletcher, Joseph. *Situation Ethics: The New Morality.* Philadelphia: The Westminster Press, 1974.

"Focus on Associate Degree Nursing" (Overview of ADN education in 5 articles). *Nursing Outlook* 25, no. 6 (August 1977):496-513.

Frankel, Charles. "The New Egalitarianism and the Old." *Commentary* 56 (September 1973): 54-61.

Frankena, William K. *Ethics,* ed. 2. Englewood Cliffs, N.J.: Prentice-Hall, Inc., 1976.

Friedrich, Carl J., ed. *The Philosophy of Kant: Immanuel Kant's Moral and Political Writings.* New York: Random House, Inc., 1949.

Gortner, Susan R. "Strategies for Survival in the Practice World." *American Journal of Nursing* 77, no. 4 (April 1977):618-619.

Gargaro, William. "The Tuma Case." *Cancer Nursing* 1, no. 4 (August 1978):329-330.

Gargaro, William. "Update on the Tuma Case," *Cancer Nursing* 1, no. 6 (December 1978): 467-468.

Gardner, John W. *Excellence.* New York: Harper & Row, Publishers, Inc., 1961.

Gordon, Barbara. *I'm Dancing as Fast as I Can.* New York: Harper and Row, Publishers, Inc., 1979.

Grissum, Marlene, and Spengler, Carol. *Woman Power and Health Care.* Boston: Little, Brown & Co., 1976.

Hadley, Arthur Twining. *The Conflict Between Liberty and Equality.* Cambridge: The Riverside Press, 1925.

Henley, Nancy and Jo Freeman. "The Sexual Politics of Interpersonal Behavior." *Women, A Feminist Perspective,* ed. J. Freeman. Palo Alto: Mayfield Publishing Co., 1975.

Hollingshead, August, and Frederich, Redlich. *Social Class and Mental Illness.,* 1974.

Hott, Jacqueline Rose. "Updating Cherry Ames." *American Journal of Nursing* 77, no. 10 (October 1977):1581-1583.

Illich, Ivan. *Medical Nemesis.* New York: Pantheon Books, Inc., 1976.

Imbus, Sharon H., and Zawacki, Bruce, E. "Autonomy for Burned Patients When Survival is Unprecedented." *The New England Journal of Medicine* 297 (August 11, 1977):308-311.

Isaacs, Marion. "Toward a National Health Policy: a Realistic View." *AJN*, May, 1978, Vol. 78 (No. 5), pp. 848-851.

Jonas, Steven. *Health Care Delivery in the United States*, ed. 2. New York: Springer Publishing Co., Inc., 1981.

Kalisch, Beatrice J., and Kalisch, Phillip A. *Politics of Nursing*. Philadelphia: J. B. Lippincott Co., 1982.

Kinlein, Lucille. *Independent Nursing Practice with Clients*. Philadelphia: J.B. Lippincott Co., 1977.

Kohlberg, Lawrence, and Turiel, Elliot. "Moral Development and Moral Education." In *Psychology and Educational Practice*, edited by G. Lesser. Chicago: Scott, Foresman & Co., 1971.

Kohnke, Mary F. *The Case For Consultation in Nursing: Designs for Professional Practice*. New York: John Wiley & Sons, Inc., 1978.

Kohnke, Mary F. "Nurse Abuse—Nurse Abusers." *Nursing and Health Care* 2, no. 5 (May 1981):256-260.

Kohnke, Mary F. "The Nurse's Responsibility to the Consumer." *American Journal of Nursing*, March 1978, pp. 440-442.

Kohnke, Mary F. "Do Nursing Educators Practice What They Preach?" *American Journal of Nursing*, September 1973, pp. 1571-1575.

Korda, Michael. *Male Chauvinism: How It Works*. New York: Random House, Inc., 1972.

Korda, Michael. *Power: How to Get It, How to Use it*. New York: Random House, Inc., 1975.

Kotelchuck, David. *Prognosis Negative*. New York: Vintage Books, 1976.

Kramer, Marlene. *Reality Shock: Why Nurses Leave Nursing*. St. Louis: The C.V. Mosby Co., 1974.

Krawezk, Rosemary, and Kudzma, Elizabeth. "Ethics: A Matter of Moral Development." *Nursing Outlook* 4 (April 1978):254-257.

Lambertson, Martha, et al. "Peer Review in a Family Nurse Clinician Program." *Nursing Outlook*, January 1977, pp. 47-53.

Law, Sylvia. *Blue Cross: What Went Wrong*. New Haven: Yale University Press, 1974.

Levinson, Richard. "Sexism in Medicine." *American Journal of Nursing* 76 no. 3 (March 1976):426-431.

Maas, Meridian, Specht, Janet, and Jacox, Ada. "Nursing Autonomy: Reality, Not Rhetoric," *American Journal of Nursing*, December, pp. 2201-2208.

May, Rollo. *Power and Innocence*. New York: W.W. Norton & Co., Inc., 1972.

Mill, John Stuart. *Utilitarianism, Liberty and Representative Government*. New York: E.P. Dutton and Co., Inc., 1951.

Page, B.B. "Who Owns the Professions?" *Hastings Center Report* 5, no. 5 (October 1975):7-8.

Partridge, Kay B. "Nursing Values in a Changing Society." *American Journal of Nursing* 78, no. 6 (June 1978):356-360.

Poulin, M. "The Nurse Administrator: Survival in the Executive Jungle." *Journal of the New York State Nurses' Association*, December 1975.

The Pregnant Patient's Bill of Rights and the Pregnant Patient's Responsibilities. International Childbirth Education Association, Inc. (Complimentary copy can be obtained by sending a self-addressed envelope to Box 1900, New York, N.Y. 10001; bulk order can be obtained from ICEA Publication/Distribution Center, P.O. Box 3825, Brighton Station, Rochester, N.Y. 14610.)

"Pulling Back From Permissiveness." *Time* 111 (March 27, 1978):76.

Redman, Eric. *The Dance of Legislation.* New York: Simon & Schuster, Inc., 1973.

Schlotfeldt, Rozella M. "The Professional Doctorate: Rationale and Characteristics." *Nursing Outlook* 26, no. 5 (May 1978):302-311.

Schoenmaker, Adrian and Radoswich, David. "Conflict Between Expectations and Reality." *Nursing Outlook* May, 1976, pp. 298-302.

Sensterheim, Herbert, and Baer, Jean. *Don't Say Yes When You Want to Say No.* New York: Dell Publishing Co., Inc., 1975.

Smith, Ralph R. "Bakke's Case vs. the Case for Affirmative Action." *New York University Education Quarterly* 60 (Winter 1978):2-8.

"State of the Profession" (6 articles on nursing today). *Nursing Outlook* 26, no. 1 (January 1978):28-55. (Especially valuable are the articles by Margaret McClure, "The Long Road to Accountability," pp. 47-50, and Donna Diers, "A Different Kind of Energy: New Powder," pp. 51-55.)

Swerling, Israel. *Racism, Elitism, Professionalism: Barriers to Community Mental Health.* New York: Atheneum Publishers, 1976.

Toffler, Alvin. *Future Shock.* New York: Bantam Press, 1970.

Tuma, Jolene. "Professional Misconduct" (letter to editor). *Nursing Outlook* 29, no. 9, (September 1977):546.

Yarling, Roland R. "Ethical Analysis of a Nursing Problem: The Scope of Nursing Practice in Disclosing the Truth to Terminal Patients." *Supervisor Nurse* 9, May 1978, pp. 40-50, and June 1978, pp. 28-34.

INDEX